# The Technology of Policing

# The Technology of Policing

*Crime Mapping, Information Technology, and the Rationality of Crime Control*

Peter K. Manning

NEW YORK UNIVERSITY PRESS

*New York and London*

NEW YORK UNIVERSITY PRESS
New York and London
www.nyupress.org

Library of Congress Cataloging-in-Publication Data
Manning, Peter K.
The technology of policing : crime mapping, information technology,
and the rationality of crime control / Peter K. Manning.
p. cm. — (New perspectives in crime, deviance, and law series)
Includes bibliographical references and index.
ISBN 978-0-8147-5724-6 (cloth : alk. paper)
1. Crime analysis—United States—Data processing. 2. Information
retrieval—United States. 3. Crime prevention—United States.
4. Digital mapping. I. Title.
HV7936.C88M356 2008
363.250285—dc22                2007037271

New York University Press books are printed on acid-free paper,
and their binding materials are chosen for strength and durability.

Manufactured in the United States of America
10 9 8 7 6 5 4 3 2 1

*For Annie*

# Contents

# Preface

Books leave more unsaid than said; more to be imagined than to be read; more in the wholly created than in the created. I began the work that in time became this book, as Heidegger might say, as a wanderer along a path rather than a focused and directed researcher. An opportunity arose and fieldwork ensued in an available and convivial police department; I transferred my interest to the Metropolitan Washington Department, moved to Boston, and walked across the street to the BPD. The uncritical and rather naïve idea that crime mapping-in-use was the cause of a crime drop arose during the course of the study and was neither the impetus to nor the result of my research. The axial and organizing idea that there are several contesting rationalities, and not just one—modes in which we relate to the world of others—emerged over the course of the study. I assumed initially that crime mapping (CM) and crime analyzing (CA) is a "technological package," a means by which work is accomplished, that has symbolic (the way it is represented and thought about—its meaning) and instrumental (what work it actually does where and when) facets. However, while it is that, a pragmatic tool, it is above all a stimulus to systematic imagining.

As the work unfolded I narrowed my interest to the way, in a traditionally structured organization, social change emerges. I called the organization the music and the practices, some of which changed, the dance. Because organizations rationalize all that they do and do what they know how to do, they treasure institutional accounts, or explanations for why what is done is that which best accomplishes what they set out to do. Such tautologies are powerful. Technology stimulates; it mediates relationships and elaborates complexity. It can disrupt power balances. Technology produces new social objects, and information technology in particular reflects upon itself, creating reflective loops and conundrums. Social objects produced by information technology, crime maps and their impedimenta, can be made real to police—lasting, enduring, and a thing-in-presence. This is true even as it remained a matter "ready to hand" and obscure by great clarity and unexamined properties for police. They did not question its workings. Here, again, I echo Heidegger (1977). How are these new objects grasped? What forms of collective sense making (Weick 2000) are required to order this new information? In due course, I began to see how a rationally intended project thrust into the police world became just another tool. In spite of the competing and contesting rationalities in the organizations I studied, the organizations changed little. The epilogue suggests that by the time the present book was published the fad that was crime analysis had been either radically transformed or abandoned some ten years after it walked on stage. It came and left.

In what follows, using my field data, I draw out similarities and differences based on six dimensions of comparison and describe the emergence of rationalities based on police-used information technology. Most of the fieldwork was accomplished between 1996 and 2002, in two large American cities (Boston and Washington, D.C.) and in one medium-sized American city (called by its pseudonym, "Western"). The work was done up to and including December 2003, when the commissioner in Boston, Paul Evans, resigned to take a position in the Home Office in London.

The three case studies (Details of the methods of study, the site selection, and rationale for the choice of sites are found in appendix A.) resemble a series of snapshots of three organizations at quite different "stages" of development. Only one of the studied police departments, Boston, has a well-developed crime analysis process, including department-wide semipublic meetings. They are partial studies, and they are pictures of organizations in flux, as seen at the periods observed. The case studies are intended as an illumination of, or tessellation upon, rationality as it is situated and described in organizational context. Rationality is a mode of relating to the world as given and no more. This is a study of some rationalities.

The materials are presented in the ethnographic present—or as they were at the time of the study. Events shaping the department since that time are mentioned in footnotes but are not evaluated for their impact on the rationalities studied here. I would have preferred to use pseudonyms for all three of the sites, but doing so would have been meaningless given the descriptions necessary to locate the cities politically. To protect individuals, I use coded names for police department employees.

The exceptions to this practice are the commissioner in Boston, the chief in Washington, D.C., and high-ranking people named in newspaper stories.

My analytic categories stood out, or were "thrown to me," and emerged early in my fieldwork. Reexamining my field notes, I found that they were viable in each of the sites.

- The key actors involved in making the decisions to make the transition to crime analysis and crime mapping and their social roles. This included the teams that emerged (groups that shared secrets), their audiences, and third parties or onlookers.
- Salient political networks, within and without the police organization, and their connections—these may include networks or players outside as well as inside the police department.
- The most relevant information-processing and storage systems: extant databases, data outputs and their various social forms, texts, maps, figures, diagrams, tables, charts, and lists. This set of systems also included the resident hardware and software configured for use.
- The nature of the links between databases and systems—electronic, physical, paper, oral, or other modalities, including how often they are used and by whom.
- The secondary key players: experts and staffs who are the database minders, processors, and analysts, as well as the repair and installation groups.
- Data users, clientele, and relevant examples of field application and results, if available.
- The ecological configuration of the components of the management information system, e.g., terminals, mapping machines, mobile digital terminals, cell phones, electronic devices for scheduling, entertainment, and communication, and notebooks or laptops.

The crime mapping/crime analysis programs studied in the three organizations varied in their coherence, functional capacities, and utility. While the programs were the core concern, other abiding fringe issues arose. While the programs are the focal object, they exist in what Bourdieu (1993:30) calls a field of political forces. A field is a set of positions and relations that are both hierarchical and replete with struggle and competition. The police use strategies of resource allocation and rhetoric to sustain their position in the political field of a city. These strategies were combined with other programs in the organizations. The high politics of the cities (governance and business interests) and of the departments (internal politics and power struggles) shaped decisions and possibilities. The technologies employed, as will be seen below, varied. The key information flows, both formal and informal press releases, meetings and press conferences, and related feedback loops, ranged from simple to complex.

Some changes in the political field had wide ramifications outside the organizations because they were attended by the media. While I was not concerned with bookkeeping and budgeting processes per se, I discovered that they affect and shape decisions about acquiring equipment, paying overtime, estimating the cost of projects, and printing the requested maps. Washington, D.C., for example, had set crime reduction goals (see the website http://mpdc.dc.gov/). Given goals (desired end states such as crime reduction) and objectives (what percent change is to be expected in what indicator), some modes of auditing, quality control, and evaluation should be in place to assess whether the objectives are met. These modes existed precariously in the three organizations. The flows of information were located ecologically so that the consequences of spatial distribution (or maldistribution) of information became problematic. Flow charts of communication among key players involved in deciding were collected. What is called "information" is a thing that is shaped and determined organizationally. My interest in information was in the distribution of information, both its form and its content, but the relevant information needed was always contextually defined.

The case studies presented here are phenomenological— they examine the structure of meaning that embeds CM/CA as a technology in organizational context. The structure of meaning is revealed by displays, actions, *practices*; ways to show how something is grasped, taken on, and brought into being. In effect, maps and tables are social objects that must be "made sense of"; they do not "speak for themselves"; they may be worth a thousand words or not; but they are not obvious in their implications. They contain a series of signifiers or partial signs that point to something else, but they do not themselves finish the story a map might tell. All such signifiers are incomplete and must be completed by connecting them to some social referent such as offenders, offenses, or criminogenic environments that are relevant to the viewer. Since people use technologies to achieve many ends or purposes (amuse themselves, get help, communicate to others, appear to be working, buy and sell commodities, find dates, and etc.), there are many kinds of rationalities. My concern was to capture the manner of police accounting for the deciding used to allocate resources and the rationalities that arise as the CM/CA approach and related technology are introduced to the organization.

It is important to note that I did not study the filtering down of this information, only the way in which CM/CA was embedded in traditional police perspectives. There is little or no reason to believe that any change in the basically undirected and entrepreneurial work of patrol officers changed in Boston—the only organization studied that implemented the CM/CA approach. Short-term reallocation of officers by shift, saturation patrol, authorizing additional ad hoc allocation of overtime pay, and other exercises in traditional police tactics predate World War II and cannot account for brief up or down tics in reported crime. The actual impact of CM/CA on crime, disorder, or services rendered has not been and cannot be established at present because the data on the "success" or "failure" of the given allocation of resources has not been tracked, measured, and used to evaluate the decisions made. Variations in the short term of officially recorded crime statistics (ORCS) cannot be used to establish causation. This is not a book about the impact of these technologies on police work seen as the activities of officers and investigators. That is another book, not this one. Since some version of the CM/CA process remained in place in 2006 in many departments, and crime continues to rise, no claims have been made by the police that they are masters of the streets or the like, claims trumpeted widely by the police and the media late in the last century. (See the epilogue concerning the fate of Boston's CAMs (crime-analysis meetings.)

The book is divided into three sections and ten chapters. The first section concerns theorizing. In chapter 1 I examine rationalities in a dialogue with Weber. In chapter 2, I lay out the dance of change, some innovations in policing over the last twenty years. The third chapter concerns the obdurate structure of policing, the music; this is the background against which the book unfolds. Chapter 4 describes what is done in policing, in part as a result of new information technologies. The second section of the book, chapters 5, 6, and 7, is composed of case studies carried out in Western, Washington, D.C., and Boston. To illustrate the constraints of the organizations in their environments, these chapters include data such as city population and ecology, the size of the department, and the crime burden. In the third section, chapters 8, 9, and 10, I reflect and summarize. Chapters 8 and 9 outline the unseen ordering factors in Boston, and the complicated matter of collective seeing and saying found in the Boston crime-analysis meetings. Chapter 10 is something of a summary: in the end, the steps of the dance remain the same. Section 4 contains two appendices: one contains details of the field studies, while the other contrasts policy papers, faery tales, and scientific research. I conclude with an epilogue that comments on changes in Boston since 2003, including the termination of the CAMs and the stripping of the Research and Development Division of its crime analysts.

## Acknowledgments

Sponsorship is both a burden and an opportunity. I am grateful for the support of the Defense Security Research Center, formerly PERSEREC, Jim Riedel, and the late Ted Sarbin, the sponsorship of Carolyn Nichol, Sampson Annan, and Sam McQuaid, at that time with the Metropolitan Police Department in Washington, D.C., the chief of Western, and the many officers in the several departments who gave of their time. I owe a great debt, accumulated over the course many years, to Mike Chatterton, former director of the Henry Fielding Centre at Manchester University. Mike has been a loyal friend for over thirty years, sponsored me in the late nineties to several constabularies and to Bramshill Police College, and offered consistent warm support and facilities during my several visits to the UK at that time. I was enabled by the funds associated with the Brooks Chair at Northeastern University to complete the research, draft portions of the book, and have it published. A fellowship in practice-oriented education from Northeastern University from September 2003 to September 2004, and support for the summer of 2004, are gratefully acknowledged.

In the course of events for which this text is a surrogate, I have incurred many obligations, fulfilled a few, and passed on a few others that remain. I thank some of my colleagues and friends for their tolerance. Keith Hawkins has endured my uneven efforts on our decision-making book. Recently, I have been supported and encouraged by Jack Greene, Jack McDevitt, and Eva Buzawa. Anne Rawls has been a colleague and friend through difficult times, and her ideas resonate throughout this book. I have learned a great deal by impulsive wandering through, in, and around the Boston Common searching for cabs, and I now understand the proximity of Chinatown to all Boston points, as well as the centrality of Waltham to driving in Massachusetts. I am grateful to Claire Rambo, Maria Marcucilli, Stephanie Saia, Isabel Cancel, Garrett Warfield, and Elizabeth Farnham, who undertook diverse tasks with consistent good humor. I thank Marion Sullivan, Marilyn Kearney, Shirley Davis, and Courtney (Clifford) Bitto of the College of Criminal Justice at Northeastern. Husky Express did the necessary, and friends at Conor Larkin's, especially Chris, Brent, Conor, and Paul S., were variously good company. At Our House–East, Paul Benko and the "little Benkos" looked after the material side of this effort. It does take four-plus years, Paul.

# PART I

# Theorizing

# 1

# Rationalities

The contention of *signification* and *being* which has caused such mischief in religion would perhaps have been more salutary if it had been conducted with respect to other subjects, for it is a general source of misfortune to us that we believe things are in actuality what they in fact only signify.

—Georg Christoph Lichtenberg 1990

## *Résumé*

Consider now the police. On the one hand, they function as they have for some 177 years: they stand poised, ready to react to the emergent, the unexpected, and the unpredictable, that which cannot be fully anticipated, prevented, nor planned for in detail. On the other hand, they are being dragged into the information age, an age that imagines the future prior to executing it. Are they caught up in the global western European movement Max Weber (1947) called the rationalizing of society? What is known about how policing is being affected by the daunting and rapid changes in applied information technology? Is this technology being applied? Are the police being shaped by a more rational, goal-oriented management and making better, more information-centered, decisions? What is known about these matters presently is more descriptive than analytic, eagerly ameliorative in tone and not grounded in a sociological tradition.[1]

One highly praised system of information processing, crime mapping and crime analysis (CM/CA), has been seen as a fundamental window into the transformation of policing (Willis, Mastrofski, and Weisburd 2004, 2007). Meetings featuring these displays achieved great popularity after the crime drop in the early nineties was attributed to management (Bratton 1998) and to crime analysis and mapping techniques initially developed and refined in the NYPD. Yet, no convincing evidence or logical chain has been shown to support this claim of a direct effect of

CA/CM. The process by which ad hoc traditional tactics suppressed crime, including homicide and other largely private conflicts, has not been explained. The workings of the meetings producing the putative results remain more or less a "black box." They are opaque at best. With the exception of one case study (Willis, Mastrofski, and Weisburd 2004), little is known about this "window" into the rationalizing of policing.

My focus here is on the rationalizing effects of an applied information technology, CM/CA, taken together as a pair. This pair is a fact-based, generalizable, reproducible source of information that appear to challenge the traditional logic and practices of policing. Crime analysis (CA) is a family of techniques designed to gather information on the temporal, spatial, and social aspects of crime (offenders, victims, and their social characteristics such as race, class, age, and gender); describe their patterning (basically, show variations indicating increases in everyday street crimes—burglary, robbery, homicide, assault, and some indications of disorder such as shots fired, noise complaints, and "gangs"); make them available generally; and direct police resources in order to reduce the levels shown. These analyses, prepared by civilian analysts, are quite simple, showing variations in reported crime and other matters of interest for brief periods of time. Once gathered and recorded by officers, entered into standardized computer files, and shaped by software to include text, pictures, or graphics for dramatic data presentation, they are combined with detectives' records for the reporting, investigation, and disposition of crime and presented in summary form without the complexities of the events reported—their substance or context, the local knowledge of patrol officers or detectives, etc.—and aggregated as problematic. The screens present. With the current speed, memory, and data capacity of computers, materials can be dramatically configured and shown in maps, tables, graphs, and other colorful iconic displays. The data can be quickly distributed, discussed, and referred to across units and divisions and are in some departments essentially "online." In many ways, these crime maps are modern versions of the pin maps first used in nineteenth-century London, refined in Chicago in the 1920s, and long a staple of police information systems. The maps are of course the surface manifestation of a very complex infrastructure. But it is important to keep one's eye on what is out of sight.

What follows is an inquiry into the features of a CM/CA capacity, and the process of sense making surrounding data presentations. In the following chapters I ask to what degree and how crime mapping and crime analysis (CM/CA), as implemented, reveals rationalizing forces, how they are accounted for or explained, and what effects these changes, if any, have upon power relationships within police organizations. By "effects," I mean changes in the everyday police practices, or police administration, the cognitive and sense-making processing of information that is prior to police work "on the streets." I begin with rationality, examine how it is seen in the context of policing, sketch an outline of police and organization and technology, and then present the analysis based on three case studies. Boston's crime-analysis meetings require extended treatment because the BPD had the only operating version of CM/CA.

## Variations on a Theme of Rationality

A characteristic of our chaotic times is the contest of rationalities, a struggle between adherents of particular ways in which means are related to ends in a rational-legal organizational context (Espeland 1998). While Weber used a single term, "instrumental rationality," he included in this a wide range of "methodical suiting of efficient means to widely embraced social ends" (Merelman 1998, interpreting Weber 1978b: 24–26). Technology, more than any other means, has been elevated as the source of efficiency in the modern age. The introduction of new technologies raises questions about why and how it works and its impact on the organization. It may erode a pattern of organizational legitimacy, a mode of stability and compliance. Even in a rational-legal bureaucracy, many interests may lie behind apparent submission to an order (Weber 1978a: 37–38). There are thus many rationalities linking ends to means and many ways to think with such ideas. The rationalities found in police organizations are in part a function of the development of the modern bureaucratic form, and in part a function of their traditional mandate. The patterns of conflict, loyalty, and submission are situational, and reflect contesting rationalities. While the notion of the bureau seems to imply unity and coherence rather than conflict and confusion, there is no reason to assume that human confusions, passions, and self-serving performances have been eradicated by modern organizational forms. It may be that modern bureaux are the most important context for passions, envy, revenge, lust, attachment and alienation, politics and power (Herzfeld 1992).

## The Long Shadow of Max Weber

In studies of economic and social development, Weber's concept of rationality is a dominant icon. Weber (1947, 1978a, b; Gerth and Mills 1958), on the basis of his elaborate historical and comparative research, emphasized that if a form of rationality consistent with capitalism was to emerge, the end, accumulation of wealth, should be ideally connected to the means by rules and procedures that ensure that the end will occur. His strongest point here was the necessity of sustained, close monitoring of the modes of deciding and of the outcomes produced. Whatever the end—to suppress crime, capture a market share, serve communities better—the means must be evaluated with respect to this desired end state. The connection between the ends sought and the means used must be consistently evaluated and audited for success (Weber 1947: 186–202). Those matters, such as personal preferences, religious beliefs, loyalties to families and friends, as they did not elevate the importance of organizational goals and might deter their pursuit, were to be set aside. "To be set aside" in this context meant that they were not to be taken into account in evaluation of organizational functioning. As organizations became more rule and procedurally guided, more objective, they were seen as "more rational," or as rationalizing their operations.

This broad concept of rationality was contrasted with another social form, irrationality. Rationality, in Weber's view, referred to action, a means that is oriented to the achievement of an end. This conception of rationality pervades modern life, shadows all its institutions, and is a dominant vocabulary of motives, or way of explaining why something was done (Mills 1940). To function collectively, a means-ends connection must have a general tacit reality. This is achieved via public enunciation and rhetoric, symbolized by such things as mission statements, values, and formal statements of purpose. Rationality as an explanation for why something was done is a useful story that guides actions and reflections upon it. Businesses, universities, armies, and charitable institutions are governed by the notion of rationality, a careful and persistent gauging of the means by which resources are developed, deployed, and allocated with reference to ends or mission statements. Irrationality, on the other hand, is a term that references action that is oriented to the sustaining of a principle, an end, or a belief that is habitual or affectively based. These distinctions between rational and irrational action, as Weber noted, are perspectival: the definitions depend in part on the point of view of the actor or organization. While devout Christians may believe that floods and other disasters are best avoided or reduced by prayer, rituals, and offerings, a nonbeliever would reject these measures, favoring planning, emergency procedures, and scientific analysis of the causes of such disasters as floods. Habits and customs are critical to this latter formulation because the believer acts as those before him or her have acted, and feels emotional connection to the reproduction of the traditional ways of doing. But, individuals and organizations sustain and develop alternative modes of subjective rationality over time, and these are the source of change.

Weber (1947) sought to explain the conditions under which "subjective rational action" obtains or governs decisions. An action is "subjective" insofar as it refers to the meanings that are attached to such action, not the overt behavior itself. Instrumental formal rationality is thus subjective and refers to action or means oriented to achieving ends. On the other hand, value-oriented rationality refers to actions that seek valued ends in themselves. It is action intended to sustain what is valued.[2] In any organization, both sorts work actively and beneath observation—they decline into invisibility.

The tendency in modern societies to value formal rationality has become institutionalized in a pattern, reinforced by rules, procedures, and techniques within given institutional areas such as music, art, literature, religion, or public administration. This attachment and legitimation of policies and practices is what Weber (1978: xxx) called the "iron cage of rationality" because such a process of institutionalization drains away the appeal of other modes of acting, feeling, and expressing. These forces have powerful rooting and legitimation in other institutions as well so that they complement each other in operation (Merelman 1998). While ends differ, rationality, or the connection between means and ends, remains salient in all modern bureaucracies. That having been said, it is also true that police organizations are unusual, perhaps similar to the armed services, the fire service, and religious organizations, because a core of sacredness remains as an alternative source of order and compliance. Let us consider this further.

Weber distinguishes between organizations based on charisma, rational-legal compliance, or bureaucratic compliance and those based on loyalty to a patron, or to persons. These competing organizational forms do not vanish in the course of development, but remain viable in the world, even as formal rationality tends to destroy and flatten alternative modes of reasoning and evaluating action. Police organizations manifest a mixed or dualistic mode of organizational compliance. The modes of loyalty and leadership in reference to grounding legitimation, or achieving the police mandate, are in conflict. Weber writes that rational bureaucracy is a reversal of the patrimonial model of routinization; it is, as translated, "patrimonialism transposed into rationality." This is true because in the patrimonial form people perform routines, or what might be termed behavioral sequences, as a result of habit and loyalty. On the other hand, in the rational bureau, routines are based on well-established procedures and rules that stabilize these preferred routines (Gerth and Mills 1958: 245). The police department, as we shall see, remains a two-sided and awkwardly integrated organization precisely because it combines uneasily the patrimonial model of loyalty to the patriarch, whether to a rank superior, to senior officers, or to a member of the top command, with immediate here-and-now actions conforming loosely to established practices. These are nominally rule based. The icon and target of this loyalty is the chief, the patriarch of the police department. The rigid rational-legal bureaucracy requires loyalty to rules, procedures, and routines; the patrimonial bureau requires consistent unquestioning responses to the "irrational" commands of a chief. This heritage is a troubled inheritance of the police from the military with its collocation of ideas of loyalty, honor, and duty, matters that are almost totally in contrast and conflict with formal rationality. As Weber points out, of course, subjective rationality can be an essential element in achieving a rational goal such as winning a war or subduing a riotous situation. In other words, the basis for compliance differs fundamentally: in one mode, loyalty to rules and procedures drives action, while in the other, loyalty to persons and groups is the basis. One sort of rationality achieves a goal by means of loyalty to persons and groups, another by means of rules, procedures, and calculative rationality. These rationalities are in conflict from time to time, even when they are not verbalized openly.

Within the rational-legal model or mode of organizing action, a tension remains among the means that obtain. There are connections made in the organization between ends and means in which the putative ends are the same or at least equivalent, but the means differ. Organizations operate on what might be called notional or imagined goals that are often unclear, contradictory, or unexplicated. Actions become displaced to the imagined means to these ends, not the means themselves. Consider a university that wants to be better known and respected according to *U.S. News & World Report*. It might reduce class size, but this is not necessarily a sign of increased quality of education; it can increase retention rates of students, but the students may be of less ability, and so on. In addition, all these measures are means, not ends, and they reify the process of education. Thus, while a university can rise in some of the indices, the evaluation by other university faculty of the research and publication of the university in question can fall as the other variables in the index rise. None of these variables of course measures the central aim of a university—the development, dissemination, and analysis of credible knowledge. As we shall see in chapter 6 on Boston, ministers were asked by the police department to hold services, to walk the streets in displays of piety, and, in effect, to pray for reduced crime (McRoberts 2003). The effectiveness of this effort was gauged by crime statistics. These are based on various means used by the police, patrol, 911 responses, and investigation of crime to assess the effectiveness of those means in reducing crime (an end). The effectiveness of prayer, devotion, service attendance, and belief in God is given in the doing; these are intrinsically valued matters. Within the police, there were devotees of this approach to crime reduction while others favored "crackdowns," crime-attack models, threats, and abundant arrests. These are conflicts or contests surrounding means to an unexplicated end.

However, the most important tensions arise, in a contest of rationalities, when ends are not clearly stated, or the ends stated are surrogates, symptomatic, or displaced from effectiveness. In policing, as noted above, many tactics or means are afloat, and they are accounted for in statements and public documents. Policing now includes community policing, problem-solving policing, and crime mapping and crime analysis —all tactics relating to the ill-defined goal of improving the quality of life in our neighborhoods (this is the Boston Police Department's mission statement as found in the *Annual Report,* 2003). These tactics are rational in the sense that they are stipulated means to this end. However, the debate over means that takes place in policing obscures the reality that there is no clearly stated end and that whatever end is assumed is out of sight—a value such as security, high-quality life, coproduction of order, control of the streets. To these value-laden ideas are added statistical paraphernalia such as tables, charts, and graphs (see the annual report of any large police department) that measure not the quality of life, security, or disorder but calls for service, complaints against officers, reported official crime, and so on. Even crime figures alone, whether high or low, do not indicate the quality of life or security of an area as those are measured by other means and instead measure other matters such as sense of security, safety, and degree to which the area is seen as a high-crime area (Mastrofski, Reisig, and McCluskey 2002). In this sense, crime figures do not serve to audit, evaluate, adjust, or assess the achievements of the organization, as Weber would require. These are surrogate measures not of an achievable end state, but of a value. This creates a form of substantive rationality.

Policing is characterized by rationalities, not rationality, for the reasons outlined above. Any police organization could be seen through two lenses, or in term of two conflicting images—as a rational-legal bureau at some times, and as a patrimonial bureau at others. Conflicts exist among the means advocated to achieve policing's mission or mandate. These conflicts are sometimes resolved or discussed within the context of an operating patrimonial bureau and sometimes in the context of a rational-legal organization. This means the context of deciding varies and is occasioned or evolves and appears in a situation. Decisions can be made and justified or accounted for on the grounds of loyalty, duty, and honor (shorthand terms for personal obligation)—an approach sometimes criticized as being a function of the occupational culture if the behavior is that of an officer of sergeant level or below—or on the basis of procedures, rules and regulations, and legal standards. In either case, the operative rationalities are grounded quite differently in history and tradition. The debates within the overtly rational-legal model are accounts based on expertise, planning, information, new technology, and the like. These grounding ideas are modern "professional policing," supported by experts, consultants, and researchers and rooted in the idea of scientific, even experimental, research.

## Vocabularies of Motive as Institutional Accounts

Rationalities are not self-explanatory or even visible. They come in and out of organizational functioning and discourse. The way one goes about achieving an end in an organization is problematic; many modes are possible, and they are often debated. In a sense, the "operational" status of principles of rationality must be established and sustained. One version of this establishment of rationalities is that it takes place through the acceptance of a vocabulary of motives. Motives in this sense are explanations for actions, or "institutional accounts." Motives do not drive action from "inside the heads" of people; they are explanations for what has been done. Life is lived forward and explained backward, as Kierkegaard once wrote.

Let us explore this idea further. C. Wright Mills, in a classic article (1940), argued that motives are ways of coordinating action in situations. This argument had much influence on social sociology and is reflected in Goffman's (1959) masterful synthesis of performative actions. "Motives may be considered as typical vocabularies having ascertainable functions in delimited social situations. . . . The differing reasons men give for their actions are not themselves without reason" (Mills 1940: 904–905). Vocabularies of motive coordinate social action by being typical, repetitive, and anticipated. Motives are social and are indexed by what is said when, in a given situation, an account is requested, or answers to questions interrupt acts. Why did you . . . ? They are "accepted justifications" that shape and provide grounds for mutual accommodation. While there are terminologies or taxonomies of motives, such as the Marxian or Freudian view of motivation, motives are best studied in situations, when they are present. They must be studied as "vocabularies of motive in historic epochs and specified situations" (Mills 1940: 913). Motives are typical of organizations, occupations, and current ideologies, and are preferred in these contexts as plausible explanations. Finally, the virtue of using a vocabulary of motives as a conceptual window into organizational rationalities is that they account for both the past and anticipated future actions; they serve to organize social interactions; and they anticipate future consequences of conduct (Mills 1940: 907). They must, in Mills's view (1940: 913), remain grounded in situations, and not simplified into abstracted terminology of a general sort.

Vocabularies of motive, or accounts, are rationalities insofar as they link what is done, has been done, and will be done to present deciding. This formulation requires that the interactional dynamics of organizational action be connected to longer-term plans, rationalities, policies, and everyday decisions.

We can begin with Mills's argument for attending to situated conversations, and assume that this holds for organizational vocabularies. These might be called institutional or institutionalized accounts. Mills supplies us with a vocabulary for studying vocabularies of motive, or stated reasons for doing something. If we are to follow these dictates, we must uncover *how* such motives order and coordinate interaction. A situational approach to this matter means that we consider a situation as an occasion in which an account is rendered and that, furthermore, if an account is rendered, it is the determining feature of the situation. In the case studies, the situations of use, especially in the crime-analysis meetings in Boston, we find minitheaters in which the situated rationalities are being tried out in presentations. In the accounts, responses to questions asked are found in the often unclear assorted reasons for practices, or doing policing. Because they are partial, and cannot include all the imaginable reasons police might list for doing something, they are indexical, pointing to a variety of things, given a context. As we will see, when someone asks a presenter in a crime analysis meeting, "What sort of gun was used?" the question calls out to the other, the person questioned, to respond. The question calls for an account, but it points to a list of possible interests—caliber, type, stolen or not, age and function, semiautomatic or automatic, registered or on a list of guns, erased serial numbers or not, types of bullets it might fire, and more—not all of which could possibly be asked about. The question, nevertheless, goes to a shared concern or to reasons why it might be asked, and it calls upon the trustworthiness of the participants to react to the question even when much of what was asked is not asked or stated. The shared interests of the collective, the police in the meeting, in crime and order are touched upon but not stated.

Rationalities, in the present argument, are accounts, vocabularies of motives that are used in the course of meetings to discuss crime and disorder. They are ways in which connections between implicit means and ends are made public. They are more assumed than used, and they pass muster as adequate to the matters at hand. Awareness of their utility may not be present in the meetings. We might say that they are everyday rationalities in use rather than scientific statements of rationality (Garfinkel 1967: 269).

Why is this argument based on actions within situations necessary in order to understand the rationalities and the process of the development of crime analysis and crime mapping displays? Because the facts are various and uncertain and there are multiple stimuli active in the setting—because deciders "satisfice," or make the most of what is known. These modes of "satisficing" vary and have to be indicated by actors to each other by words, gestures, pauses, or explanations in order to "work."

Here are some reasons for the emphasis on the *situational argument* explored here.[3]

Without the described, detailed, and presented interactional dynamics, it is not possible to see how the decisions are produced—for example, the tactical decisions to assign more patrol officers to an area, to gather forensic evidence, to approve overtime, or to assign a special squad to surveillance.

The means of policing that are discussed are not assessed for their efficacy; they are assumed to be efficacious.

The vocabularies of motive, rationalities in action, are glosses on the process of being accountable in institutional-organizational terms.

The everyday character of the meeting is punctuated by questions that cry out for accounts and accountability, one of the consistent themes in the development of compstatlike meetings (Bratton 1998).

The rationalities are visible aspects of a contract, or implicit trust, and they ramify and activate mutuality and collective obligations (Garfinkel 1967: 173).

These questions and accounts are a kind of dance, and also are steps in a dance. This metaphor of "dancing to the music" is developed throughout this book.

## The Music

Is an organization musical? I use the metaphor of music to suggest that the constraints upon policing as a structured organization are powerful, lasting, meaningful, and enduring. A metaphor is a way of seeing something in terms of something else, so the music of policing suggests constraint: it is difficult to samba to a square dance tune or waltz to a hip-hop sonnet. If we think of the abovelisted innovations as steps in a dance, they are patterned by the structure of policing, the features of which are discussed in chapter 2. The structure is the music. These innovations are multifaceted and significant; they are not one-dimensional. They are attempts to achieve stated diverse aims, allocate resources to an activity, and evaluate efforts. They are cast as evidence-based practices, or matters about which one should reflect; as a result, they encounter resistance from those adhering to the traditional ways of doing things.

Rationalizing takes on several forms and styles, as does any dance.

We might say many dance, but few have distinctive style. Unlike the picture in Yeats's poem, the dancer *can* be distinguished from the dance. Rationalizing efforts are also attempts to move policing to consider its impact on the environment rather than merely reiterate largely empty "efficiency" claims or means-oriented justificatory data (figures such as arrests, calls for service, and reported crimes). These data are surrogates (partial, indirect, convenient, and sometimes misleading indicators) that divert attention from actual impact on the distribution of types of level of crime or disorder, or on criminogenic processes. Efficiency-based ideas such as providing rapid response, covering the workload for a shift, reducing officially reported crime figures, or "putting more officers on the street" are aspects of a presentational rhetoric (how the police present their mandate or public legitimacy—Manning 1997: 85). They beg the question of actual proven impact of or consequences of police actions. They cry out for legitimation, validation, and support, not confirmation by fact.

To follow the dancing metaphor a bit further, any given rendition of a dance, its steps with accompanying music, is an instance, or a case. This study draws together data from three case studies to create a rendition of policing in transition. I am suggesting that if one can "write choreography" one can reproduce a dance. Sociology as an investigative mode could be seen as a kind of search for choreography. Because the fulsome, multifaceted aspects of rationalizing cannot be fully grasped, any research must be sharpened and focused. My primary window into rationalizing is an examination of information technologies (IT) or, more explicitly, a study of the role of crime analysis and crime mapping (CM/CA) in modern policing.

## A Window on Rationalities

### Maps

There is a rather deep background that foreshadows the present interest in the use of spatial distributions to array crime and disorder as incidents. Social scientists from the 1920s understood that all manner of social activities are patterned ecologically, and that cities shaped them in powerful and even predictable fashion (Park and Burgess 1926). The most salient example of this was the innovative work of Shaw and

McKay in mapping juvenile gangs in Chicago (1942). The dynamic aspects of these processes, first indicated by Park and Burgess, were elaborated first in studies of value conflict and its role in generating crime (see Short 1963) and later by the work of Robert J. Bursik and Grasmick (1993) and Sampson and Groves (1989). These works showed how powerfully space shaped crime and its impact. The work was analytical, theoretical, and deeply embedded in the ecology of the city, and in many respects it was nontechnical (see Sampson 2002 for a useful overview). In large part, the commitment of the "Chicago School" was to sustaining the quality of urban life, sympathy for the marginal and exploited, and a view of crime as a mode of adjustment and accommodation to the ravages of new and very abrasive city life. The victims of urban life were not simply the middle-class citizens who encountered the homeless and hopeless, and the idea of a single ordering of life, implied by zero tolerance, was simply unthinkable to these scholars of urban life.

The mapping of crime became a more practical tool in the period between 1980 and 1990. It was nurtured as a research technique by a generation of social scientists (such as Brantlingham and Brantlingham 1981; Maltz 1991; and Rossmo 2000). In time, the technique evolved from a descriptive, geographically based way to present data spatially to a means by which one can analyze these data and apply them to practice. The burst of studies on crime and place have redirected and refashioned concern from theoretical and analytic to "practical" interventions designed to reduce disorder and crime.

## Maps and Crime

Crime mapping and analysis has also been used for fifteen years or so to augment and/or refine police ideas (Sherman, Gartin, and Buerger 1989). Sherman's work stimulated descriptive studies of the spatial distribution of repeat calls for service, clusters of crime, or other indices of disorganization with the aim of reducing them on the grounds that they were burdensome (Sherman 1987). This later focus was refined into a series of studies designed to show that crime-attack tactics were much needed (Sherman 1990, 1992). Studies claiming to combine problem solving, spatial analysis, and crime reduction were published (see the entire issue of *Justice Quarterly* 12(4) 1995). In a useful and clear example of the application of experimental design to the reduction of disorder, Braga et al. (1999) used a variety of tactics, including focused police saturation, to reduce calls for service and reported drug crime. Some ex post facto statistical analyses of crime in various selected places have been carried out to simulate experimental methods (Weisburd et al. 2004). This research, from Sherman's first insights in Minneapolis through to the series of works now featured in the *Journal of Experimental Criminology* (see Springeronnline.com), features increasingly elaborate statistical methods with a variety of surrogate measures of the quality of life in neighborhoods. This technique has been refined to a concern for dynamics over time (Weisburd et al. 2004). In these works, there is no human presence, no people, no life situation, no semblance of urban life as a moving, culturally embedded process. Urban life as mapped is a police theater, a cartoon of methodological pretense.

With the appearance and development of what have come to be called "compstat meetings" after the NYPD version (Bratton 1998)—meetings at which crime and disorder data are presented to police officials in order to press them into crime crusades—spatial analysis and visual presentations were elevated to sacerdotal level. There was a hope that spatial analyses and problem solving would result not only in focused management that would produce crime reduction using official police-generated figures but also in a lean and "smart" police management style. It has been claimed to be the fundamental cause of a crime drop in New York City (Maple 1998; Bratton 1998; Kelling and Coles 1996; Manning 2001a). Crime mapping, when combined with meetings, has been studied as an innovation in policing by Weisburd, et al., in two publications (2003, 2004). By the turn of the century it had become a major police fad and was diffused widely (Weisburd, et al. 2003). While not all of the eight elements were present in all the organizations studied, and the focus on crime-attack tactics was not salient in all, they found no substantial change in policing.

In this way, a theoretically grounded idea based in the catabolic and anabolic processes in city life and reflecting systematic notions of culture, economic pressures, and lifestyles that were given authenticity and integrity was stripped of these concerns, made merely pragmatic, and converted into a tool to reduce crime by increasing arrests. Spatial analysis moved from an analytic, theoretically grounded, scientific theory of urban processes, including crime and other disorder, to a shorthand tool for reducing crime using a variety of surrogate and second-hand data sources such as calls for service and reports taken by officers (themselves a part of the experimental team). The aim of the quasi-experimental research, which is brief and focused in duration, mirrors the police ideology that their job is suppressing crime quickly, by direct reactive tactics that reveal results in the short term, cheaply, without reflection, in an identified, political, defined space. The actual drops are small and last for brief periods, according to systematic evaluations (e.g. Eck and Maguire 2000; Weisburd and Eck 2004; Weisburd and Braga 2006).

## Crime Mapping and Analysis

An operating system of crime mapping has a number of essential elements that constitute it. As used in policing, crime mapping has a number of salient features. Crime mapping is a technique based on software (usually ERSI, ArcView, or MapInfo) that converts geo-coded addresses or locations (one set of files) so that maps, tables, and figures can be merged with them and maps created. These maps can display an array of signs (tables, graphs, or other figures) on maps of a city or political area, combined with pictures, sound, drawings, and diagrams. A wide range of facts can be included, such as fire risks, demographic characteristics, indices of disorder and quality-of-life offenses, addresses of those on parole, registered sex offenders, and more conventional police-generated data concerning juvenile gangs, patterns of adult crime, and traffic. A range of other sorts of data has been added by some departments, such as addresses where restraining orders are to be enforced and turfs of gangs, as well as demographics of social areas in the city. Variations in density by location, types of crimes, or days of the week can be mapped, as can offenders' residences and patterns of co-offending (Bottoms and Wiles 1997). Anything that can be plotted spatially can be represented. In effect, almost by default, these displays have created a context for problem solving and reflection—what is loosely called crime analysis.

In policing, crime analysis covers a wide range of practices. At one level, it simply means examining the patterning of types of crime by time and space. This analysis may include crime's corollaries, such as age, sex, and ethnicity, as well as its temporal or episodic nature. Police then ask what can be done by the police, citizens, or other agencies to prevent, reduce, eradicate, or displace this identified crime or disorder. Most of these analyses give rise to short-term interventions by police such as crackdowns, saturation patrol, or raids. More sophisticated versions of crime analysis may require models of the dynamics of areas, including disorder, crime, and their correlates, as a prelude to longer-term planning or interventions.

Crime analysis, and crime mapping as an adjunct, has at least three components that may or may not be present in a given police organization. The first is the *technical* component: the software and knowledge needed to make tables, graphs, figures, and models. This is the arena of the experts, the technicians, the repair people, and the often civilian analysts. The second is the *implementation process,* the capacity to fit such materials into organizational planning, strategic plans, unit objectives, evaluations, and operating procedures. The third is the *integration in daily police operations* of crime mapping. All of these components must be examined in context to see what effects CM/CA has. The focus here is primarily upon the implementation and the resultant meeting-based uses of the data. In this sense, this study taps into the ritual and expressive aspects of the work rather than the consequences of introducing the CM/CA process into the organization's work in the city at large.

Crime mapping and crime analysis have been readily adopted as described (Weisburd et al. 2003). They fit the conventional police focus, crime, the police's interest in decisive, short-term interventions, and the belief in magic that they associate with technology. Police are drawn to the public position that through systematic analysis of crime patterns they can prevent, anticipate, shape, or avoid spikes in crime, especially the most common crimes of auto theft, burglary, and robbery. The practices of given departments under the rubric of "compstat" are based on a simple or minimalist definition of the technology in use in police departments. As noted above, many urban police departments now possess the required software, databases, and geo-coded records, although few use them. The key concepts used to describe CM/CA's focus, such as "hot spots," are left undefined and are used as and when—indiscrimately. The term "hot spot" essentially refers to any visible cluster on a map regardless of its source, consequence, origins, dynamics, meaning, or reference. There were and are also practical appeals. CM/CA software is inexpensive to acquire, and the software (that which does the GIS work as well as the graphics packages that produce elaborate and elegant maps) is standardized and easy to install and run. With lightweight laptops, now possessing enormous memory capacity, a visual display can be mounted almost anywhere at any time. These laptops or notebooks can be linked in parallel, and large datasets can be accessed and used quickly and efficiently. On-line presentations of a wide range of records—whatever is on-line in a police department—can be presented, drilled down, reconfigured, and again displayed in seconds. Data, once aggregated and disaggregated, can be distributed to any terminal—in the headquarters of a district or a vehicle. The maps and graphics have enormous appeal, both expressively (jokes, cartoons, funny voices over the visuals, little video snippets, etc.) and instrumentally (they are compact, colorful, dramatic, and simple). The visuals are both convincing and misleading in their simplicity. The results can be stored, reviewed, used again, redisplayed, and so on so that evaluation and data-based feedback are readily at hand. Good or bad work becomes memorialized, called up again, and enjoyed or criticized. This distinguishes the CM/CA approach from the traditionally strong oral culture so highly regarded in policing. Some history of events, actions taken, and even outcomes accumulates as a result of the experience of the regular participants in the meetings. Acceptance of the approach and public acceptance of the prima facie credibility of the idea as crime, as measured by the official, police-kept rate, has dropped means that it is seen as an efficient and effective innovation. The software, the hardware, the imagination of utility and its fit with the policing view of the world, and its relatively low cost and efficiency potential (production, reproduction, creation, distribution, and use) make it very useful. It also amplifies, as it is reported to be used, the core value of police: crime control or suppression. A final source of support for the innovation and its diffusion has been the strong and consistent financial backing of the National Institute of Justice for CM/CA. This support includes providing grants for crime mapping and its assessment, funding national conferences on crime mapping, establishing a national institute for crime mapping with a Ph.D. director within the institute itself, and funding a number of publications (LaVigne and Wartell 2000, 2001). In many ways, this research has been a powerful reproduction of police ideology, unquestioning, supportive, and technically complex. While the ideas have swept through policing and been widely adopted, no research has examined *how* and *why* such meetings unfold as they do. I suggest later that they are a form of ritual celebration, a kind of secularized magic and staged authenticity.

## *Signwork*

The workings of an approach to orienting policing, such as CM/CA, are not simple, nor are their ramifications obvious. My perspective on this has been suggested above, when I referenced the importance of displays, practices, multiple rationalities, and the construction of meaning. I want to sketch my approach to my observations and interviews.

Crime analysis and crime mapping (CM/CA) are modes of representing crime-relevant information (I rely on a vague term here), and they rely on signwork. That is, they rely on the actors' (collective or individual) cognitive effort, which is necessary to interpret an expression (what is seen) with a content (what is connected mentally with an expression). A sign is thus created—the combination of an expression and a content in a context. This connecting may be done in a flash, unreflectively, like speaking generally, or it may be laborious. Signwork, or sign-based analysis, is based on semiotics, the science of signs (Hawkes 1977; Manning 1987), and in a sense can be deconstructed from semiotics to practical actions.

If we think of a gun as an expression, it can be linked to many contents to make a sign. These might include technical factors such as make (Colt, Ruger, Smith and Wesson), kind (handgun, long gun), caliber, mode of operation (automatic, semiautomatic), emotional impact (fear, confidence, potency, security), part played in a uniform (present or absent distinguishing "flashlight cops" from publicly sworn officers), and so on. The connections made are mental, or one might say sociocultural, and are based largely on context, or what is brought to the expression and later to the completed sign. Even a complete sign is essentially incomplete without the presence of other signs and an audience. From a semiotic point of view, crime maps are awash with *expressions* that must be connected to a content in order to make sense. This is the process of producing a sign, or something that means something to someone in a context (to paraphrase C. S. Pierce—see Eco's overview, 1979).

Semiotics will assist us in making sense of crime mapping and crime analysis, because they are essentially signwork. For example, if a neighborhood is shown on a map, perhaps projected by means of Power Point software, with streets, parks, and alleyways displayed, and at each place where a robbery has occurred a large red triangle glows, this is a set of iconic representations, or set of expressions. The glowing triangles (expressions) do not have explicit meaning until they are connected to a content—in this case, for example, to the official crime category robbery as defined by the UCR (Uniform Crime Report) and/or state and local law and departmental standards. It is this work of "connecting" or sense making that provides a window into rationalizing and the situated nature of rationalizing in policing.

## Conclusion

The iron cage of rationality described by Weber is not one cage, but many. The contesting rationalities present from time to time are visible and give rise to accounts and rationalizations that are in turn the basis for power within the organization. Police organizations strive to maintain a rational face, a professional face, in spite of deep fissures in practice and belief within them. The concatenation of a crime drop and the introduction of crime mapping and analysis in the early nineties created a powerful trend, a fad in which the two rather discrete aspects of "crime control" were conflated. Sponsored by foundations, government grants, and progressive departments, and used to direct crime crackdowns and other brief and focused interventions, CM/CA became an icon of scientific, crime-focused police work. It was thrust into the operational heart of policing by top command and became a media favorite. Nevertheless, while no research established its impact internally or externally, it dramatized and elevated those aspects of policing most appealing to the police themselves—their capacity to intervene and reduce officially recorded crime.

# 2

# The Dance of Change

## Introduction

The structure of policing, to be discussed in more detail in the following chapter, is a kind of music. The practices are a kind of dance. Organizations can dance, usually with less or more skill, so they have a style. Even elephants can dance. The cases found in chapters 5–7 are about the dance of change—how three police departments adapted to and made sense of innovations. A dancing style is the way the given organizations carry off the dance. To see style is to compare it with something that is other. And as with anything, style and substance tend to cohere.

To speak of change in police departments—these grounded, conservative organizations thought of as polluted by their proximity to evil, violence, and crime—as an emerging dance may seem odd. Yet, the metaphoric language of these chapters is intentional. Technology has many ways, it is part of a process of rationalizing with many faces, and the faces are strongly determined by the situations in which technologies are used. What is elevated to the foreground in this discussion may be background to the participants—they may not understand in an abstract sense what they are doing or why. The utility of technology is unquestioned publicly. Nevertheless, members of the organization must do the work of interpretation and be seen to be doing it by others. Participants, members of organizations, carry with them assumptions, attributions, values, beliefs, and shorthand recipes for explaining situations, even as they change and emerge before them. Transformative moments of change are like a new dance, but are always shadowed by the past, foresee the future, and move without direct rational guidance. This book, too, is a kind of dance between the past, present, and future; so like a dance, it repeats itself in the course of the performance.

To carry the metaphoric baggage somewhat further, it is useful to think of policing (as opposed to the police organization) in an organizational environment or field. Within a limited context of rules and traditional practices, policing does not dance alone, and it is always in some relationship to other organizations. Policing is an integrated bureaucratic reflection of and response to social-control processes generally—it cannot be seen outside the context of politics, power, authority, and social ordering. One can dance alone, but social action is collective action, a grand ballroom performance requiring multiple interchangeable partners. Nor can the internal rationalizing dance be seen in isolation, organizationally or politically. Consider the police one figure in a shadowy, sometimes dramatic performance that implicates a political and economic environment indirectly. It rests in a culture, and so one can speak of a culture of policing or of how policing is valued and described in moral terms. This is called the culture of policing (Loader and Mulcahy 2003). This chapter and the next examine policing broadly, both democratic policing and Anglo-American policing, while chapter 4 takes up police information technologies. Chapters 5–7 are the case studies.

## Rationalizing as a Situated, Iterative Process

The police are a rather quaint kind of rational-legal organization built over a traditional core of values and practices—namely, visible patrol, "working the streets," and investigating class-based, nineteenth-century street crimes. That is, the focus has always been upon regulating simple crimes of stealth and violence committed on the streets by those with few options and choices. A core of police values is composed of medieval ideas of duty, honor, personal loyalty to superiors, and obedience that are partially revealed in practices. This core radiates a kind of sacredness that extends throughout the organization in spite of the overlay of command and control that is an inheritance from the military origins of policing. This "overlay" includes the elevation of the chief as an honorable position, hyperelevation of rank and deference to command (the zone of indifference vanishes, to be replaced with compliance), and strict rules and regulations capriciously enforced. On the other hand, police organizations revere personalized authority relationships (feudal loyalty and honoring) and have an often baroque politics based on competition between segments (clusters of rank-related positions), cliques (upwardly oriented, ambitious small groups), and cabals (resistant status quo advocates) resident in networks. While authority ostensibly lies in rank, the differences in skill, political will, and insights, and particularly the sponsorship by one generation of the upcoming one, mean that power is based on the current alignment of networks with the present chief and her or his allies.[1]

Inevitably, an organization is an arena is which power struggles take place. Key players may not share the assumed rationality or reciprocity of perspectives that characterize the bureaucrat resident in the Weberian ideal type. The organization is segmented into top command, middle management, lower participants (uniformed patrol), and detective work, with each level entertaining a different definition of its authority, the meaning of the work's rewards and career options, the risks entailed, and its audiences (those whose respect they most seek, both in and out of the organization).[2] When change is introduced it may disrupt the patterns of exchange and reciprocity among the segments (Gouldner 1960). The fundamental consequence of this change and power drama is the elevation to attention of repeated circumstances in which differing standards, aims, and preferences are displayed and come in conflict.[3]

Displays of power are seen in the following case studies, and they are in effect yet another face of rationalizing. Rationalizing alters patterns of trust and exchanges that stabilize relationships across the widely dispersed, ecologically based police organization. The traditional and stabilizing features of policing, spelled out in more detail in the case studies in chapters 5–7, are in intermittent conflict with processes of rationalizing described in the case studies.

Bureaucracies, of course, feature different sorts of technologies, but those that deal with people, which some call "street-corner bureaucracies" (Lipsky 1986), require "people skills"—verbal and nonverbal means of persuasion—to achieve their ends. Even when a particular technology is dominant, be it an assembly line or the queues of a welfare office, it must be interpreted and used in spite of its often invisible workings. Think of the invisible magic workings of computers that are the cynosure of most modern offices.

Clearly, technologies, especially information technologies, have been the prime movers in organizational change in the last one hundred years. Yet, information systems alone do not change organizations; they must be attuned to simulate, stimulate, and respond to reflexive practice —the ongoing application of knowledge by people to their present and future decisions. This process cannot be restricted to a single goal, objective, or short-term aim or political mission. It is not captured by idle rhetorical claims such as "our mission is community policing." It is not simply a matter of setting goals and objectives. It may come in conflict with leadership fantasies, political campaigns, media orgies, and feeding frenzies of either the positive or negative sort, or with the short-term goals of the chief and his/her staff.

The emphasis in the following case studies is upon the many *faces of rationality* and how what is taken to be rational is explained and made sensible in key situations. Rationality comes and goes, yet appears repeatedly and curiously retains its power as a family of approaches (see Wittgenstein 1961) rather than a single kind of deciding. It is manifested in situations in which breaches, mistakes, or anomalies arise. These adaptive moves cannot be predicted but continue to arise as organizations change and reflect on these changes. Anomalous situations continue; they reappear; this repetition and response is a series, or a re-iteration, or, in broader terms, part of the dance. The dancers usually sway in time to the music they hear.

Think of the process of change metaphorically—like a dance with several partners at once. Labeling innovations as "dance steps," movements and responses with reiterations, does not imply a refinement, or closer approximation of an ideal; these innovations merely are much like the previous version of the same situation and response. If one thinks of a poem as dancing an attitude (Burke 1960), responses to these problematic situations constitute a kind of dance in which the dancer and the dance become one or at least are blurred. Words that strive to capture these subtle interpersonal struggles are verbal icons, incomplete pictures. In many respects, it is a moot point whether the environment is in reality changing or the organization is merely better able to adjust itself to itself. Most deciding situations are complex, especially those that involve groups of participants; they are often over- or under-studied and replete with errant facts (Feldman 1986). Yet decisions must be made (see March and Simon 1993, the classic statement of this position; and Weick 2002). The complexity of the longer-term consequences of deciding and the need to organize and make sense of them over time is signaled by ideas like "situational" and "iterative" in the subhead above.

Rationalizing is multifaceted, and its forms are variable. It certainly includes written policies and procedures and mission statements that are explicitly designed to have an impact on some selected aspect of the external environment (as well as the internal organizational environment). It might include establishing sets of goals and objectives, assessing them, gathering feedback from the results of these evaluations, and applying them to current practice. The detailed analysis of the Boston crime-analysis meetings suggests that it is situational and interactional. In other words, as examples, cases, instances arise, they are responded to, made sense of, and understood by the displays of talk, interaction, and negotiation in the crime-analysis meetings. The faces of rationality appear in the same settings over time, but no single rationality such as "reduce crime with the assignment of more personnel" is always used or justified as such. The relevance of this kind of rationalizing to modern policing is addressed later in this chapter. The background against which rationalizing is a foreground is the "professionalizing" movement of the last eighty years or so in America. The rhetoric that occupations use to elevate their status, gain respect, and solidify a mandate are presentational strategies or mini-ideologies, and require close examination to weigh claims and realities (Hughes 1958).

## The "Professional Model"

While the police force is a traditional bureau, it has been changed somewhat internally since the 1920s. This transformation has been seen as the rise of professional policing, or the professional model of policing. The term "professional" is an ideological claim that draws upon the aura of other professions, but uses the word as a rhetorical upgrading device. Unlike traditional professions such as law, dentistry, medicine, engineering, academic life in general, and the clergy, policing has no abstract theory, no control of its market or clientele (it serves all), few internal modes of assuring quality, a very short training period (sixteen-plus weeks), and no requirements for sustained higher education. As this listing of the absent implies, much is concealed and revealed in the rhetoric of the "professional model" of policing (see Wilson 1968; Bittner 1990). American policing "sells" itself by emphasizing scientific crime solving and its efficacy in controlling crime; dramatizing official statistics (that it controls and maintains); and playing up its sacred and honorable past (associated with the traditions of the military and the army), its association with the law and "law enforcement," and its neutral, apolitical position. The police force is in many ways a traditional, conservative (in both senses of the word), stealthy, secretive organization that overvalues its secrets and its unrevealed backstage machinations (doings out of sight of the public). The police have developed rhetorical or presentational strategies to set out their claim to legitimacy—the official line that is used to describe and characterize the organization in ideal, positive, and unambiguous terms. They also deploy resources in strategic and tactical fashion to achieve their goals. Because the police are a kind of sacred entity, awesome, distant, and secretive, they have been insulated until recently from pressures to be efficient, businesslike, and budget driven in their deciding. The skills and competence of police are not without virtue. Civil society requires that strangers sustain distance and a sense of security and that predatory violence be condemned and punished, and the eruptions of disorder and crime require a sophisticated competence. Of their tools, it is this violence competence, not its application, that the police most value (Brodeur forthcoming).

While pressures upon the police from city governments to become more efficient have increased, technology has become faster, cheaper, more mobile and compact, and more "user friendly." The emphasis on scientific work, technology, and efficiency, aping the clichés of business, is the current reflection of much longer term police reform and the professionalism movement that began in policing the late 1920s.

American police reformers August Vollmer, O. W. Wilson, Bruce Smith, Harry E. Fosdick, and V. O. Leonard assembled in their writings the key elements of scientific policing. Trained in law, public administration, and public service, they sought not only to alter the corrupt and violent police of that time but also to chart a new and more respectable course. In part reformers, in part visionaries, and well invested in the role of the police as the core of democratic polity, they fashioned in writing and in policy papers and while holding police office the modern surface or most visible features of policing.[4] Histories of policing in the period, especially during the Depression-Prohibition era, do not suggest that the basic venality, violence, and corruption of policing was much altered (Reppetto 1977).[5] The public standing of the police may have benefited, and in time the phrase "professional police" became a cliché.

From the beginning, the professional model included a commitment to science and technology, as well as the shadow of official data on reported crime. This commitment was the basis for claiming solid cases brought to court on the basis of valid evidence, mobile, skilled, more educated, and well-trained officers, and an organization administered rationally on the basis of a management philosophy drawn from contemporaneous theories of public administration. It implied better and more scientific control of crime and modern criminals. It also combined emulation of the ideology of the "higher professions" (altruism, service, ideals, and abstract knowledge) with claims for a scientifically based crime-control mandate and the pay and respect associated with these prestigious occupations. This model, part of a professionalization movement, became known as "professional policing" in America, even though it took very different shapes in local and regional contexts (Lane 1967; Reppetto 1977; Monkonnen 1981, 1992). This regional diversity continues, even though the research literature in police studies reflects studies done primarily in large urban police departments in the United States. At the federal level, J. Edgar Hoover masterminded and marketed the facade of the Federal Bureau of Investigation: an efficient crime-fighting organization, its agents civil, dapper, and tidy, and an active and effective army in the war against of crime, communism, or civil rights. Hoover also gathered to the FBI control over crime statistics (the Uniform Crime Reports assembled by the FBI from local police reports) and most-wanted lists and distributed them widely. While he was an intensely political man with great skill, he built the reputation of the FBI by insisting upon a contradiction: the FBI is politically neutral and loyal to the elected government of the day.

This professionalizing movement, in part an honest attempt at upgrading standards and performance, in time was shaped by a cynical, job-oriented ideology of the lower participants. It was not originally a cynical one but has become so through the influence of police unions and the harsh, often punitive approach to "management" taken by top command. Emphasis on mobile and scientific policing was well adapted to the changing population of the United States, which was becoming increasingly urban and mobile. Professionalizing in the police context was as much a matter of status striving and "occupational uptake" as an adaptation to vast urban growth, the density of urban populations, the mobility of populations, including criminals, and the differentiation of the population by ethnicity, education, and generation. Urban sprawl and "suburbanization" complicated these forces, along with increased immigration to the United States (Reiss 1992a). At the same time, progressive politics increased the viability of an objective, neutral form of policing unfettered by politics and political machines, and thus less vulnerable to corruption (Monkonnen 1992). In time this mandate, its validation by the public notwithstanding, became means focused—focused upon doing the job as tradition demanded without reference to consequence, rather than focused on impact on the environment or outcomes produced (Goldstein 1990). It was dominated in time by job control by patrol officers, especially as the unionization movement gained strength within big-city policing. In the last ten years, an accreditation movement has arisen, organized to increase police status and insulation from lawsuits. It has been argued that accreditation procedures will achieve the long sought for status and respect accorded other professions. Calls for civilian review boards and increased accountability to the public continue to appear and fade, but they also contribute to dynamic pressures on policing to change. These calls for reform usually are touched off by a media-amplified event such as a shooting, beating, or spike in crime, especially homicide.

So began a series of dominolike alterations, elaborations, and transformations that altered the surface features of policing, not the deep and entrenched modes of police work that remained much as they had been for some sixty-plus years since the "professional reform movement." The pressures for change that have emerged in the last twenty to thirty years have been in part internal and in part precipitated by external changes.

## Pressures for Change

The professional model of policing, a kind of surrogate for careful thinking about its components, is featured in every textbook on criminology, criminal justice, and police administration. It has been radically shaped in the past twenty to thirty years, and it is perhaps misleading even now as an ideal type of characterization of the broad features of Anglo-American policing (reviewed in chapter 3).

The period from the end of World War II until the midsixties was a quiet period in American society, and policing changed little. The revolutionary riots of the sixties and the antiwar protests of the early seventies were stimuli to many changes in policing, perhaps best seen in the themes of community policing, increased education of officers, and a reduction in the overt use of violence. These themes concern reducing social distance from publics, especially minority communities or, more specifically, people of color; creating partnerships in the control of crime and disorder; reducing hierarchy; and increasing flexibility in tactics and uses of resources, both public and private (see Trojanowicz and Buqueroux 1994). But these issues are less salient to the narrative developed here than the impact of the eighties on management and businesslike practices in American policing.

A number of external political and economic pressures forced change upon American policing following 1980, the most significant of which were the dramatic collapse of the economy, high interest rates, and the mounting awareness of the success of the Japanese model of business enterprise (Forst and Manning 1999: 72–77). Large city budgets were devastated, and in Detroit, police were laid off. These pressures, combined, were wed with privatization pressures, public-private partnerships for providing security in semipublic places, and the glorification of the "wisdom of the market" in allocating public trust and confidence. Neoliberal thinking associated with privatization, deregulation, "outsourcing" of previously restricted public functions, and decentralization of functions became seductively acceptable, in part because of the promise of reduced taxes and costs. With these external constraints, as crime figures rose and public concern increased, a variety of inconsistent reforms and changes within the American police occurred. State and municipal budgets, and with them the police budgets, shrank, as did public confidence. There were internal changes of a modest sort within policing. Some changes in education and diversity slightly altered the culture within police forces. There was a new awareness of the virtues, in times of economic distress, of management, of careful planning and budgeting, of proper use of "human resources," and of high-tech information technology designed to facilitate and make more efficient the work of the organization.

Recent changes in policing, as in other public-sector agencies, are in part stimulated by these market-driven ideas about public service. Although what the police do in theory is endlessly elastic, they are now expected be more sensitive to "the customer" (this being a ghostly figure that sometimes means the good citizens who support and value the police in general, sometimes means those who are victims of crime and their families, and sometimes means the criminals and villains they target for arrest and surveillance). They are also expected to "compete" for a market share (Moore 1997) of the security-providing business. New forms of third-party policing were recognized and the overlap in functions noted (Bayley and Shearing 1996), even as the movement to privatize more of the public functions gained momentum (Jones and Newburn 1998).

Policing is presently converted into a business by way of new and rather crude rhetoric, snappy epigrams such as "we are changing the way we do business." Police chiefs are called "chief executive officers" (Metropolitan Washington, D.C., website 2002). They are smart managers, leading lean and fit organizations. The vocabulary of the marketplace and of private security has penetrated the rhetoric of public policing. Here, I include in addition to vague notions of "customer service" and "value for money," auditing for efficient use of resources, "smart technologies," and "information services" (as well as ideas long abandoned in business such as Total Quality Management and Quality Circles). These slogans are often made public by a media office and media spokespersons that react to crime events and explain them as well as being proactive in promoting the accomplishments of the police (Mawby 2002). The police are expected, in the absence of a product, market, or measures of quality, to be more efficient.[6] In many respects, they avoid the onus of inefficiency by elevating their role in crime control, something of a time-tested rhetorical strategy. If crime decreases, as it did in the 1990s, crime reduction can be attributed to and accepted by police on the basis of their own flawed statistics (Kelling and Coles 1996; Bratton 1998; Manning 2001a; Blumstein and Wallman 2000). The rise in crime since the turn of the century has never been attributed by the media to police failures, incompetence, inadequate practices, or malfeasance. If police practices had eradicated crime, why does it rise and fall in spite of their touted best efforts and practices? Bear in mind that what is said and what is done are rarely connected in organizational life, and invoking the rhetoric of efficiency is no exception to this rule.

The present pressures and urging of the police to somehow be more efficient and effective, with no recognition of the irrelevance of those matters absent definitions and measurement of them, has been a burden of the twentieth-century urban police. The public police have long sought technological solutions to their vexing problems but are now faced by the transition into newer forms of control that are yet another form of undigested pressure to change. These include video surveillance, simulation, and anticipation. These new forms reproduce in other surface features the same empty rhetoric of control and security with no evidence of their efficacy. They imply increasing concern about the power of information technologies to scan, gather, and digest information about tastes, choices, lifestyles, and other matters seen traditionally as "private."[7] Representative of these trends are the various screens by which communication is mediated—monitors, video cameras, webcams, and mobile cameras linked to satellite systems (Crawford 1998). In Boston during the Democratic National Convention, cameras were trained on various strategic sites, entrances, and exits (*Boston Globe,* July 2004). These were in addition to the already abundant hidden cameras that are trained on buildings, citizens, and waterways in Boston itself (*Globe,* July 2004). These cameras were complemented by "smart machines" that read the irises and eye blinks of frequent business flyers at Logan Airport (*Globe,* August 2004). The Metropolitan Washington, D.C., police now have a contract with "Axis" to provide

> video feeds from various locations around the District of Columbia to the MPDC's Synchronized Operations Command Complex via a series of digital security cameras. Using a video link, the cameras send the video feed to . . . video servers, which in turn seamlessly relay the video images to the command center at Police Headquarters.

(What will be done with these seamless feeds, how they will be analyzed, stored, coded, or reproduced and for what purpose, is not noted at the website.)

While government shrinks or is hollowed of some functions, and increasingly includes a network of semiprivate contractual arrangements, policing as a function, both public and private, is growing in size and budgets (Bogard 1996; Staples 1997; Lyons 1999; Ericson and Haggerty 1997; Garland 2000; Johnston and Shearing 2003). This development has been escalated to a previously unknown degree after September 11, 2001. The creation of the Transportation Security Agency (TSA) and the creation of the Homeland Security Agency are two of the dramatic and visible changes associated with semiprivatizing security functions. The idea that policing is a service is making its way across the Atlantic as well as in this country. The Royal Ulster Constabulary is now the Police Service of North Ireland. The Toronto police are now the Metropolitan Toronto Police Service. These euphemisms have several functions for the police. They suggest that the police are flexible and market oriented, thus able to shift foci and direction to improve their service; they suggest having a market orientation to clientele rather than being a distant coercive force; and they conceal the violence and the obligation of the police to jail, physically constrain, confine, and control known "dangerous groups." The extent to which policing has been reformed, fundamentally recast in this fashion, remains an empirical question.[8] These developments, in short, suggest the ongoing shaping of demand for police services and their complexity.

## Management in Policing

The developments of modern management, especially since World War II, had little effect on policing until the last twenty years or so, as suggested above in the overview of externally sourced pressures to change. That is not to say no change has occurred. While policing was metaphorically sleeping—or, perhaps more accurately, burdened with a series of quasi-revolutionary movements in cities and rising official crime figures—a series of management-oriented books argued for innovations that were introduced in time to policing.[9] To some degree, these changes were reflected in new management courses, seminars, and short courses held at police institutes (Southern Police Institute, Southwestern Law Enforcement Institute, and the Law Enforcement Institute at Sam Houston) around the country. The Kennedy School of Harvard in the Reagan era dominated management discourse in policing with a series of seminars, publications, and promotional announcements funded and supported by the National Institute of Justice within the Department of Justice (DOJ). Broader ideas about policing were also advanced—ideas that added to the abilities traditionally claimed by police chiefs management skills, public leadership qualities, pride of purpose, and a somewhat more far-sighted grasp of organizational change and adaptation. Police chiefs now claimed status honor as managers, CEOs, and responsible public leaders in addition to well-accepted notions that police chiefs had command and control at all times over their widespread, ecologically displaced officers; had diverse, intimate, and close knowledge of their workers' duties (and their mistakes, errors, and frivolities); could alter practices and policies at the stroke of a pen; and maintained full awareness of their obligations and duties (see Mastrofski 1998 for a sympathetic alternative view). Ironically, there were continued calls for policing to develop more democratic work environments, be less punitive and harsh, permit innovation and challenges from "the bottom," and lead in a consultative manner (Guyot 1991). In some ways, community policing is an attempt to reshape police organizations into less tightly integrated, hierarchical, closed, and secretive organizations even while highlighting crime control.

These developments brought to police attention basic innovations in management that had been in progress for the previous ten-plus years in private industry: zero-based budgeting, management by objectives, mission statements, total quality management and quality circles, and decentralization of decision making and budgeting. Police innovators also sought to define police ethics and to train the trainers to raise awareness of ethical issues. As in many other matters, and like "country music," policing is at least a generation behind the cutting edges that are touted in the slick magazines of business, the *Wall Street Journal* et al. This conservatism is not a function of denials or ignorance but rather of the sacred nature of the social organization of policing and its devotion to the notion of rank-determined actions and choices, harsh, punitive management style, and the myth of command and control.

The police are, however, acutely aware of the neoliberal cant of market-driven, efficient service provision. While the period prior to the 1980s had been rich in research innovations and guided and evaluated projects (Manning 1979), this research-rich tradition was abandoned in the Reagan years. Violent crime and its control became thematic (Moore, et al. 1984). In time, the popularity of the term "community policing" meant that this label was applied to anything and everything pertaining to local policing sponsored by the federal governments during the Clinton years. Almost the same could be said about innovations in local policing carried out across the country, many of which included acquiring and using military weapons and tactics and training in making violent interventions (Kraska and Kappeler 1998). While community policing is a broad-based reform movement, in many respects it is simply an effort to reduce social distance between the police and their respectable, supportive publics.[10]

## Community-Oriented Policing and the "COPS" Office

The Clinton years, however, changed policing and policing research significantly. The Clinton Crime Control and Safe Streets Law of 1994 was the most significant recent source of pressure for change, and it was backed by vast resources. Although it masked the kinds of changes and the way they were integrated into the ongoing routines of police work, much like Law Enforcewment Assistance Administration (LEAA) before it in the late sixties and early seventies, the crime bill spilled resources to police organizations for which they were ill prepared. The Community-Oriented Police Services Agency (COPS) was created within the Department of Justice and given a huge budget that by 2003 had exhaled some $8 billion. Although the ostensible aim was broad, including evaluating community policing, sponsoring programs, training, and partnerships with industry and universities, and supplying direct and indirect salary support, the strategy quickly became one of pushing money out the door.

This was done via small grants and programs but featured a thematic well loved by the media. This was the theme captured in the promise to increase the number of police officers "on the street" by one hundred thousand.[11] It was also claimed in the early nineties by the COPS office that community policing would reduce "fat organizations," making them "lean," reducing the number of ranks, increasing decentralized operations, and spreading the availability of officers on the street. A brilliant political coup, it was reduced in the end to a paper exercise rather than a "body count." Claims were made on the basis of some evidence that these monies reduced crime (Zhao and Lovrich 2003). The effort was a significant aspect of the politics of law and order; it augmented police budgets for brief, focused projects, raised salaries, and perhaps lifted morale and the horizon of expectations for police of themselves. Police chiefs supported a democratic presidential candidate, Bill Clinton, in 1996 for the first time in recent memory.

## Recent Research-Based Innovations in Policing

In general, external and internal innovations do not cohere, and they arise in spurts and apparent innovative outbursts such as the announcement of a new program or policy. The resistance of policing to deep change while it claims modern scientific status is but one of the anomalies of the last ninety years or so. While the big movement and trendy options in policing—community policing, tactical crackdowns, and problem-solving policing—have been much featured, they are tactical in nature, and are combined in various ways in police departments across this country. Crime mapping and crime analysis combine scientific and information-technology notions in creative ways and are recognizable practices, and because they are public and managerial in character, can be observed in action and evaluated by independent criteria. They are not programs so much as specific information-based practices.

## Management Innovation

Technologically driven innovations are in apparent abundance and are striking in their relative superficiality. Here are some found in the Anglo-American[12] policing world. The police are

- laying out longer-range planning schemes and short-term goals and objectives and exhibiting greater awareness of the need for detailed and manageable plans for crisis management. This includes developing written and public plans covering many aspects of both strategic and day-to-day or tactical operations and establishing sets of goals and objectives as a framework for comparing progress toward goals and as the basis for routine assessment and richly rhetorical mission statements. Some have considered making formal the ethical principles and value premises of policing for use especially in training. This theme has been elevated in importance by the establishment of the Homeland Security agency in the federal government and by fears of terrorism.
- acknowledging publicly the limits of local democratic policing in regard to monitoring, tracking, or investigating terrorism. This includes resisting federal urgings to investigate or interview people from Middle Eastern cultures (excluding Jews and Israelis), sharing and exchanging data, and engaging in high policing (Brodeur 1983) and national security–related activities (Thacher 2005; Erickson, Carr, and Herbert 2006).
- assembling more integrated databases and systems to guide personnel deployment. This may include adopting software and geocoded databases and computer-assisted dispatching (CAD) data that facilitate crime analysis and crime mapping. Tactical deployment may include using short-term efforts directed to identified problems, e.g., street dealing of drugs, panhandling and the home-

less, jaywalking, and monitoring pornographic outlets, or "operations" based on longer-term, carefully considered problem solving.

• adopting tools for career assessment and monitoring to identify high-risk officers and guide supervisors in their tasks.

• funding a modest internal research capacity. Police now feature research and development units, some of which innovate rather than produce routine reports. These include assessments of programs and projects, and reporting some results of this research in a publicly accessible fashion.

• supporting more explicit public relations policies, personnel, and offices. This is designed to communicate with media and the public routinely and in a non–crime-focused as well as in a crisis modality. This effort may include use of newsletters, public relations firms, and press releases as well as designated sworn or nonsworn media officers and media offices. Some police departments have institutionalized communication channels for publics to contact police, such as providing business cards, e-mail addresses, and voice mail for uniformed officers as well as for police to contact villains, victims, or witnesses on a case-by-case basis. Most large urban departments have introduced programs to target groups, neighborhood associations, corporations, and other governmental agencies (Mawby 2002).

• developing some information-based operational infrastructures. This includes transforming management information systems into networks linking electronically created and sustained databases; making these networks accessible wirelessly; and seeking integration of various nonlinked (typically) paper databases such as criminal records, juvenile records, CAD data, and social facts about neighborhoods (Dunworth 2000).

• increasing civilianization in part as a result of the information-based systems of management. Such a complex infrastructure cannot be managed by officers merely finding a niche. It requires hiring support groups such as computer specialists, consultants in information needs, and experts who repair, smile at, and replace outdated equipment. The present composition of police departments shows about 27–30 percent of their employees are civilians (Reaves and Goldberg 2000 survey). Using internal electronic communications devices such as e-mail, visuals guided by Power

Point, and videos is a parallel development made possible by this emergent infrastructure.

- deploying resources briefly to achieve a given aim, program, or policy. A variety of new tactics, such as the many associated with community policing, have raised questions about the effects of changing the dominant paradigm and strategies of reactive policing based on nineteenth-century ideas.
- innovating in thinking about crimes that are planned, politically imagined, organized, and belief based, such as terrorism and other threats to homeland security. This has been the result of massive infusions of money through federal and state-based grants.

Each of these examples is built upon a core of information processing. They operate, however, according to a structure, strategies, and values largely unchanged since the 1920s. There have been no structural changes, setting aside computer-assisted dispatch (itself a means), since the mid-nineteenth century when detective work was added. The rest are add-ons to the basic model developed by Sir Robert Peel prior to 1829—the model featuring reactive, uniformed, visible, full-time patrol.

Although each can be adopted in a force as a unique program, or combined with any of the nine others, they all feature a few key points that define their frugal purchase on change:

- They are based on data gathered and analyzed in addition to that generated directly by police calls for service.
- They tend toward intelligence-based actions, or use knowledge gathered prior to the events reacted to or the programs mounted.
- They call upon various levels of abstraction that rise above "street smarts," or what every street officer knows, involving concepts, tables, figures, maps, statistic above the descriptive level, and in some cases rather elaborate modes of evaluation (Weisburd, et al. 2003; Braga, et al. 1999; Manning 2003: 220–28).
- They rely on the diffusion and distribution of information of a public sort rather than the usual mode of highly secretive and personally retained oral knowledge of the craft. An example of this is the compstat process and related meetings described briefly below.
- They suggest a temporal dimension to problems and their solution rather than the "clear the call and get back into service" mentality that dominates the urban patrol officers' perspective on the job.

- They suggest that policing may properly be about order and ordering rather than about crime control in the narrow sense. This does not mean that the two are not deeply intertwined—only that they are related but independent dimensions. Crime is a specific feature of particular places and groups in urban areas (Sampson and Raudenbush 1999).

- They require, or perhaps demand, that random patrol as the chief public means of policing, its total hegemony in resource allocation terms, and the related "blue mouse syndrome," chasing after calls for service, be questioned as to results or value.

- They clash rather dramatically with the ideology of the police—the view that the real work is individualistic and entrepreneurial, carried out alone, largely undirected, by an isolated patrol officer doing the job, making unreviewed, low-visibility decisions and commanding his or her turf.

These innovations have a similar basis in a reorientation of policing toward some manifestation of results and away from reiteration of ritual positions, theme, and focus, as noted in the introduction. They do not all precipitate the same kinds of changes in organizations because they stimulate power struggles among ranks, segments, and specialties. I am focusing in this book on the impact of combining crime mapping with crime analysis. This combination may induce broadly based problem solving, but it need not. Community policing, as a tactical matter, may or may not utilize crime mapping or crime analysis. Problem solving and other generalized approaches are far too vague to have direct impact on policing. Each of the three organizations studied announced its commitment to community policing, but the reality of how this was done varied quite extensively (see chapters 5–7). They intended to create a crime mapping and analysis capacity. The icon for this was the imputed success of the NYPD's compstat program.

## Compstat

Because the NYPD's version of this was the first, has had consistent favorable publicity, and influenced other departments to imitate it in some fashion, compstat requires some extended description.[13] "Compstat" was a filename given to a program developed to compae crime data and became a general term for the meetings and process of crime analysis based on mapping. Although it began in the NYPD, it is now a general term.

The most celebrated example of CM/CA is the NYPD's compstat meeting and process. It was created by William Bratton and his inner circle of management people and his advisors, including George Kelling and others. Bratton's description is candid and includes a series of pressures and innovations that lay behind the emergence of the compstat process: Jack Maple's memory for detail, use of maps, focus on crime spurts, and commanding presence; Bratton's wish to hold precinct commanders accountable for their performance in crime control; an officer's development of a crude software program to compare crime statistics (Bratton 1998: 233–39); Bratton's linking crime control suppression to rewards and promotion; and his ability to mobilize and reward patrol officers with cars, radios, semiautomatic weapons, and smart uniforms. The meetings were the high point of the vertically integrated process of gathering data, displaying them on a large screen in an auditorium-meeting room, and calling precinct commanders to comment on crime, disorder, and other trends. The NYPD process is the model for other processes of this sort, now widely used (Walsh 2001; Weisburd, et al. 2003). The features emphasized, as well as when and how the process is run, vary widely (Weisburd et al. 2003), but the meetings tend to be arenas for the display of crime-control tactics.

The NYPD's version, the stimulus to emulation and diffusion, was described by Kelling 1995: 9–10). According to Kelling, the NYPD's versions was a three-hour, twice-weekly meeting mandatory for all seventy-six precinct commanders, superchiefs, deputy commissioners, and borough chiefs. It was held in the command center of the NYPD, and a lectern was placed in front of a large projection screen facing a U-shaped arrangement of tables. At the side of the U sat the four or five precinct commanders and the detective lieutenants from the borough that would be presenting. At the end of the U sat the closest associates of the commissioner. Around the edges sat the representatives of schools, district attorney's offices, and the parole department, along with members of the NYPD's special units and support staff. Outside observers stood at the edges of the meeting. The meetings began with presentation of data, including complaints, overtime, and unfounded service calls. The display included the precinct commander's picture and his background information.

The meetings were run by the late deputy commissioner of the NYPD, Jack Maple, who set the tone and pace of the meeting by his questioning. From the descriptions rendered by a number of observers (cited above), the meetings were often harsh, accusatory, and embarrassing to those grilled. The focus was on current crimes, although quality-of-life matters were discussed. Descriptions suggest that some deconstruction was going on, e.g., of the nature of the relationships in reported rapes (Kelling 1995: 10) and of types of burglaries, and also included the pattern analysis of robberies (mode, descriptions of suspects, number of offenders, etc.), for example (Kelling 1995: 10). The assessment tended to be quick, querulous, and concrete with respect to the simple character of the crime, and an implicit pressure was mounted to do something, to have done something, or to plan to do something quickly.

The claims for this meeting and related data gathering and police response are uniformly uncritical (see especially Kelling 1995; Kelling and Coles 1996). Three monographs (Henry 2001; Silverman 1999; McDonald 2002) assume, without explicating the logic of the process, that it served to reduce officially reported crime. The examples given are either programmatic descriptions with quotations from police taking responsibility (with no other evidence given); ad hoc single instances (Kelling 1995: 11); hypothetical examples (Henry 2001); or post hoc, ergo propter hoc reasoning (McDonald 2003; Henry 2001). The compstat meetings have stimulated wide interest, been given credit for crime reductions (Manning 2001a), been diffused widely, and been seen to fit well with the trends in management and rationalizing discussed above. They are also well suited to the NYPD's crime-fighting rhetoric, police culture, and command from the top down, as well as to the motives and rhetoric of uniformed officers in particular, and are highly consistent with the zero-tolerance, disorder-oriented ideas about policing partially adopted from the Wilson and Kelling (1982) broken windows article (Moore 2003: 480–83). While the idea is described as strategic and is associated with broad organizational-change and transformation-management ideas (Bratton 1998; Kelling 1995; Silverman 1999; Weisburd, et al. 2003; Willis, Mastrofski, and Weisburd 2004, 2007), Moore (2003) argues quite correctly that it was a crime-focused means to pressure performance, reward conventional police tactics (arrest-based coercion), and hold precinct commanders responsible. The primary thrust has been internal, with compstat being used as a management tool, and the claims for crime control a growing cottage industry nurtured by the media.

The question of the research reported here is not about the environmental impact of the practices, nor their focus per se.[14] It is an analysis of how a technology, including the meeting, the talk, the ecology, and the information-processing equipment, was understood to be working to enhance and advance policing. The research in two organizations did not entail observations of the "trickle-down" effect of crime analysis and mapping on patrol work because the meetings were not mobilized. In Boston, the focus of this research was on the rationalities demonstrated in the meetings by those attending, the solutions and approaches offered, and the justifications or accounts that were used to discuss the options available.

## Conclusion

Policing as action is a dance to music and as a set of processes is a configuration. It manifests much rationality that arises as situations require responses. The introduction of information technologies has played an important part in the changes in the police dance steps in the last thirty years. These technologies are part of the rationalizing process now ongoing, perhaps unevenly, within the context of the "professional model" in American policing. This model is the background against which recent changes in management rhetoric and market-based pressures to change should be seen. This book features crime mapping combined with crime analysis (CM/CA) as a source of organizational change in policing. CM/CA is an information-based innovation, and has been associated with the NYPD's 1995-96 development of the ingenious compstat meetings and associated process. This background is needed to understand the examples found in chapters 5-7, which describe the stylistic efforts of three police departments to develop a crime mapping/crime analysis capacity and to encourage the management-level officers, the featured dancers, to learn, rehearse, and carry out a new dance and new steps.

# 3

# The Music and Its Features

## Introduction

The various rationalities that have emerged around information technology and its effects on policing are generally seen in relation to a model adopted from the German sociologist Max Weber. These are historically grounded abstract ideas about what bureaus are meant to accomplish and by what means. Yet, in many respects, the traditional police bureau, which combines personal loyalties—loyalties to friends, kin, former partners, and other work associates—with a rigid hierarchical ordering of ranks and role obligations, is a special case of a compromised bureaucracy in the modern world. It does not easily conform to generalities derived from other organizations such as industries, academe, or loosely integrated dot.com-like aggregations. It is not unique, a special case of exceptionalism, because it conforms to the general model of a service organization with a concentration of efforts, resources, and personnel "on the ground" or at the "sharp end," such as schools, welfare organizations, and the military.

However, the past thirty years have seen a number of changes in policing, the most important of which are CM/CA, problem-solving policing, community policing, and short-term tactical crime-attack suppression modes of policing. At the end of the previous chapter, I suggested that semiotics, the science of signs, is a useful tool for unpacking the significance of the maps used in police work. Maps and crime tables do not speak for themselves. They must be interpreted in the situations where they are used and according to the common-sense assumptions brought to them. What results is occasioned usage, not a universal, repetitive, and redundant display. This view of maps and the role of IT is the necessary background for understanding the case studies.

This chapter considers the definition of policing in general and Anglo-American policing in particular. It then introduces the concepts of mandate, contingency, theme, and focus with reference to Anglo-American policing, and describes features of policing in the United States. These features provide the music, organizational structure, mandate, and license. They produce metaphorically the traditional dance. The relevance of this exercise in definition, revealed more clearly in the case studies, is that the requirements of democratic policing as a type of policing with a long and distinguished history and traditions are moral and political, not solely pragmatic. Much that can be done is not done and should not be done. This is why asking pragmatic questions like "What works?" or arguing that something works absent a clear rationale for the process by which its goal is achieved and for its moral and political consequences, an argument begging for a pragmatic approach, is specious and misleading. Experimental method, for example, is stripped of moral meaning and can be used to design effective gas ovens as easily as it might capture the impact of arrest on reducing domestic violence. What works, as the history of fascist and totalitarian societies such as Nazi Germany or Stalin's Russia show, is unacceptable in Anglo-American democracies. While external pressures may lead to costume and surface changes, and organizations can change costumes, if the style and steps are the same, little change will actually have occurred. Dancers cannot create new dances if their music remains, and their repertoire is restricted to military waltz steps, tempos, and rhythms. What is the current dance of the police?

## Definition of Democratic Anglo-American Policing

### Definitional Problems Arising

An unfortunate tradition in police studies has been to take the definition of policing for granted and to move to examples, analysis, or proscriptive statements, e.g., policing should do this or that. Even careful summaries of the literature avoid analytic definitions in large part and are organized topically rather than theoretically (see, for example, the chapters on policing by Newburn in Newburn 2004, and by Reiner in Maguire, Morgan, and Reiner 2002). This approach leads to either quoting a previous definition, usually from Bittner (1990), claiming that policing is the situational distribution of force as needed (paraphrase), or to drawing on clichés like policing is law enforcement (only partially), policing is peace keeping and law enforcement (yes, and more), or policing sustains law and order (these are distinct and separate entities) in a society. These are misleading glosses that overlook several important facts:

- There are many *types of policing* worldwide: Islamic-religious, authoritarian, democratic, Asian, and continental types (Bayley 1985; R. I. Mawby 2004; Dammer and Fairchild 2006). Even these types are blurred and reshaped by economic and political developments such as wars of conquest (Iraq); genocide in Bosnia and Kosovo; private war-making corporations (Singer 2003); the exporting of community policing as a commodity (Brogden and Nijhar 2005;) and transnational policing (Bowling 2006; Scheptyki 2000; Deflem 2002).

- All *policing systems* are divided to some degree by their interest both in ordering populations, especially marginal, feared, or newly acquired populations, and in maintaining national security. The former requires an overt respect for and constraint by law, and the latter obviates these concerns, trumps them in fact, on the basis of the expediency of protecting national security at all costs.

- Two functions of policing, democratic or low policing and high policing (Brodeur 1983), remain in contest, especially in democratically elected régimes. However, while police in theory possess rather wide and sometimes secret powers, democratic societies have sought, except in times of extreme crisis, to limit police powers via law, civil traditions, and supervisory mechanisms such as commissions, special judicial inquiries, and civilian complaint-processing systems. The police possess far more power and authority than they exercise.

- Policing, as a form of control via sanctions, includes many forms, public and private, and ranges from the most passive (guard-station screen watchers) to the most proactive (guerilla forces, hired mercenaries) (see Wakefield 2003; Button 2002; Johnston 1993; Johnston and Shearing 2003). While there are reasons for restricting the definition of policing to publicly funded state-based public police, this distinction is increasingly difficult to maintain, and perhaps is misleading.

- Formal, full-time policing is always in conflict with other forms of social control such as self-help or revenge (Black 1983); associational and part-time policing of groups; and vigilantes, rangers, and *posse comitatus* groups. There are also conflicts between public and private policing (Forst and Manning 1999; Rigakos 2002).

- In times of crisis, the mandate of the domestic police expands to include high policing and secret operations, as in the cases of antiterrorism efforts. This flexibility is itself characteristic of democratic policing.

- Centralized democratic policing differs from decentralized democratic policing (Bordua 1968; Bayley 1992) because of the delegation of security to armed national forces under central authority.

## Requisites for a Definition of Democratic Policing

The police are naturally dramatic, violent, and visible. They easily become targets and representatives of order, danger, and mystery. They are a quasi-sacred entity in a secular society. They inspire awe, distance, deference, and feelings that differ from those generally felt. They mark the boundaries of civilized order as well as being boundary markers themselves, standing between the known and the less known or unknown. The police are unique as a domestic organization, more like the army in some sense than like other civil servants. They are violent, constrained, politically important actors, and organizers of collective responses, and are constrained to act in the interests of others more often than their own. They have enormous power in the form of legal resources; weapons, both fatal and nonfatal; vehicles, some specialized such as armored and insulated personnel carriers; present and reserve personnel; and agreements for mutual aid up to and including federal troops. They have dramatic potential and actuality, and vibrancy in the context of the politics of the modern democratic state. The drama of policing, it seems, requires both opposition and negation to survive without being submerged in revenge, or anarchy (Black 1976). A dominant and violent police force, if it becomes too dominant, is a threat to a democratic society. This implies also that violence or force can be and may be applied as needed, but the degree of force should be moderate and moderated to the minimum required to control. This of course is the abiding problem of policing in a democracy.

Liang's historically grounded work on the development of European policing is provocative (1992: 2) and sound. He argues that democratic policing should be legalistically guided; should focus on individuals, not groups and their politics; should eschew terrorism, counterterrorism, and torture; and should strive to ensure minimal damage to civility. He argues, in addition, that marginal types of policing highlight and sustain what is required for democratic policing. These marginal types of policing—high or political policing that focuses on what is termed state security (Brodeur 1983); self- or voluntary policing; and counter and parallel policing (such as private security and regulatory agencies)—are much needed. It would appear that the existence of these sustain the tension that permits the general strategies of democratic police to work over time. The democratic police, as noted above, do not hold and have never held a monopoly on legitimate force. They hold it in law, but states within the United States vary widely in respect to the conditions under which self-defense is permitted, and differences in firepower are only known when the police display automatic weapons, riot shields, and bulletproof vests in shows of force. It is the very absence of this monopoly, among the other features noted by Liang, that makes a police "democratic." If we think of police organizations as carrying out their mandate via strategies and tactics of allocating resources, police have a repertoire that has served them well. These successful democratic tactics, according to Liang (1992: 14–17), include using potential and actual direct violence, employing the tactics of divide and conquer, using lies and deceit, and preserving sustaining myths to ground their legitimacy. These have worked, he argues, since the early part of the nineteenth century. It should be added that the use of dramaturgical rhetoric (selective presentation of mission, values, and core functions in public) as a presentational strategy (Manning 2005) and the creation of symbolic assailants (enemy others who represent a danger or risk to the society, e.g., "terrorists," "criminals," and "drug users") incorporate the powerless into compliance.

Policing certainly has three primary elements that can be seen as variables in cross-cultural work (Mawby 1999: 20): their structure or pattern of organization (centralized versus decentralized, focused on national security or on more local concerns); their function and routines; and their legitimacy. As Bayley and Shearing point out (1996), the source of the legitimacy and the sponsorship may vary. More importantly, perhaps, is that distinction that makes a difference: the public police can employ the criminal sanction and enter cases into the legal system. This power is unavailable in general to citizens in Anglo-American societies, private police, and other organizations, although the law can be mobilized via civil suits. As Black points out correctly, the mobilization of law in the criminal framework is reactive, and the police in general are ambivalent about enforcing "victimless" crimes (Black 1976), while the civil law system is open to litigation and provides remedies. In analogous fashion, high policing, policing concerning national security or imagined threats or plots against the state, since there is no victim and no crime without clear evidence, is a task treated gingerly by local police (see Thacher 2005; Erickson, Carr, and Herbert 2006).

## A Definition of Police

There is no generally accepted definition of police or policing, although many important works imply such (Bordua and Reiss 1966; Bordua 1967; Reiss and Bordua 1967), and a few definitions have been advanced (Cain 1979; Bayley 1985; Reiner 2002). In most research and writing the definition is assumed to have a pungent clarity and unassailable obviousness.

Consider this definition of police: democratic police, constituted of many diverse agencies, are authoritatively coordinated, legitimate, and trusted organizations that stand ready to apply force, up to and including fatal force, in a legitimate territory to sustain political ordering. They accomplish their aims via surveillance, tracking, investigating, and monitoring incongruities.[1]

Ordering and trust are interconnected. Ordering can be produced by force or fraud, violence, and coercion, or it can result from social processes for which the police, for example, are merely surrogates. "Ordering" is a fundamentally political matter, and arises when questions about trust and order come to the fore. The police represent trust, assess trustworthiness, and are expected to be trustworthy. They are surrogates for the rest of us in assessing risk and trust. Thus, they are always vulnerable to allegations of corruption, violence, and the rest— they are expected to meet an imagined higher standard although the question, higher than what? is left unexamined. "Political ordering" has no fundamental definition but rather a contextual and historical one. It arises when the threat of force appears. As Bittner (1990) correctly points out, any action or group from which resistance might be imagined can be the target of policing. This shifting locus of concern, or of symbolic assailants or threats, provides those distractions necessary to avoid the consolidation of power. In summary, democratic police are not neutral, nonpolitical forces absent their own motivations, interests, and ideological readings of events. They employ narrow, self-serving tactics when under threat, but often compromise in the interest of maintaining public trust and respect. This spirit of compromise is best revealed by close study of the practices of the police in crisis situations—demonstrations, strikes, parades, riots, disasters, revolution, and war. It is in these situations that the absence of accountability, when one organization acts on behalf of another one, is most visible.

A powerful exception to the usual practices of democratic policing occurs when it is exported by force or conquest. This situation reveals the powerful unstated limits on domestic policing in the "home territories" that do not obtain in the course of disciplining resident colonials, whether in Latin America, Asia, the Indian subcontinent, or Africa. In these situations—for example, the German police and army in East Africa (Strachan 2004), the British police and army in the Sepoy rebellion, and the everyday policing organized by the British in Ireland, India, and the remainder of the empire (Enloe 1973, 1980a, 1980b)—policing differs. When the military police police nations postwar, they cannot sustain the military tactics of "total victory"—occupy the territory, eradicate the enemy's will to fight, and monitor outbreaks—because such tactics produce insurgencies and rebellion. In these situations, the line among war, civil rebellion, crime, and "lawlessness" become blurred, and extreme measures are often taken and concealed. Policing in colonies is guided by very different assumptions and practices. The British historian of the empire, David Carradine (2001), has shown in text and remarkable pictures how the empire was based on coopting the others, people of color, into acceptance of the empire through granting titles, giving honors and awards, staging elaborate rituals that mimicked those of the "host" country, and so on. These tactics were only manifested in high drama and scale in the countries of peoples of color; such was not deemed as necessary in areas of the empire where the native populations were sparse, removed, or killed off early. In effect, the hierarchy of the British nation was reproduced grandly abroad, but the limits on the resident colonials' actions were those of colonial powers, not of domestic ordering.

This abstract discussion is essential to understanding the unexplicated limits on surveillance, tracking and watching, spying, and intelligence-led policing. Democratic policing strives to be just and to avoid producing more inequalities. This discussion places the changes in American policing that have resulted from the introduction of IT, especially CM/CA, in theoretical and historical context. It also underscores the importance of comparison, historical, cross-cultural, and national, and the emerging horizon of possibilities for change that such policing exhibits.

The progress of rationalizing in policing, of which the later chapters are cases in point, must be seen in light of the subtle, less visible developments in policing in the United States and, to a lesser degree, in the U.K. Now, arguably, police are constrained by their successes in shaping, selling, sustaining, and obfuscating the utility of the idea of random patrol and responsiveness and are, as a result, increasingly engaged publicly in media stylistics (R. C. Mawby 2002) and demand management.[2] In many respects the pressure of heeding calls for service retards any other program that requires time and resources. This restraint is amplified by the police unions' insistence on tight job control and control over promotions, hours, and tasks, and their efforts to shape wages. Demand management is discussed in more detail in chapter 3.

## *Contingency, Mandate, Strategy, Tactics, Theme, and Focus*

The shadow of democratic policing in the Anglo-American tradition is present. It is important to consider how the idea of democratic policing shapes rather indirectly the American police mandate, its strategies and tactics as well as its theme and focus (Manning 1997).

All occupations are in some way directed to a fundamental contingency or uncertainty in a social system. This is the societal need for which an occupational mandate may be constructed. Uncertainties are matters that are neither soluble by fact (How many officers are on duty at a given time? What time is it? How much money is in the current budget?) nor completely impossible to know (Is there life on Mars? Will terrorists strike the Democratic convention? When will cheap underground oil be exhausted?). Some contingencies are matters that groups seek to control in spite of their universality: sin, disease, property and its continuity, ignorance, and crime or deviance (perhaps more generally social order and formal ordering processes). These are socially developed means of coping with the contingency, not eradicating it. The contingency remains. Occupations that have formed around tasks and roles may claim a right to control the attitude toward that work. However, the mandate (a valid or accepted moral claim to carry out work) and license (delimited tasks and duties) are always in some dynamic tension in a democratic society. The mandate claimed by occupations, the right to define the nature of the work, if validated, leads to further efforts to circumscribe the tasks and duties associated with that validated claim (Hughes 1958). This seeking and validation is a dialectical process. The mandate in effect is an occupation's rendering of the societal contingency, an elaboration of its connection to the central concerns of the society. It is a sign of the moral division of labor as well as the division of tasks and duties in any society. Once a mandate is granted, however, occupations sustain their claims variously—by appeals and control of a market, by association with the sacred and holy remnants thereof in Western industrialized societies—or they can claim expediency: someone needs to do it. The ability of an occupation to control its practices and the costs of its services are indications of its power and authority, or indices of the strength of its mandate. Some occupations rise and gain status, such as computer technician or crime analyst, while others fall in public esteem, such as blacksmith, journalist, or cooper. Other occupations, such as chimney sweep, coal miner, lobsterman, and deep sea fisherman, flutter to the ground like dying leaves in the autumn.

The primary contingency or uncertainty of concern to the police, it might be said, is negative: unwanted risk. They claim to supply security and political ordering in the face of uncertainty. At best, the police rely on the trust of their publics, the publics trust the police, and this trust binding in theory extends to public trust of each other in their civic roles.

To review or summarize this argument, the police mandate, often obscured by crime-control rhetoric, is a validated claim to public trust in this regard, and to a metaphoric license that grants them the right to use fatal force and restricts others from similar violence. The police also select and perhaps have cast upon them a theme. A theme is a matter of how the work is done in general terms. While a contingency might be considered a general analytic aspect of an occupation, a theme refers to how the occupation carries out its tasks and what it does to render its services consumable, needed, and, indeed, necessary. While all professions claim to be of service in some way to the society beyond the virtues of money, and to give more than they receive, policing has touted a responsiveness theme in this last century and has refined it conspicuously. The claim ensconced in the theme is simply that the police are ready to serve at the call of any citizen at any time for virtually any problem. The salience of this theme varies in terms of public definitions in the Anglo-American world, but the public position is much the same. Now, given this contingency, the mandate and license, and the responsiveness theme, the police have narrowed their focus (or strategies and related tactics [how strategies are carried out] of resource allocation —see Manning 1997: 44) to three: random patrol, responding to calls for service, and investigating crime. These are now seen and dramatized in the media and locked in the public mind as the essential sources of "crime control."

The focus of policing—random patrol, investigative work, and response to calls for service—dramatizes the strengths and weaknesses of the professional model by focusing on the theme of responsiveness and actively promoting it with the public. It is possible, of course, to alter the distribution of resources into the strategies that comprise the focus. At present, somewhere between 60 and 80 percent of all police personnel and resources go into patrol, for example, and the distribution between warranted officers and other "civilians" stands at about 27 percent in large U.S. departments (see discussion below of the features of American policing). As organizations grow, they tend to increase their administrative component, and specialized staffs and units, but policing seems to resist this tendency (Maguire 1997).

From the early 1970s on, with the introduction of computer-assisted dispatch, the police encouraged demand via the telephone. In due course, the police were perhaps overly successful in "selling" the idea of demand-led policing to the public, thereby persuading the public that response-to-calls-based policing was both a service and an effective means of controlling crime and criminals. The American version of this persuasion is perhaps seen most clearly and visibly in the way people are encouraged to call 911 via advertising on billboards, television, radio, and other mass media, and on police cars themselves. Because this persuasion makes the overt response to calls the core of the day-to-day work, in fact, while "crime control" is claimed, the police remain "demand-led." The level of demand, uneven as it is in cities, may not constitute a crisis, but because most police are committed publicly to this definition of the job even as they claim to be doing community policing, it matters little whether they are actually, in fact, daily "overloaded" or not. What is central is the power of the idea—that police serve best by rapid responses to calls for service—in the mind of the public, the politicians, and the police. This matter is further discussed in chapter 4, because solutions to the demand issue are linked to crime prevention and to the transformation and rationalizing of policing. This issue of demand management and focus on the incident is a microcosm of modern policing's dilemma. In short, an occupation can expand its mandate through service, but it cannot serve all who call and still retain control of the nature of its work and the obligations entailed in it.

## The Features of Policing

The general features of American policing in this century are a powerful constraint on change (Reiss 1992a), and they are grounded in the mandate forged in the last eighty years or so.[3]

### Size and Its Correlates

Policing in the United States resembles the Anglo-American model with respect to legal authority and its relatively local nature.[4] To summarize these features, we must draw on research. The bulk of the systematic research in the police field concerns white patrol officers in large-city police departments, and little research is available on state or federal police, specialized police and regulators, or rural policing, whether small-town chiefs or county sheriffs, is available (Weisheit, Falcone, and Wells 1996). Little is known still about private policing (Johnston 1993; Jones, Smith, and Newburn 1996; Rigakos 2002; Wakefield 2003).

Public police number approximately seven hundred thousand, but the figure is not precisely known. There are probably about 680,000-plus serving full-time public officers (Bayley 1994; Maguire, et al. 1998). Because definitions are inconsistent—for example, of part-time, reserve, full-time, and sworn officers—because samples of agencies include varying numbers (Maguire, et al. 1998), and because policing functions themselves are left undefined—for example, omitting agricultural, Occupational Safety and Health Administration, and EPA inspectors, but including the investigative officers within the armed services—there is little hope of precision. For example, all law enforcement officers do not carry guns, and all who carry guns are not law enforcement officers. The number of police agencies is also debated. Maguire, et al. argue (1998: 109–10) that a total 21,143 agencies exist in the United States: 14,628 local, 49 state, 3,156 sheriff-headed, 3,280 special agencies, and an estimated 30 federal enforcement agencies. Others have estimated forty-three or more federal specialized agencies, depending on how they are defined, e.g., whether the police carry guns or not (Geller and Morris 1992). Quoting the numbers of public police is misleading, in part because the number of private security officers probably exceeds the number in public employ. Within police organizations, there are many groups employed and their proportion varies as well. The occupation is not the organization. The larger the organization, the more likely it is to have an administrative component composed in part of "civilians." Police organizations are composed of many occupational groups: forensic scientists, computer experts, lawyers, and research and development personnel. Civilians constitute 27 percent of police employees and have increased by 161 percent as a ratio to the population (O'Brien 1996a: 197, cited in Reaves and Goldberg 1996). By tradition, if not by law, the top administrative cadre of a department is composed of sworn officers.

Public policing has uneven entry requirements, training, and qualifications. Police are trained in cohorts in local academies, and formal training can range from a few days to over twenty-six weeks. Training typically involves apprenticeshiplike relationships with field training officers. Hiring and promotional standards vary widely, and are little influenced by educational attainment. Promotions by rank arise when exams or boards are offered. There is no national training center or police college, and no national system of executive or management training, although efforts have been made to certify the quality of policing through accreditation. Police officers above the level of sergeant are autodidacts in the arts of management.

## Police and Politics

Public policing is grounded in local politics and responds to overlapping governmental authority. It enforces a wide range of local, state, and federal laws as well as municipal regulations concerning parking, traffic, and the environment. American policing is shaped by known and applied local law and by highly selected federal and appellate decisions rendered concerning civil liberties and liabilities. It is somewhat "insulated" from the rulings of the courts and of legislatures because of its special authority in the use of violence. The line between violence, coercion, persuasion, and "excess force" and abuse of authority is drawn by custom, not law. Policing powers, de facto, are quite widespread, and are shared among individual citizens, private investigators, citizen self-help groups, private policing agencies, and, occasionally, the military (the National Guard, reserves, and regular forces). The degree of independence of the organization from the "environment," especially the police role in politics, and in political policing or "high politics" (Brodeur 1983), is a central and largely unexplored question in police studies.

While the community policing movement emphasizes benign cooperative actions, public policing organizations remain highly armed, militaristic, violent, and dangerous. The state holds out violence as a means to coerce compliance only if habit and expediency fail. They are expected to use the level of force needed to control a situation, yet not escalate disorder. In practice, little violence is routinely administered (Mastrofski, Reisig, and McCluskey 2002). While police are increasingly heavily armed in America, the absence of visible police coercion is a sign of legitimacy and of the effectiveness of informal controls (Banton 1964; Black 1976). A variety of means to regulate police, to provide remedies for complaints against them, and to review and evaluate their performance have been applied but have never influenced policing long and often have had very short histories.

As Robinson and Scaglion (1987) have argued very persuasively, the emergence of democratic policing is contingent on several developments of unequal significance, including legal specialization, the division of labor, the emergence of a surplus controlled in large part by elites, and the shaping of the modern nation state. As elite dominance took the form of control of government, the police were converted from a local, community-based, kinship-shaped force into an enforcement body whose obligations were defined by more abstract, distant, and formalized rules such as law and religious canons. Consistent with this is the emergence of an ideological canopy that defined police as public and public as police; emphasized their reactive and supportive role, their visible presence (not secret and secretive); and, in effect, emphasized their benign function in ordering society (Robinson and Scaglion 1987). This is itself a reading of the functions of police, and as Bittner (1990) correctly notes, the police occupy a slightly archaic, even quaint, place in modern societies because they are violent and intrusive and value traditional things such as loyalty to group obligations and yet must act violently in the collective interest. It is the belief-based trust in policing as rendered that permits their violence to be seen as secondary to their supportive, nonpolitical, neutral, and nonintrusive style and activities.

## Contradictions Arising

This intellectual proposition can be extended further to note that the fundamental contradictions of policing in democratic societies are thus blurred, obscured, and seen as mere background to the foreground of democratic policing (See Manning 1997: 106–10; Manning 2003: 53–58). These contradictions include policing equally and justly in a highly divided society in which exclusion and marginalization of people of color is omnipresent; being accessible while remaining a secretive, closed, and secret-based organization; acting occasionally quickly on short notice in a militaristic, coordinated fashion to control disorder such as crowds, riots, and demonstrations, while acting as a dispersed, ecologically separated, entrepreneurial, and individualistic set of agents in everyday practice; sustaining order and ordering nonpolitically when the idea of order is fundamentally a political one; and enforcing the law when law enforcement is the least of their duties when time and effort in practice is considered.

As part of their ongoing dramaturgical performance, the police present many contradictory public and private faces, back stage and front stage. Internally, or back stage, the police, especially the command segment, emphasize control and service as central to their mission, but this rhetoric clashes with visible policing practice and the sentiments and concerns of the lower ranks. The basis for compliance to command is a mix of charismatic or "personal" authority based on respect for the individual rather than or in addition to the office held and rational-legal authority based upon expertise and experience. Often, tensions arise between these modes of authority, in part because they are unevenly distributed throughout the organization. Considerable autonomy and conflict exist within each of the divisions (usually patrol, administrative, and investigative), within the segmentalized occupational culture (management, supervision, and lowest ranks), and between civilians and police within the organization. Unionization adds another important source of internal conflict that can further divide ranks. These factors shape the sort of rationalities at play in a given issue (Magenau and Hunt 1989).

## Patrimonial Loyalty and Internal Tensions

On the other hand, the police share understandings about the deeper nature of their work that are nuanced and redefined within the segments. These are such assumptions as the following: we are marginal to the society and misunderstood; people's motives are unclear and they typically deceive, prevaricate, and dissemble to others and themselves; there is little one can do to change society or the police organization; the job is okay but the organization is not (unfair, rigid, punitive, malleable by political forces). As Van Maanen (1973) writes poetically, uniformed patrol officers see themselves as pseudo-kin, identifying with each other, backing each other up on calls, sharing affection and dislike situationally (not consistently), and demonstrating solidarity in rituals such as funerals, roll calls, parades, and action in mass, potentially violent public occasions. Detectives share a slightly more nuanced and less threatened role because they act on behalf of society and its victims, in their crime-clearing practices, appear in supportive roles to most of the public, and appear in court and are granted respect there. The issue of trust reverberates differentially in the segments because while the middle managers seek to be trusted by the "troops" and by top management, top management is oriented more to the external audience than to the rest in the organization. Therefore, they are mistrusted by the rest of the department. The final irony perhaps is that police act to assess trust in others; they are agents for trust assessment in the mass society. They are distrustful, sensitive to incongruities and things out of place, and even of colleagues. They are told and learn that they must trust their "gut" yet are in a constant dialogue with the formal rules (procedures to justify actions taken) of the organization. Their view of themselves as trustworthy extends to other matters as well, such as sustaining this position even in the face of charges of perjury. These shared misunderstandings fill in to provide for each other a façade of solidarity in the face of the contradictions and segmentalization noted above.

The police organization is an odd bureaucracy, quaint in that it combines a rational-legal format with unresolved tensions associated with earlier forms of rational organization. It is often said that the police are a paramilitary bureaucracy, yet they also display features of the rational-legal bureaucracy described by Weber. In the rational-legal organization as an ideal type, specific offices in a stated hierarchy are designated; the occupants are full-time and salaried and consider their work to be a career; the role is specified in detail; the work is defined to be routinized and bound by written procedures and rules; and the occupants act in ways that depersonalize their activities. They serve in a neutral way distinct from the material interests of the organization. Bureaucrats are competent, but under strict control and discipline in accord with the office held (Weber 1947: 329–36). In other respects, the police organization is a patrimonial bureau characterized by alternative features. It is as if it were two organizations living under a single mandate.

In a patrimonial bureau, loyalty is owed to the patron, or the lord, the owner of the land or resources on which the life of the organization is based. The relations are not contractual but personal and are simply renewed yearly or at the will of the patron (Bloch 1961). There is no administrative structure to carry out technically defined duties (such a bookkeeping, records keeping, or supplies acquisition). The cohorts in such arrangements, often called feudal (Bloch 1961), work "absent a code of obligation." Nor do they have stated limits on their private acquisitive activity. These characteristics make the organization ill suited to support the growth of capitalism, especially the absence of a specialized administration. Rules and regulations cannot be salient because the peculiarities of the loyalty vary from person to person in the arena; and there is a tendency to substantive rationality, or situated reaction to the problems, rather than long-term calculative activity. As Weber (1947: 354–55) writes, a wide range of arbitrariness and expressly personal whims characterize the actions of the chief and his staff.

If this pattern of a dualistic organization is applied to policing, we can see that it is in functional terms divided by loyalties based on past friendships, partners, cohorts in the academy, and sponsors and patrons who support younger colleagues' advancement. This causes rule enforcement to be colored by past relationships, personal relations, even kin relations, and by loyalties that obviate the neutral processing of violations; as Weber says, it introduces whimsy and personalistic bases for bureaucratically defined relationships. The blurred line between the office and personal acquisitive activity is seen in the different lines police departments draw concerning second and third jobs, some of which are sponsored by the department and some of which are not. Police departments lack adequate staff and typically groom or train most of the skilled people who work within the organization, such as computer operators and experts in ballistics, finger printing, or the handling and use of weapons of all kinds. The percent of the organization devoted to research and planning is very small in comparison to other organizations. Furthermore, the chief's office, which is the most expertlike ensemble, is constituted by appointments off the list of union rules concerning seniority, and typically includes a few people with higher degrees and a few bodyguards, drivers, and others whose loyalty is to the chief, not the office or the organization.

There is a further problem in viewing the police as a standard rational-legal bureau. The loyalty question raised above, which has to do with compliance within the organization, is complicated by the fact that the organization is partitioned into at least five distinct segments, and interaction within each segment is greater, more frequent, and more expressive than it is between segments. These segments can be labeled the detectives, the civilian operatives, the top command, the middle management,and the lower participants (uniformed patrol). They have distinctive views of their authority and its source, their primary audiences, their most sought after rewards, and the sources of risks to their careers or jobs. Loyalty runs primarily laterally, towards peers of the same rank and/or specialization in a police department, with some orientation up and down. These loyalties are often in conflict with the neutral, routinized role obligations and routines of bureaucrats. The exchanges that take place between or across segments rely on tacit tolerance, and semiformal and formal rewards, while within segments quite different things matter.

## Power, Authority, and Change

Power and authority relations within police organizations are thus complicated, and any attempt to introduce change, technological or otherwise, encounters resistance. This is so for several reasons:

- The union contracts define all job-related matters such that any change must be bargained for. If something new is to be added or required, such as a civilian review board, some other constraint must be lifted, or a pay raise granted.

- Civilian and sworn personnel are governed by different rules. While civilian employees can be disciplined and fired fairly easily, police officers are almost impossible to fire short of an admitted criminal act on duty.

- Exceptions to rules are decided by the chief, and in spite of the severe limits on firing, suspension, fining, or other disciplinary action is almost unlimited and immediate. Furthermore, much discipline is not done by formal means but by transfers to unwanted or obscure jobs, or transfer to unfavorable districts in which to work (however that might be defined).

- The organization abides by a "rules paradox" insofar as the work is one of interpreting rules in respect to compliance, violation, and the like and the relevant response to such. Officers make decisions largely on their own, with little supervision or feedback on their performance, and they are largely supported in their routine, day-to-day decisions. This means that allegation of an internal violation always has a context of interpretation; the lower participants see it intentionally pointed to them in a global fashion while "top management" or command sees it as a failure of duty and obligation.

- Patterns of loyalty shape internal and external enforcement practices. These in turn run counter to both bureaucratic rules that are designed to deal with routine, repeated processing of like cases in like fashion, and legal rules that call for procedural sensitivity and fairness of enforcement. This is what Weber would call a conflict between formal, rational, rule-bound actions and actions that are oriented to substantive, or here-and-now-situated, rationality.

This list is yet another way of underscoring the competition among rationalities that is ongoing in policing and that is the structure within which technological change is introduced. The ways in which technologies are introduced, used, responded to, abandoned, redefined, reintroduced, and made to "fit in" to organizations is situational and varies by the ways in which the objects (technology) perform in given situations that bear on the work routines. These contradictions and power balances are potentially disrupted within the organization. The question is, who gains from a new IT?

Low-Tech Organizations

Police organizations are very "low tech" when compared to other modern organizations such as universities, corporations, and federal agencies. They are dependent on citizens for compliance, information, assistance, and tolerance. To appear to control information, policing can and does occasionally employ information-processing tools, yet relies basically on interpersonal relations to maintain public trust. In many respects, the police are embedded in the social life of communities, but this embeddedness, or responsiveness to local community politics, varies according to the social composition of the area, its density, police strategies and tactics, and traditions. A few innovations, such as investigators' use of computers, seem general, but the impact on clearing crime is unknown (Harper and Watson 1988; Harper 1991; Innes 2003).

While police are linked or networked to a considerable degree via mobile digital terminals, radios, and PDAs or cell phones, they are ecologically isolated and work alone, in partnerships, or in small groups. At times, they join in performance-oriented short-term teams to serve warrants, cordon off an area, make massive traffic stops, or conduct sweeps of areas. In most cities they patrol, ecologically separated in time and space, linked via communications networks, and are rarely directly supervised (Jermeir and Berkes 1979). The degree and kind of supervision varies widely (Chatterton 1989, 1993, 1995; Van Maanen 1983). Police workloads, the proportion of "free" or uncommitted driving-around time, and the composition of work tasks vary widely by time of day, day of the week, month, and year, as well as being shaped by local budgets, traditions, and weather conditions (Bayley 1994: 39–44).

The past thirty years have produced changes in police organizations, but perhaps less in policing as a practice. What changes are taking place in policing as a result of the introduction of new information technologies? This is the theme of coming chapters.

## Conclusion

Some basic and essential concepts and definitions—policing, democratic policing, and the features of American policing—have been detailed and the origins of policing have been outlined. While many pressures to change, outlined in the first chapter, remain, and some internal readjustment can be seen in the changes in the last twenty years, the contingency, mandate, theme, and focus of professional policing in the United States has not changed significantly. The organization is a dualistic one, combining the patrimonial and rational-legal types. The bases for political tensions are not only rank and specialization but also personal loyalties, sponsorship, and cliques and cabals that form across rank and specialization-based lines. These are the bases for realigning power relations. While changes have been introduced, the primary technology of the police is symbolic, words and persuasion, and in that sense policing remains a "low-tech" organization. These contradictions and conflicts are revealed in deciding and in the links between the internal politics of the police and external networks and links to political bodies.

# 4

## Technology's Ways
### Imaginative Variations

### Introduction

Having defined police and reviewed the features of police organizations, and some bases for conflict and power imbalance within them, I can now place technology as an idea and a functioning apparatus within the context of the music. This might be called setting technology to music. The idea of technology is more important than the materiality of technology because it is ideas that drive its installation, social shape, aesthetics, and uses (Thomas 1994; Suchman 1987). Technologies are complex, semimagical means to accomplish ends, with both symbolic (they stand for something else) and instrumental (they do things) consequences. Information technology in the narrow sense is not the fundamental technology, or means of accomplishing work, of policing. The primary technology of policing is talk, or interpersonal skills. Considerable research shows that policing works best when deciding is combined with restrained, respectful listening and talk (Mastrofski, Reisig, and McCluskey 2002). The legitimacy of street policing seems contingent on the appearance of fairness and procedural adherence. Policing is about establishing and maintaining trust, and assessing trustworthiness. This in turn is rooted in the fundamental interpersonal realities of our differentiated, mediated life. The technological infrastructure of policing, the speed and efficiency of information technologies, is in every way a tertiary question with respect to the quality of police work because it does not foreordain what is done but creates a number of channels for rationalizing it. The speed and efficiency of policing are in every way ambiguous properties of the practices. The practices that both shape and are shaped by IT are of interest in that they may alter the contours of the job, and add to the appearance of modern management techniques.

As argued in the previous chapter, the features of policing, the contingency, mandate, focus, and responsiveness theme, shaped by the professionalizing movement and by some innovations, are quite resistant to change. We can expect to hear the same music repeated, yet the last thirty years have been dynamic in reshaping society's modes of communication, and information technology has been in the forefront of police presentational rhetoric—the way the police explain their work to others—since computer-assisted dispatch was introduced in the early 1970s. Because the narrative of this chapter begins with organizations, moves to the role of information technologies in organizations, and then proceeds to the particulars of policing and its ambivalence toward IT, the chapter is something of a broad and inverted pyramid. To discuss technologically induced change in policing, it is necessary to define and characterize an organization and its relationship to technology, especially information technologies. Technology is a chameleon: it simulates its environment.

The literature on information technology and organizational change is as extensive as it is thin. Several important limits are encountered when one reviews relevant studies of information technology. The literature seeks to summarize, gloss, and compare very different organizational contexts (in reference to their structure, features, external and internal pressures, and the resultant organizational dance). In addition, the definitions are "top-down" attempts to define technology apart from the practices through which work is accomplished. When these are considered in detail, it is clear that the practices are the levers through which change takes place. Unfortunately, with some important exceptions, such as the work of Suchman (1987), Thomas (1994), Chan (2001), and Barley and students (Barley 1986, 1988; Barley and Orr 1997), there is little published work based on close ethnographic observation that places work-based practices in the context of organizational change.

In this chapter, the role of technologies in organizational change, the rules and routines of policing, and the limits of the present police information-processing systems are introduced. The most prominent element in police information processing is that it is not properly a "system" because the various databases are not linked to form an integrated, bounded whole. They are a midden heap of disparate and unconnected, layered facts. Policing is demand led in the sense that responsiveness to calls is emphasized, even though more than half the time spent in random patrol is spent simply driving around. Calls for service trump virtually all other forms of data for management and supervision. Intelligence gathering and analysis is virtually nonexistent. Technology becomes a mode of relating and working that little modifies the actual practices of policing.

## The Information Problem

American policing's mandate, including the theme of demand production, responsiveness, and the management of calls for service, continues to constrain efforts to adopt and adapt to new information technologies. The information problem is that while police store abundant facts, they have little interest in converting, or capacity to convert, these facts into useful, actionable information in the future. They have virtually no intelligence or facts gathered in advance of their current utility. The organization locates itself in the here and now almost exclusively. It is awash with facts and stores its information in many places, most of them inaccessible by standardized means—written records, electronic files, or archival repositories. IT works within an organization to convert facts or "raw data," into *information*, or facts placed in a context. Facts, raw data, once placed in some context with a purpose, can be stored, distilled, elaborated, analyzed, and retrieved in new forms. In a context, information becomes something, a distinction that makes a difference. It can be used to decide. A fact must be placed in a context if it is to be understood and acted upon. A call for service is a fact; a series of calls for service may be a pattern such as a spatial location with disorderly character. When a series of facts is converted into a pattern, it becomes information. As long as it is not put in any underlying set of processes and outcomes, it has little utility. One might say, to push the matter a bit further, that the present policing style of aimless wandering, followed by running after one call after another, is fact-based, not information-based, policing. Intelligence or information-based policing requires another step back to examine problems in advance of their occurrence. To do this, police are largely unwilling, if not incompetent. If and insofar as the organization can store, retrieve, and alter its practices in the future as a result of this information, it is beginning to be knowledge based, or able to apply generalized information to recurrent problems. The abiding focus of American policing and its basis in local knowledge, personal insights, past experiences, anecdotes, semipublic rumor, and gossip, in part captured in the oral culture of policing, means that any abstract system of deciding without immediate and transparent utility will be opposed.

Information technology is a multisided mirror. It ingests data, shapes and stores it, transforms it via coding, formats, software, and hardware, and then produces the texts, screens, files, images, and sounds used to interpret the work and the nature of the "outside world." It is reflexive —it is the primary way in which the organization sees itself, speaks to itself, and stores its memories. Its very reflexivity is an enigma because while it is a way an organization talks to itself about itself, it is also a conduit of new information. All information must be repeatedly reframed and recontextualized or else it is not information.

The American police have accepted publicly the ostensible capacity of IT and have framed many processes as instrumental, rather than exploring its inherently problematic features. They have promoted 911 and calls for service without modifying the nature of the response to these calls. Increased calls have not led to changes in what police do on the ground. When IT is used rationally to enhance police work, it is brought to bear on the work as a result of a stimulus, and is contingently relevant or occasioned. Like violence or coercion in policing, it is used when an occasion or situation requires it. In this sense, it produces and reflects situational rationality, rather than long-term rationality directed to transcendental or formally defined objectives. The faces of technology appear and fade, much like the moon on a cloudy night.

When IT is combined with the demand-management-incident focus, the cloying idea persists that policing is (only) about clearing the present call by whatever means necessary and returning fairly quickly to service (meaning not busy or otherwise engaged!) and that investigative work is about clearing the current case. There are as a result strong sources of tacit and unrecognized resistance to an integrated system of information processing and deployment of resources.

## Technologies and Change

Technologies are a background for imagining.[1] This is glaringly obvious in the case of information technologies, which work silently, invisibly, and magically. Work practices must be watched and displayed, shown and learned, and then repeated so that imagery remains of the work, sedimentation of how the thing (work) is done here. This demonstrable aspect is particularly powerful in policing because it is a cohort-based, apprenticelike craft learned by watching and emulating and reinforced by story telling (Shearing and Ericson 1991). The lingering symbolic images of the craft, of good work, or stories that encapsulate what is done and why, are important for sense making (Weick 1995: 171). Warnings, cautionary tales, and "cock-ups" mark what is to be avoided, but their generality is always dubious. Tools of the trade shift in and out of importance, and are reified in the oral culture of policing. Cars, weapons, communications equipment, strategies, and tactical lines (Bayley and Bittner 1986) vary in utility. IT lurks, emerging from time to time, but is obscured by the obvious and traditional means by which the craft is carried out.

## Technology

"Technology," like most concepts in the social sciences, is a sponge word that soaks up meaning as it is used. It is often reified, or given a concrete reality independent of the context or the cues and gestalts that surround its uses. This is misleading. Let us begin with a basic definition and work "outward" to more complex shadings. "Technology" is defined in *Webster's Collegiate Dictionary* (ninth edition) as "a particular means for achieving ends." This is a denotative definition glossed as the totality of means employed to provide objects necessary for human sustenance and comfort. It is the means of converting "raw materials" into "processed outputs." It connotes instrumentality, a focused, direct, and visible end or product. However, what is "raw" and what is "processed" or "cooked" remains complicated when both are human beings in complex social relationships. Academic definitions, taking into account that much technology is information based and involves manipulation of symbols or people, deemphasizing the material, range widely in their focus and detail (Roberts and Grabowski 1996: 141 provide a daunting list).

Framing technology in a narrow instrumental sense avoids the larger question of its values and purposes, the hopes and dreams of those who use it, and the connotations of its workings. Technology must be imagined, and is therefore always more than what is seen, more than the material, and more than the routines it requires.

Information technology, as a type of technology, or means of accomplishing work, is perhaps the most difficult technology to evaluate because the input and output are both symbolic, and it reverberates and affects social relationships subtly as well as altering structures via feedback loops (Orlikowski 1992; Poster 1990).[2] Does the IT cause change or does it merely reflect other forces at work? Does it make work faster rather than easier? IT is also shaped and affected by organizational change of other kinds: downsizing, reducing middle management, altering production processes. This ambiguity of cause and effect, stated in terms of the question, Does technology cause, facilitate, or merely reflect change? is perhaps not remarkable, given the great flexibility and adaptability of formal organizations, and the ambiguity that surrounds the plastic concept "technology" (Orlikowski 1992, 1996, 2000). These ambiguous generalizations hold for studies of IT in policing (Greene 2000; Dunworth 2000; Abt Associates 2000; Manning 1992, 2005).[3] To put this in positivistic terms, we might say that technology in every case is the dependent variable, not the independent variable.

"Organization" is an abstraction, a concept.[4] It is in some ways a rational overlay upon the messiness of human interactions, decisions, and preferences. While organizations try to structure uncertainty by routine and rule, they are also fluid, meanings-generating, and meanings-based systems. That is, the collective actions that take place are like a cartoon —they must be interpreted. Formal organizations are authoritatively coordinated systems of interaction in which the density of interaction is greater within than between members and other organizations, and they typically occupy an identified spatial-ecological niche. That being said, one must recall that rational organizations are developed to cope with abiding social uncertainties. The center of an organization is sense making, or the ongoing, social, plausible extracting of cues that order experience retrospectively and serve to enact a sensible environment (Weick 1995: 17). The enduring ground of the work is moral and political. As noted above, work within police bureaucracies is embedded in processes of moral exchange and reciprocity that may be disturbed but never totally effaced by technological innovations (Gouldner 1965; Crozier 1964; Thomas 1994).

Technologies are multivocal—they speak with many voices. As Weick (1995: 171) writes, almost in passing, "running the technology is an art form." He means that responses to events cannot be fully predicted, that new responses emerge from crises, that events must be connected to formal goals and rules, and that the more complex and covert the workings of a technology, the more creative the working must be. Yet, dealing with unpredictable departures from plan and routine, common in every organization except a high-reliability one (Weick and Roberts, in Weick 2000), requires collective imagination. What is unseen is the necessary. Departures from routine, events and responses to them, are particularly indicative in IT because they induce what might be called the invisibility paradox. As work is more shaped and structured by technologies, especially information technologies, what is done is out of sight, and what is required is to orient practices to *abstract concepts*. The observer must keep her eyes on what is out of sight. As Weick (2000: 157) notes, two invisible processes are at work—that beneath the surface of the machine and that beneath the surface of the human actor (body and mind). This implies, of course, that all work is collective, social, and, in some sense, rooted in sentiments and practices that must be displayed. The meaning of technologies within this framework takes its contours through the vocabularies of talk used in the work-ideologies (beliefs about the work), work-talk (talk about how to do the work), and specific machine talk (talk about how to use a particular machine) (Suchman 1987; Weick 1995: 107). What is not seen (for example, what is indicated by error messages and failures of computer-based machinery) must be imputed and interpreted collectively (see Suchman 1987: 121–63).

## The Current Technology

Let us consider some of the properties of current police-used information technology.

Technology in use, whether in the communications center, on patrol, or in investigations, produces pressures to reduce the time available for deciding and reflection. Operators are surveilled by several means to coerce them to rapid processing of calls for service and to precise, categorical, "by-the-numbers" dispatching (Manning 1988). Patrol officers are encouraged to keep up their numbers, to be productive, e.g., by running number plates, making traffic stops, and returning to service (Meehan 1994, 1998). Detectives are pressured to "produce" clearances and so focus on the few cases that can be cleared (Waegel 1981). The greater the time constraints on action, given ambiguity in technological human interaction, the greater the tendency for coping on the basis of collective cues and signals (Janis 1972; Janis and Mann 1977). Technology so used compresses deciding time, and simplifies complexity.

Police organizations shape their responses to technology. These responses suggest a continuing response, and it is likely that organizations shift modalities from crisis to routine and from logics of practice to rule-based definitions. Crisis and routine are fundamental conditions, always implicit or shadowed, one by the other. Crises can arise internally as a result of a succession crisis in an organization such as the naming of a new chief, or externally, when a fatal shooting, chase, or accident involving police occurs.

Work arises to fill the time available to do it. In every police department, detectives claim they are overloaded regardless of the workload; patrol officers complain of the same. As MDTs (mobile data terminals) are installed in patrol cars, officers increase their inquiries to databases (Meehan 1994, 1998).

Technologies touch off shifting modalities within organizations, not single, stable responses to a stable environment. The police environment is fraught with uncertainty. The most important oscillation is between routine and emergency. The influx of information about a riot, a disaster, or a flood of calls for service may require changes in command authority (it moves up in emergencies), resources available ("assets"), and deployment.

In an emergency mode, the organization communicates internally and externally quite differently (Manning 1990: 141)—more quickly and with less reflection and anticipation of outcomes. In other words, from a rhetorical perspective, organizations in crisis act differently than organizations in a routine mode. They are almost two different organizations.

As the police organization increases its capacity to make short-term surveillances and interventions, it increases the use of "high tech"–based activities, e.g., heavily armed and elaborately uniformed SWAT teams or "dynamic entry" teams for relatively benign incidents. These encounters increase the chances for a mistake in judgment, a bad shooting, a false entry, a response to an exaggerated risk.

Technologies stimulate and shape routines. While routines are malleable, subject to change and reorganization (Feldman and Pentland 2003), they persist. The segments of the organizations, e.g., top management, middle management, and the lower participants, tend to be loosely connected, one with the other, through routines that are occasioned. For example, e-mails are typically monitored and suppressed when sent to the top command, and paperwork rarely rises to the top; routine change almost always occurs as a result of communication from the top down.

While IT produces material constraints—it occupies space, has weight, and possesses other physical properties—IT also produces symbolic verbal responses and counterresponses that are attempts by those in power to stabilize the organization. The time frame of introduction and response to new technology will shape the types of responses the organization makes to and with technologies (Manning 2003).

When IT violate the zone of indifference at the bottom, that is, when monitoring and surveillance are seen as "big brother" activities, the relevant IT will be sabotaged, damaged, turned off, not used at all, and resisted. This takes place in connection with audio and video monitoring of patrol officers (installed in cars making traffic stops), transponders, and GPS devices used to track the movements of unit (Meehan 1998).

Technologies dramatize differentially routines and practices. Rules in police organizations, perhaps more than in other organizations because they are designed to reduce temptation and corruption and provide a basis for punishment, are complex, opaque, and seen as capricious in their application. Police organizations are "mock bureaucracies" designed to provide flexibility in sanctioning and punishing workers, not give them prospective guidance (Gouldner 1955, 1965). Technologies with features that decrease effort in respect to valued routines—checking data from traffic stops, running field stops data, or running credit checks—are used and praised; those that are associated with unwanted efforts or disvalued routines—with "paperwork," whether electronic, typed, or handwritten—are ignored, sabotaged, or seldom used.

Technology adds to uncertainties; it does not reduce them. The central uncertainties remain because exceptions are omnipresent. Policing is a process designed to deal with complexity and with exceptions. Rules for organizing are bureaucratic until such matters as "exceptions" must be handled. Exceptions fall to the top management to define and resolve; thus, what top management does is define into the routines those matters that are in fact outside of their control.

In summary, while the managers of organizations struggle to produce orderly processes through rules, routines, and procedures, and by adopting new technologies that are intended to control the worker, they constantly fail to achieve their overt public aims. On the other hand, the rationality of the worker, poised between work control and rate busting, persists and determines production, e.g., responses to calls for service, clearance of crimes, and visits to schools and neighborhood meetings.

## Technology as Caricatured

By referring to technology as a caricature, I mean that the situational, adaptive, and creative aspects of using technologies are ignored, while the managerial profiles are highlighted and dramatized. If we follow the usual instrumental caricature, the portraits of technologies will have the following character. They will always

- possess intrinsic meaning, purpose, and consequence;
- affect and shape social roles and tasks, work routines, and ideology;
- symbolize such matters as power, status, and control, and generate fears, dread, and loathing among those who do and do not use them (Manning 1992);
- appear to work like magic (it works, but we know not how or why) and be embedded in belief systems within the organization;
- be differentially perceived and labeled (Some of its effects may be overlooked, discounted, or ignored, while others are emphasized and dramatized.);
- be shaped by and shape organizations and their politics (Thomas 1994; Manning 2003: 144–74; Barley 1986).

Technology, as this list suggests, indicates not only the material processes associated with the work but also the sociological and cognitive elements that are required to use the technology in a collaborative and meaningful fashion. The most sensitive of these definitional packages suggests that "technology" as an expression points to several matters: (a) what is seen and visible, the material, (b) the logical, (c) the social, and (d) the cognitive and imaginative work required to understand, fix, maintain, and use technology routinely (I adopt these categories freely from Roberts and Grabowski 1996). The imaginative and cognitive aspects are situated and situational in their unfolding. The workings of technologies, including information technologies, are best seen or revealed by looking at how people use them. This is true because information technologies, as noted above, are invisible in their interior workings. Think of interpreting messages when using the internet: "HTPP error 5505"; "Network Timeout"; "browser error"; "not a valid command"; "logging in"; "page not available or expired"; etc. At times, these messages say that something is wrong and at other times they make positive statements. The source(s) of the error are unspecified and remedies are not suggested. The way one makes sense of these breaches suggests what the underlying order and ordering is. When action requires reaction, it must be collective, and such sense making must be seen, shown, and communicated.

This view of technology means, as I argued above, that key and thematic situations must be studied in an organization in order to set out the context of technology's ways—much of it imaginative and cognitive work. Since new technology confronts old practices, ideas, and even instrumental functions, it creates anomalies. Historically, the key situations in policing are defined by the uniformed patrol officers' practices —those "on the ground," at the "coal-face," at the street level. Problems are best dealt with, it is believed, by "street smarts"—practical, commonsense decisions and actions (from the perspective of the occupation's practitioners, not the public they face). The broadening of police practices to include crime mapping and crime analysis moves not only the locus of deciding, and the key situations, but also the level of abstraction required to deal with a problematic situation.

Consider the problem of a "burglary" for a patrol officer. For the street officer, a burglary begins with a call from a dispatcher (or, rarely, a person asking for assistance). The facts of a "burglary" must first be processed at a communication center, then formatted, passed on, and responded to by an officer. Others may hear the call on the radio or the MDT and back up the call. How else could the burglary be known to a patrolling officer? If the officer on the scene decides to "officialize" (my term) the job, she must put the facts in new contexts, for example, make a note in the car's logbook (a different format), write up a report, and pass this on to investigators. Opening a case file means that it must be closed in some fashion; there are strong reasons for not opening a new case file—it may mean more paperwork. The officer may provide feedback to the dispatcher about the disposition of the case and her current location and status. Officers must put facts in new formats and new contexts. New cues are attended to by detectives. They assess the salience and presence of needed facts (e.g., any victims, witnesses, physical evidence, records of the property taken). Now, given format, and ranking of facts, there is a difference between the operators' facts, the patrol officers' facts, and the investigators' "case." There is some "information" (facts, in this context) present that may increase the possibility that the case will be cleared. If the cases solved in this way have apparent similarities—e.g., they are burglaries of small shops without security guards and/or alarms at night—and this information is made available to other officers, there may be a repository of "knowledge" that can foreshadow future "break-ins" in shops of this type. This concern for pattern moves toward the possibilities represented by crime analysis because such events can be mapped temporally and spatially.

## The Data of the Police

While many police departments have acquired new information technologies, and most departments typically possess many of them, they remain unintegrated, scarcely used beyond daily needs, and marginal to the core work as seen by officers. Consider these features of modern information systems in policing:

- There are many nonlinked databanks: national, state, and federal. Many nonlinked databases are locally sourced (CAD [computer-assisted dispatching], jail booking system, criminal records, other management data, fingerprints, visual images such as "mug shots," records management systems, in most large departments a geographical information system (GIS) that charts data points spatially, and many paper files). The range of these national, accessible, but nonlinked databases is large and growing. These include significantly the basic managerial records-management systems (budgets, personnel, workload, payroll, leaves and holidays) and various investigative records (detectives' work, case records, statements, evidence, and court decisions, if any, that are kept either in paper files or in separate databases). The latter are not integrated with patrol-generated data.
- Other used databases are nominally national: NCIC (National Crime Information Center, containing the names of those wanted, warrants, and stolen vehicles and property, including firearms),

UCR (Uniform Crime Report), NIBRS (National Incident Based Reporting System) NDIS (a DNA profile databank, run by the FBI), NICS (National Incident Check System for people disqualified from receiving firearms), AFIS (Automated Fingerprint System), and CHRI (Criminal History Record Information System). These are nominally national because not all states participate in submitting data to these databases, the quality of data varies, and they are frequently redundant and contain useless or dated information (Geller and Morris 1992). The stated capacity to gather and process data quickly, to store them in an accessible and orderly fashion, and to develop vast fact-based files of fingerprints, criminal records, lab reports, arrest documents, and cases, is considerable.

- Storage capacity and use are not calibrated. The growth in storage capacity absent access and use reveals the tendency within policing and perhaps other public agencies to acquire systems without clear standards or stated purposes, and without considering the complexity of creating usable and simple modes of interface, collocation, and analysis. At times, this burgeoning of tools and databases strains the memory capacity of departments, and computers crash, or lack functional memory for peak-time operations (Greene 2000).

- Numerous software systems exist, e.g., ArcView, for geo-coded material; Pop TRAK, for monitoring problem solving; specialized programs for workload management; many spreadsheets for accounting and noncriminal records maintenance.

- Large departments have diverse work stations, running software of various generations (several versions of Microsoft) and a sprinkling of MACS and IBM clones that do not speak to each other. Research suggests that they are rarely and poorly utilized (Dunworth 2000; Abt Associates 2000; Manning 2003) and that data transfer is awkward and flawed.

- Changes in software are seldom done well "in house" and, when outsourced, lead to confusion because training is not provided, new systems have new "bells and whistles," and the oral culture may not exist. A parallel matter is that when federal or state funding expires for a given software, it is abandoned in time because those who knew the routines were transferred or retired, and no one knows how to run it (Nesbary 1994).

- Some departments have websites. These websites display descriptive materials, some data on calls for service or crime patterns, and hyperlinks to other websites. These tend to be taken-as-read texts with no explication or guidance as to their significance.
- A variety of limited and many nonlinked access points exist. While there are decentralized terminals in neighborhoods allowing minimal data access to citizens, as in Hartford, Connecticut, and laptops to be taken home by officers in Charlotte-Mecklenberg, North Carolina, few terminals permit direct access for officers or citizens to detailed maps, selected print-out, or on-line data. The databases that can be accessed are limited to recent CAD data, and questions of privacy limit access to many databases.
- Multiple and incompatible channels of communication connect the public to the police and units within the police department to each other. These now include websites, e-mail, cell and land-based phones, "snail" mail, personal visits to stations, face-to-face encounters, networked communication via fiber optic cables, paper documents, and e-files sent as attachments. None of these channels of communication is assembled or noted for overlap, inconsistency, validity, or utility. Departments are awash with facts, and starved for information.
- Inconsistent user and backside technology interfaces are many. Departments may have several servers, diverse and uneven main frame access, and terminals with varied memory and capacity. Perhaps as a result of the ad hoc accretion of these via purchasing, the influence of grants, vendors, trends, and fads, and now-abandoned, failed innovations, police have disparate information technology clusters that are not additive or cumulative in their effects. The closets and tops of file cabinets are decorated with abandoned user manuals, keyboards, and outdated computers.
- An in-use pragmatism about the IT includes a set of contradictory themes in action: on the one hand, information is personal property of a kind, to be guarded and protected; on the other hand, the most useful generally available technologies are those that have visible, local, immediate, and consequential properties, enabling police to check on drivers' licenses and insurance; ownership and registration of vehicles; and prior stops, arrests, and criminal records of drivers and passengers. These join other reliable and trustworthy technologies such as vehicles, weapons, and everyday tools

of the job (logbooks, second gun, accident-scene equipment, cell phones, and the radio-computer when help is needed). Those technologies seen as functioning to surveil, track, and monitor (and perhaps to punish) workers, such as in-car videos, sound-recording capacities, and traffic-stop records, are to be sabotaged, turned off or on as need be in the situation, or used as self-protective devices.

It is clear that the present mode of policing shapes the data collected and used, not the other way around. An engineer might think of the police in this regard as a kind of failed information-processing system. From an information-gathering perspective, the professional model creates a powerful ecology of information gathering. The social world is differentially organized with respect to information. The information of relevance to police is located in a number of these social worlds: (1) the world of other agencies and police units, which is highly trusted and usually acted upon; (2) the alarm-based world of citizens (with home alarms or patrols) and businesses, where the signal and index are one— when an alarm is seen or heard, it must be responded to; (3) businesses; (4) the private security world; (5) the world of the citizen (nonvictim and nonperpetrator), where calls must be screened further; and (6) the marginal and criminal world. The channels of primary information gatherers are a network of officers in vehicles, at desks, and on the street, who serve as conduits of information. They are independent, are rarely closely supervised in situ, and constitute a diverse and divergent set of source points. The greater the number of channels and recipients, the greater the possibility of information receipt by the police. While the 911 system is a central collection point, officers are expected to scan the environment for the problematic, intervene when they deem it necessary, and stand ready to respond to calls for service. The ecological dispersal of officers and their latitude in responding or not responding to an incident, when combined with highly valued elicited citizen demand (which is high information and noise) mean that policing is demand led. A considerable effort is devoted to screening, diverting, managing, and reducing citizen demand. This demand is composed of facts, not of information. Police act on information. The cliché of the past was "garbage in, garbage out," but given that there is almost no quality control on what is entered into police records systems, it is not surprising that the tables, figures, maps, and graphs presented are of variable quality, accuracy, or reliability. Perhaps they are trusted more than they should be, but public trust is a powerful umbrella.

## *The Strategy of Demand Solicitation and the Mandate*

### The Strategy of Demand Solicitation

The strategy of demand solicitation linked to the theme of responsiveness has been well accepted by police in Anglo-American societies. It now generates sufficient response from the public to create periods of information overload in many large departments. This is a function both of increased tendencies to call and of the massive proliferation of telephones and other personal communication devices (ninety-five million mobile phones are in use in the United States). In many respects, as I review below, demand-management technologies have been "add ons" introduced on top of the unchanged platform of current strategies and tactics, and seen by officers as not only faddish but also potentially worrying, representing more and different work obligations.

Although departmental policy on dispatching varies, most police work is the response to calls for service, or matters processed by operators and dispatchers, turned into assignments for officers, which become jobs on the ground. Thus, calls, those dispatched or assigned, are segmentalized units within a communications flow. Some incidents entail interaction and become encounters. The process of communicating, translating, and transformating information, and attending the event (in fact or via another form of communication), is recursive in the sense that some correction of initial definitions and classifications takes place). The organizational structure, resting on information technology, converts raw data into police work.

This evolved structure has important practical implications that shape Anglo-American policing. Because the work is largely reactive, and driven by calls for service, a processing or means orientation to the job arises. The cynosure of policing, the valued focus of the work, is the incident. The phenomenology, what gives it meaning, of police patrol is based on the incident, a hub of activity responded to, defined, and managed by patrol officers. The devotion to calls might be called a mini-ideology, or set of beliefs that tend to be resistant to fact, among patrol officers. The incident focus narrows policing to the here and now and absorbs in theory the time available. The logic of incident-driven policing is a misleading and only partially accurate picture of the social dynamics of the work because what happens next is officially recorded and may require investigation.

## The Incident Cynosure and Police Beliefs

The following points outline police beliefs about the character and association of incidents. They are one of the most profound impediments to information-based, technologically driven change. These beliefs vary within and across the segments of the organization, among civilians and sworn officers, and probably vary by years of service and gender, but they underlie the powerful worldview of the uniform patrol segment, and they are in many respects the primary interface—where the organization's boundaries are maintained, expanded, or contracted over time.

- Incidents, especially those of most public importance, are randomly distributed in time and space, are semi-autonomous and bounded, and have little if any connection.
- The future alone can tell whether some level of crime or disorder will arise and have to be dealt with, but without some action, things will get worse (Bittner 1990).
- Social life is odd; "things happen." The patrol culture and cops' stories, a vague set of resources, are ill fitted to guide response to a given incident confronting an officer.
- Society is what it is, and changes little. Such lasting and troubling things as homelessness, mental illness, poverty, crime, and inequality are beyond the scope of policing, and beyond the understanding of the average police officer. This is not a hindrance but a logical necessity, given the demands of police work as now done.
- Policing is about practical, decisive action that minimizes the consequences of the visible and present, here-and-now incident.
- The incident orders work. Thus, ratiocination, reflection, and paperwork are secondary to real police work on the ground. They may in fact impede accomplishing this work.
- The core incident is itself a matter of definition, as many events in

which the police intervene are truly multidimensional, could be handled in a number of ways or avoided altogether, and are governed by forces largely out of the control of the officer in any case.

- Once defined, the incident as defined shapes the needed information: that which is accessible and useful in the incident at hand, and arrives "just in time" for active use by an officer.

- The extent to which the incident extends to other matters is problematic and an information search, if undertaken, is guided by interpersonal trust.

- Inquiries from patrol officers or investigators tend to be restricted to referring to or querying a handful of trusted (external) data sources: vehicle registration and driving licenses, outstanding warrants and/or criminal records, and other field stops.

- The incident and its contours drive the records kept. Officers emphasize "keeping up the numbers," "output," or "the counters," processing calls, moving on quickly to the next, making the odd traffic stop and citation, and showing that one is part of a team.

- The technologies and related information sources required or used are matters for the officer at the scene to best determine.

Taking this list into account we see that the precise range of facts needed to convert to organizationally valid and reliable information cannot be fully and explicitly defined in advance. Thus, all police technologies are embedded in a horizon of possibilities, and their use is not determined by the presence of a technology but by current practices.

Technology's uses are *contingently relevant* (Meehan 1998). There are of course technologies that are actively circumscribing action—the mobile digital terminal in the car, the cell phone if used—but technologies employed by the officer are used not for the intrinsic merits ascribed by computer scientists, sociologists, or other experts; they are used when an occasion is fraught with its potentialities. They are used as determined by the needs of the moment, the level of interpersonal trust, and a subtle assessment of the audiences to which the information might be presented. The audience to which the presentation is directed shapes the face of rationality that is adopted. If the paper and record associated with a technology is to serve the immediate situation, one's partner, citizens, and onlookers, it may have a lower horizon than something written for the sergeant and others. If it is seen as having broader, media-based attention, it has a longer and broader horizon of possibilities. This process of imagining the horizons of use is, of course, a corollary of the many faces of rationality. The way problems are defined, approached, managed, and disposed of is situational and situated, governed by context, and what is seen as a resource shifts as contexts change. Policing is a traditional occupation in which the modes of doing are highly fixed and officers, like Chinese peasants, do things as their ancestors did them and as they were taught. But innovations do occur.

## The Power of the Incident Cynosure

Let us now see how the incident cynosure, or valuation of what is done in the occasion, leads to other matters that shape the perceptions of the public and in that sense reduce the likelihood of open channels between the public and the police. This is relevant because the amount and kind of data or fact gathered from the public will alter the orientation of the organization to change possibilities. Consider these beliefs:

- The focus on "doing something" shapes interactions with the public, and is based on a distrust of the public. Police are often lied to, misled, and subjected to provocative dramas. They learn to keep some distance from what is said.
- Public fears, insecurities, and concerns are generally inconsistent with police interpretations of these problems. The police are obligated to act, as Bittner (1990) writes, in spite of the citizens' natural attitude (citizens' requests and definitions of solutions to the situation) toward a solution. The *Dragnet* line, "Just the facts, ma'am," is a poignant rendering of this perspective.
- It is assumed that what is written is just enough and just in time to accomplish what the officer anticipates accomplishing, and no more. This often limits radically additional comments, asides, observations, and other matters that might be pertinent to linking this incident to others.
- The ideology of the present and the incident is not restricted to the patrol segment. It is revealed in the focus of detective work on the case and its clearance, and the ideology of crisis management at the command level. In general, management, if it takes place at all in policing, is management by crisis; it is focused on rapid

response to the current problem, often taking the size and weight of a refrigerator, which in turn prevents dealing with the day's routine work and virtually destroys any contemplative approach to planning beyond tomorrow. This urgency perhaps drives all organizations, but it is ideologically supported in policing. There is no question that the media's intrusive, self-serving claims and ponderous narcissism burden the police with irrelevant pressures to solve crime that the mass media considers heinous, and distorts the capacities and limits and suppresses the tedious, boring, dirty work of everyday policing.

The mandate, contingency, theme, and focus give policing its force and legitimacy. They make visible to the public what is being done to and for them. These resources are also powerful limitations on what is seen and responded to. The readiness of policing, and its vast, slack resources are its great strength (Thompson 1963; Clark and Sykes 1974). The vast resources therefore held in readiness are essential yet in everyday operation produce bored employees, a slack and indolent organization, and the phenomenon of "doing nothing" for long periods of time. The police organization is structurally inefficient and intended to be so. The mandate, contingency, focus, and theme do not change, but rhetoric, announcements of programs, and press releases do. Policing is therefore ill prepared to anticipate and act in concert toward most problems except mass disorder or disaster at a given time or place. In general, the police stand ready to act in the event, as anticipatory and premonitory agents, rather than as preventive or even ameliorative agents. While they employ a variety of control modes, ranging from the educational to the penal (Black 1976), their focus is the here and now. The importance of this, the incident cynosure, is that it reduces the value of information as a basis for action and shifts fundamental deciding to the "ground level" in order to reduce the emergent consequence of undetected and detected acts. Those things (persons, technologies, programs, and policies) seen as contributing to (rapid) response are valued, even under the misleading rubric of "putting more police on the streets." Conversely, things requiring abstract thought, planning, policy, and innovations that complicate the job are resisted. New information technologies, when linked to problem solving and crime analysis, complicate the job.

## Conclusion

This chapter is meant to connect the theorizing of the first chapters and the case studies following. It lays out the background of the music (the structure and features), the dance (results of internal and external pressures toward change), and the steps (case materials) seen. Beliefs, habits, and practices of individuals also pattern the introduction of any information technology in policing, and are the ground against which sense making takes place. The public acceptance of a license and mandate provides a cover for dealing with the practical demands. The police emphasize the theme of responsiveness and sustain their traditional strategies. Technology has many ways, and combines in a deceptive way the logical, the social, the imaginative, and the instrumental aspects of its work.

Looking at policing and the police's uses of technology, we see that even the most advanced forms of communicative technologies have been back-fitted to the extant structure and traditional processes of the police organization. No police department (that I know of) has refined a systematically integrated collection of technologies to facilitate problem solving, crime prevention, policy analysis, or community interfaces (Abt Associates 2000: 150–65). Dunworth's review (2000) suggests that in general none of these is operational in any police department and that the fundamental dimensions of community policing—interface with communities, interorganizational links, workgroup facilitation, environmental scanning, problem orientation, area-based accountability, and strategic management—are nowhere to be found in well-developed form.

Putting police work in this broader context is an attempt to see how technology in policing is defined. Describing this context is what the philosopher Martin Heidegger (1977) meant by the "enframing" of technology: it is defined in a way that obscures its unacceptable dark side, that which is not readily seen or to hand. What are the negatives, the unanticipated, the consequential that are denied or not seen of a rapid, mobile, impersonal set of units providing human services? The rapid rise of information technology, coupled with computer-assisted dispatch, has increased the demand for policing, and the perception that calls for service must be disposed of in some fashion. The core of the resistance to change is not openly acknowledged as such, and change is seen as a question of training or education. Resistance works indirectly to shape and alter plans for transforming policing via information technologies such as crime mapping. As long as policing is defined as doing the necessary at the time it is called for, major internal change will not occur.

In what follows, I discuss the several aspects of technology. I do discuss the material aspects of IT—in respect to the space taken, size, capacity, and functions of the technologies in use in crime mapping and crime analysis. I am also interested in describing the social—in respect to the interactions that take place between the users and the machinery, and between the users and the users, in connection with work. The logical aspects of the technology, what can be produced, and how, are also considered in the case studies. The most significant aspect of police technology is the imaginative or that which is seen as possible, ready to hand, something one can do with it. In many respects, although the material presence in departments is sometimes too modest (too little memory in the main frame, too few powerful notebooks, dated hardware), the hard- and software and capacity of the technologies is vast, underutilized, and far too elaborate for the actual uses to which it is put. In the case studies, the absence of imagination on the part of the users— the data minders, the support staff, and the public—most restricts the innovative possibilities associated with crime mapping and crime analysis. What is on the surface, visible, and the formal capacities of the software and hardware obscure the deeper potentialities of the information technologies. These things are not visible, ready to hand, or even manifested easily. In some ways, the material and the logical are the instrumentalist side of technologies, while the social and imaginative are the expressive or symbolizing sides. In policing, the craft focus, as discussed above, limits the social and imaginative radically, whatever the enhanced capacity of the machinery. The way these limits are played out is a function of the organizational context, which we shall examine in detail in the case studies in chapters 5–7 and the reflective materials in chapters 8–10.

PART II

# Case Studies

# Overview of the Case Studies

The following chapters present ethnographic case studies, examples of three police departments' attempts to develop and refine their crime mapping and crime analysis capacities. Although the matters of technology, infrastructure, uses, and clientele are essential to making a transformation to some sort of information-driven policing, political questions and policies are a very central part of any innovation. The chapters situate the police organization in the context of a larger *field* (Bourdieu 1977) of political pressures, objective and subjective, in which the police operate and that affect the developing police capacity to map crime or analyze it in a useful fashion. The field is generally that of social control, informal and formal, and it sits in a *surround,* the larger political forces in a city or a nation. The development of CM/CA within the organization cannot be disentangled from the impacts of the field and the surround, and the impacts of these internal changes on field and surround. A rather obvious example since September 11, 2001, is that any city police will see themselves not only in the local field of politics and issues, whatever they might be, but also within a national surround that has been shaped by fear of terrorism and concern for "homeland security." This is a new requirement for local police, and it suggests a kind of binocular vision upon the present and upon the possible. The police do not worry much about the possible.

Considerable space is given to the low politics and high politics of policing in each of the three case studies, as well as to the internal changes and struggles within the police department. American policing's top command, outside the marginal case of county sheriffs, who are generally elected officials and politicians by definition, claim their mandate on the basis of political neutrality. Political aims and interests are often denied by police agencies. Their claim is that they are politically neutral and therefore any attempt to characterize their interests in a power contest as political is dismissed, seen as discrediting, and viewed as playing "politics." Professional policing has long avoided public political statements and positions on everything except its own interests in job control and avoidance of suits and criminal charges. The police have adopted the high ground: law enforcement is apolitical, it is governed by the law, and when applied, it is neutral. Yet, clearly the law is a political force—it is created by elected legislators, it is applied by elected and appointed judges, and it is a means of altering lifestyles and opportunities differentially. Policing is political: chiefs are appointed by elected officials; they must mobilize loyalty by distributing resources, rewards, and punishments within the organization and outside; and they must retain credibility and loyalty inside and credibility outside the organization Differential enforcement, including stops, frisks, saturation patrols, and time-limited "crackdowns"—all are power moves in a political context. They alter the life chances of people who are frisked, stopped, and arrested. Even the innocent may show disrespect and be subject to further coercion and control. Democratic policing is political, deeply involved in politics and power contests, yet obligated to be just and to provide equal treatment for equal offenses. This value commitment means that policing cannot be held to the standard of business efficiency, or mere short-term pragmatism. This is the case because in general police respond to what they know, and this is the local set of people of concern, those seen frequently, "hanging out" on the street and engaged in visible problematic activities. The police are a distributive and redistributive mechanism that alters life chances, lifestyles, and fates, and restraint is its hallmark. A truly efficient police in a democracy, conducting arrests and crackdowns on this knowledge base, will further disadvantage the powerless, the marginal, and people of color.

The relevance of power to organizational change means that an ethnography that avoids questions of power is an inadequate ethnography. Too many studies of policing are stripped, empty caricatures that cast the spotlight inside the organization as if it were in isolation and politics had no role in the decisions, actions, and rhetoric of the organization. The few studies that make considerable efforts to locate the police organization in the politics of the city and the region are quite notable (see in particular Banfield and Wilson 1963; Banfield 1965; Wilson 1968; Harring 1983; Scheingold 1984, 1991; Lyons 1999; Hunt and Magenau 1993; and Cannon 1997). Following Wilson's lead concerning the way a political structure shapes policing, these studies, however, broaden his concern with patterns of arrest. These later studies connect electoral politics, law enforcement, and peace keeping and make clear that policing is about power and authority and therefore is "political." The political forces at work and their consequences are described, and the studies are fully located in a context or field of power, conflict, and negotiation over policing.

Case studies that see the policing dance as moved by powerful forces are much needed. Flyvbjerg argues in two fine and detailed books (1998, 2001) that case studies must be based on *phronesis* (Flyvbjerg 2001: 2–3), analytic thinking with stated value concerns that exceed mere technical accomplishments. He gives a useful and dramatic example in his study of an attempt to reduce traffic in the center of Aalborg, Denmark (Flyvbjerg 1998: 219–36). While city planners wanted to close the central plaza to all traffic, businesses wanted it left open with parking for shoppers. The police did not want to enforce traffic laws prohibiting a turn into the plaza because they wanted to avoid offending business owners and shoppers. Business interests dominated, and both traffic and pollution increased in the city center. Business values trumped rational planning. The conflicts between moral values and unreflective pragmatism are often hidden, since the status quo always reflects the dominant interests of the powerful. They have no need to rationalize the present. To take this one step further, it is important to note that all such value questions cry out for revelations of the power relations that shape decisions, that rationalize what is taken to be true and good, as well as of who gains by the known outcomes. Often, small matters, little tactical encounters, are more revealing than "big-bang decisions" or major shifts in known public policies (Flyvbjerg 2001: 131–32). Finally, technological innovations, such as developing and using the nuclear bomb in Hiroshima and Nagasaki, refining the massive and efficient gassing of millions of Jews in Germany in World War II, and developing biochemical weapons in this country, need not contribute to justice or fairness. Technologies are not neutral in their uses in policing or in other institutions. Technologies have their ways, but those ways are deeply embedded in organizational politics. Each of these case studies illustrates power processes.

The cases presented include data on each of the six analytic dimensions described in the introduction. The cities vary in size, traditions, symbolism, and local political and institutional governance structures. I use the six dimensions—key actors or players and their political networks, the nature of the information systems, links between databases, secondary players and infrastructure, users and clientele, and the ecology of the systems—to organize my discussion of each site. The six dimensions through which rationalizing can be tracked are ways to look at the transformative processes. They vary in their significance, coherence, and quality across the three case studies; they also reflect larger issues of the field and surround in each city. Each case highlights some generic problems in implementing crime mapping and analysis as moral tools in the rationalizing process. They illustrate variously the potential and the limits of present police practice. Each case reveals stages of development, one might say, in the sense that Western's capacity is barely operational, Metro Washington's is a shadow, an idea about an infrastructure with modest outputs, and Boston's is fully operational (criteria for selection of each are outlined in appendix A). The case studies focus on generic issues of developing and using crime analysis, given the present type of Anglo-American policing, rather than the specific issues of implementation. In many respects, the process is punctuated by and sprinkled with confusion, contradiction, and muddling through. While there are patterns, and rule-guided behavior that reflects the hierarchy of command, there are also resistances inside and outside the departments and personal agendas that confound the best-laid plans.

Situations and situated actions reveal the tensions, contradictions, and power relations emergent in each organization as attempts to install a CM/CA capacity unfolded. On the one hand, I attempt to frame a contextualized explanation for the emergence of a CM/CA capacity, and on the other, to see how and why it functions as it does if put in place. I have argued that there are six elements necessary for the capacity to emerge. They may not appear in the same chronological order. They may not take place in a predictable, given order, they may vary in their appearance, and they may come and go; however, all the elements must be present for the capacity to emerge. When present, these elements account for the appearance of the functioning system. Absent all the elements, the matter at hand is not a true or complete crime mapping/crime analysis system or capacity. Any set of elements, absent one, will not be sufficient to produce the system. The missing elements thus are indicative, and will pattern the alternative shapes that appear. Furthermore, the program has not been implemented if one or more elements are missing. In this sense, my argument is based upon analytic induction and a natural-history approach rather than statistical generalization (Becker 1970).

It should be clear, given this definition, that social surveys that rely on responses to questionnaires and even phone interviews are inaccurate depictions of the actual functioning of CM/CA capacity. It is quite clear from research (Weisburd, et al. 2003; Willis, Mastrofski, and Weisburd 2004, 2007) that while the label "compstat" is used to describe what is done, the extent to which all the elements are present is uneven and variable. For example, if rapid and precise information is a requirement for an operative "compstat"-type meeting, most of the departments surveyed did not have that capacity. By describing a system as a set of variables, such research cannot tap into its holistic, functional capacities. Observation and interviews are needed to establish this. On the other hand, given a system, as change in the information system and in the field and surround takes place, key situations will be highlighted to exemplify this change (Crozier and Friedenberg 1980: 33). New uncertainties produce problematic situations. Given this aim and my data, the question becomes, What are the conditions for the development of crime mapping and analysis, as well as the practical aspects of putting it in place and making it useful? This question is, of course, related to the question of rationalities and how they emerge. My aim in each case presentation is to use the dimensions of comparison to highlight situations that touch off, render visible, make possible the applications of these forms of rationality in police work. Therefore, the relevant materials are quotations, observations, bits of meetings, and comments made in passing that characterize the IT in use rather than archival material, interviews, or technical capacities of the servers, software, and staff.

In summary, each of the case studies follows the same format and discusses in order the key players and politics; information-processing capacities; links between databases and access; secondary key players; users of information; and the ecology and infrastructure of the distribution of information. These dimensions are not arrayed in order of importance, but it is clear that each is a necessary if not sufficient step in animating the dance of change. Each case contains a section on the practice of CM/CA in the given organization and a comment that concludes the chapter. The final section of the book, entitled "Appraising," will compare and contrast the three cases and draw some general inferences about the impact and future of CM/CA in American policing. A general analysis of CM/CA and the proceedings in Boston occupies most of chapters 8 and 9. The final chapter in the book assesses the findings and implications of these transformations for future policing.

# 5

## Western City and Police

### Introduction

The previous chapters have discussed the nature of American policing, the ways of technology, and information technology in policing. I have made a strong case for the constraints that are present in policing, what I have called the music that sets the dance. It is now possible to examine the three case studies and look for similarities and differences in their CM/CA capacities.[1]

### The City of Western

A quiet city divided by a river, long a center of heavy industry, of moderate Republican persuasion, and abutted by a university whose intellectual and sports shadows are always present in the everyday life of the city, Western is what the imagined life of the fifties perhaps was then. Western is a modest, midwestern city that can be easily characterized from the perspective of the case study approach used here. These matters of interest are population, industrial base, ecology, ethnic divisions, and politics, institutionalized and informal. Western is a fairly flat city surrounded by rolling hills and farmland. It covers some thirty-three square miles, containing 127,000 people in a metropolitan area of nearly 400,000. The city of Western has a minority population of slightly over 25 percent (about 18 percent is African American), has a large industrial and union base, and is the home of a large university and a very large two-year community college. The city has a long history of automobile production, United Auto Workers (UAW) strength, and democratic politics. The mayor (at the time of the study) had held office for two-plus terms and governed with an area-based elected city council. Crime has never been an issue in the city, nor have race relations per se. This is the case in part because the leadership of both the

Mexican American and the African American communities has been co-opted; being active in the nonpartisan city politics, they represent only the interests of the middle-class, small-business segment of the community. This position has been reinforced over the post–World War II years by a healthy auto industry that employs skilled and semiskilled union labor. The crime rate dropped modestly in 1996 (4 percent) and has dropped slightly each year since (Annual Report, Western Police Department, 2001). The city had experienced a range of nine to sixteen homicides in the previous six years and averages about twelve a year.

It has not sustained a fine or even notable history. It is a good place to live and work for skilled working people, migrants from the South after World War II and from Mexico beginning in the seventies. As an industrial, car-manufacturing town, it has union strengths, and working-class people have been active politically since World War II. It is a center of state government. The years from 1996 to 2000 were tempestuous in a subtle and perhaps erosive fashion within the city; these years saw a number of killings by police, shifts in police leadership, a critical social movement decrying violence against African Americans, and economic growth. While the city has lost population, it has gained a minor league baseball team and stadium, renewed the center city business area, reduced crime, and seen growth and specialization in its major regional hospitals.

At the time of the study period, the political network of the city was complex because it was in transition to a two-party system after long years of nonpartisan but Republican, conservative government. When the mayor at the time of the study, a former teacher and known liberal Democrat, was elected in 1990 with support from the minorities and local branches of national labor unions, it was unclear whether he would appoint a chief from within the department or mount a national search. An internal candidate, Chief A, a man with a master's degree from a nearby university, was chosen. The city council affirmed the choice, reflecting the politics of the mayor, and represented the principal majority groups within the city: African Americans and Hispanics (primarily of Mexican origin).

In the background of police reorganization in this city, always a factor in shaping the direction of policing reform, was a charismatic professor who taught in a nearby university. His father was a sergeant in a small town in the state, he was educated at the university, first as a social worker and then as a social scientist, and he remained fond of the idea of reinvigorating the policing style of the old-fashioned cop on the beat, the person he imagined his father to be. He had educated many of the top command, had a publicity agent and journalist who wrote op-ed pieces and later coauthored a textbook with him, and had a growing national and, later, international reputation as a police reformer. He won grants from the National Institute of Justice (NIJ) and from the COPS agency, and actively promoted community policing internationally (through trips to Taiwan and Brazil). From 1992 until 1996, he was an active but behind-the-scenes player in planning and actively politicking for the transformation of the Western Police Department (WPD). His agent was a key intermediary with the local media, churches, and city council members. The strength of the reform idea was grounded in part in "community policing," an ideology to which the professor and his former students subscribed, and in part in the support and resources of the mayor and city council.

When he died, still a young and active man, hundreds of uniformed police officers from surrounding departments, the state police, and out-of-state departments appeared at his funeral in his home parish, a Polish Catholic church. The police in their several colorful uniforms directed traffic around the church from blocks away, filled the quiet local neighborhood with their cars, vans, and motorcycles, and then quietly assembled outside before the service. As one, they filed into a square reserved area of the church, filled some twenty rows, and stared quietly ahead waiting. Several officers offered amusing small homilies, and when the service ended, the police were allowed to exit before the congregation. They milled about outside absent authority and looking for solace. The rest of the congregation wandered across the parking lot, into the church hall, and drank coffee and ate a tasteless meal served by the Sodality. He remained an icon in the department among the top command and the leadership coterie.

Issues of race and class have always been present in the high politics of a city. They impinge on the appointment and success of police chiefs everywhere in this country. No chief can manage a department without the fear of a major "racial" incident—a shooting, a beating, a small, visible riot or demonstration or the formation of a protest group. The high politics of American cities is something of a surround or context for the field of politics. National high politics surrounding homeland security echoes with issues of concerns, federal funding, and grants, while the local high politics seems to revolve publicly around race and race conflicts and privately around development, money, and profit taking by real estate brokers and land developers. Policing itself has a high politics, seen in its relationships with the mayor, the city council, and the powerful elites of a city as well as its internal organizational politics. Managing the mandate outside the department requires leadership—the ability to persuade external audiences and to sustain funding, legitimacy, and trust in the police. Because the transition to community policing and the development of crime-mapping and crime-analysis capacities were part of a larger rationalizing movement in Western, some background is needed.

In Western, the years prior to the study period were punctuated by ethnic/race-based incidents with powerful political significance. Western was probably no more divided along class and ethnic lines than any other medium-sized midwestern or eastern city, but an incident that remained a turning point in policing in Western took place there in February 1996. This incident highlighted the racial divide in the community. Two black men died, one in a parking lot while restrained by bouncers, and one in a jail cell while struggling with several police who were sitting on him. They "hog-tied" him (tied his hands behind his back and to his legs) and restrained him until his heart gave a great final burst, collapsed, and he died. A blurred video silently recorded his screams and calls for help. A social movement was mounted by local black ministers and in due course got considerable media attention. Responding to the resulting crisis were the mayor, city council members, and Chief A himself. In the fall of 1996, the minister who headed the movement, "A Plea for Justice," two members of neighborhood associations, a member of the police commission, and a local television pundit appeared on an "open mike" call-in local cable TV show. The content was remarkably "pro-police," and criticism was leveled at the minister for increasing tensions. Chief A did not appear on the show, nor did any members of the department. After several key events, the summer of 1996 saw the resignation of Chief A.[2] Chief B, as we shall see later, was appointed in the early winter of 1997. In December 1996, the mayor of Western responded to continuing quiet pressures from "A Plea for Justice," producing a plan to increase minority representation on the police force, insure that more officers lived in the city, add the East Precinct building, revise the civilian complaints scheme, constitute a police-community forum to meet yearly beginning in April of 1997, and create the position of deputy chief responsible for community relations. The protesting group was angered that it was not consulted on these proposals, and through July 1998 actively claimed racism and rejected the mayor's reform proposals. The police–community relations forum met in April. As of May none of the other promised changes had been realized. Two years later, yet another new chief, Chief C, instituted a series of forums on "race profiling" using a hired consultant from one of the local colleges.[3] I will return to this series of incidents later in this chapter.

## The Western City Police Department

The period between 1990 and 2002 saw great change in the Western Police Department, and I want to place these events in the past tense. This is to make clear the unfolding nature of the politics that punctuated the reorganizations and technological innovations that were put in place.

There had been four chiefs in ten years, two periods in which acting chiefs held office (both later became chiefs in their own right), four deputy chiefs, one acting deputy chief, major turnover, hiring, and loss of senior officers. The eight years discussed here in some detail, and especially the years from 2000 to 2003, were punctuated by incidents, political protest, and almost constant reorganization within the police department.

In order to see the background for the emerging CM/CA project in the WPD, one must revisit the management-succession crisis of the previous years in Western. When leadership changes in a police department, because the chief's job is personalized and loaded with at least potential charisma, the question of the legitimacy of the new leadership arises, supporters of alternative candidates are often transferred or even demoted, supporters of the new chief are elevated, and a new cadre (some formally appointed to the chief's office and others not) is assembled to advise the chief. The resignation of Chief A was followed by a national search. During the search period a former precinct captain, Mr. Sausage, popular with the "troops" and with a "street cop's mentality," was named acting chief. He subsequently applied for the chief's job and then abruptly withdrew his application a few months later. Mr. Jones, a black man who had once been an officer in a small town near Western, and was then chief in the capital city of another state, was named chief in Western. Mr. Jones is called here Chief B.

The appointment of Chief B with the mayor's support (after the previous chief had essentially been forced to resign) made it possible for him to make some political moves. In an interview I conducted in September 1999, Chief B stated that his goals were to bring some discipline and order into the organization (including rewriting procedures, rules, and regulations), to increase diversity, and to bring standards to hiring across the board (he participated directly in all hiring, from the janitors to the deputy chief). When interviewed, he said that the organization was very loose, that the "policy manual was a mess," and that "young officers needed supervision" (and by implication did not have it). He then added that he felt that the organizational culture was racist, sexist, and in need of change. In part in an attempt to tighten controls, he focused on crime reduction and more street patrol. Chief B felt the most urgent need was rationalizing the organization through more and more detailed rules. This meant rewriting and redesigning the policies and procedures of the department, and a review of the General Orders. He felt that the previous reorganization (actually a series of reorganization moves) had weakened the department. The department was below its allotted strength as a result of retirements, and there was a perception that the workload had been increased by the move to community policing. Chief B reallocated ten officers to patrol from "desk jobs." He participated in all promotional and hiring interviews and spoke in published newspaper interviews of the need for crime control and solid patrol-based service. In respect to his emphasis on command and control, restructuring of rules and procedures, and dramatizing service and crime-control functions, Chief B was a more traditional chief than Chief A. He also shook up the command cadre. The previous deputy chief, a critic of community policing and of Chief A, retired. The previous acting chief, Mr. Sausage, also retired when Chief B was named and approved by the Western city council. Chief B reassigned all of the serving captains, promoted an officer to fill a previously open captain's position, and forced one captain to retire. The retirement of the deputy chief and a captain, combined with other promotions, changed the face of command. Three of the four captains, four of the ten lieutenants, and two of the sergeants were educated at the nearby university, were advocates of community policing (CP), and surrounded the new chief. Chief B named a new deputy chief, who soon took a leave to attend the FBI academy and then accepted the chief's job in a city in another state. Captain Streets, a very active, lively, and enthusiastic supporter of community policing, and in the past supported by Chief A, was promoted to acting deputy chief. Just after Chief B took office in early 1997, two Western officers chased a young black teenager into a basement, and then sent in a police dog. The suspect shot the dog. The two officers then entered the basement and shot and killed the man. The local newspaper stated that the officers "returned fire" (there was no evidence that the young man shot at the officers), shooting him with six rounds. The subsequent FBI investigation reported that the killing followed accepted procedures. Abruptly, after slightly more than a year in office, Chief B resigned to take a job in the corrections department of another state.

Captain Streets was then named acting chief while another national search was undertaken. He named yet another acting deputy chief. Captain Streets applied for the job of chief and was interviewed successfully by the city council after his nomination by the mayor. He is called Chief C, the third chief in three years, and is still incumbent (as of January 2007). Chief C, something of protégé of Chief A, was a strong supporter of the community-oriented innovations introduced most dramatically by Chief A when Chief C was a lieutenant. Chief C, once appointed, appeared again before the city council and reaffirmed his commitment to CP. As mentioned above, in the fall of 2000, he organized a series of open seminars across the city on "racial profiling." He called on an instructor from the local college to lead the discussions. This received very favorable press in the local newspapers and on television. By July 2002, he was a popular chief who had been promoted from lieutenant to chief in the span of five years. He was part of the innovative inner cabal that has supported community policing for more than ten years in the WPD and before the city council on numerous occasions. He had an advanced degree in criminal justice from a nearby college, had studied at Harvard's Kennedy School, and was an advocate for, student of, and strong believer in the canons of community policing. He currently teaches community policing and criminal investigation, serving as an instructor at a local college. Two public events of note were given limited media attention, only two days of coverage. In the Kennedy School tradition of "fixing broken windows," the police, in cooperation with the city, in November 2000 moved out a collection of three dirty, pathetic, and homeless people from a vacant lot. Another black man died in custody in August 1999. It was reported that he suffocated on a plastic sandwich-type bag while in the back of a police car.

The command staff assembled by Chief C was highly educated, was committed to community policing, and rose through the ranks during the transitional period. According to interviews, this core as of 2002 included the chief, the deputy chief, two of the captains, two lieutenants, and three to four sergeants. There was a handful of young, college-educated officers who were keenly supportive as well. The political environment of the organization was shaped by this series of promotions to top command (about 75 percent of whom were new as of 2000), which placed those associated with the community-policing core of the department in control of the command segment. Officers at the top command level whose passive or active resistance echoed the sentiments of the "road officers" were out as a result of resignation or retirement.

In addition to changes in the command staff and the several occupants of the chief's position, the WPD was radically reorganized twice, occupied two new remodeled precinct headquarters, and was reassigned rooms and space in the former headquarters building. The former headquarters became the location of the offices of the top command, the jail, the Research and Development department, the communications center, and some administrative offices. The department was characterized by a traditional patrol–crime-control ideology and various shades of community-oriented policing.

The WPD, as of July 2002, employed some 263 officers (about 25 percent minority, 19 percent female), about half of whom had been hired in the previous five years. It also employed slightly more than one hundred civilians. About 50 percent of the officers had less than five years' service. The other large segment consisted of officers who were hired some twenty to twenty-five years previously. The WPD had a budget for 1999–2000 of approximately $25 million. The WPD had hired ninety new officers in the previous eighteen months and expected a 20–25 percent attrition rate in the following five years. Sworn officers, about equally divided between the two precincts, patrolled some twenty districts on an overlapping four-shift plan of four/ten (four ten-hour days on and three off). They were divided into two precincts, the east and the west, each headed by a captain. The precincts were "miniheadquarters." The former police headquarters adjacent to city hall, serving as both headquarters and the West Precinct, became the location of the administrative officers, the jail, the communications center, and human resources. The city was known as an example of community policing, and has been featured in textbooks and monographs on the subject. The

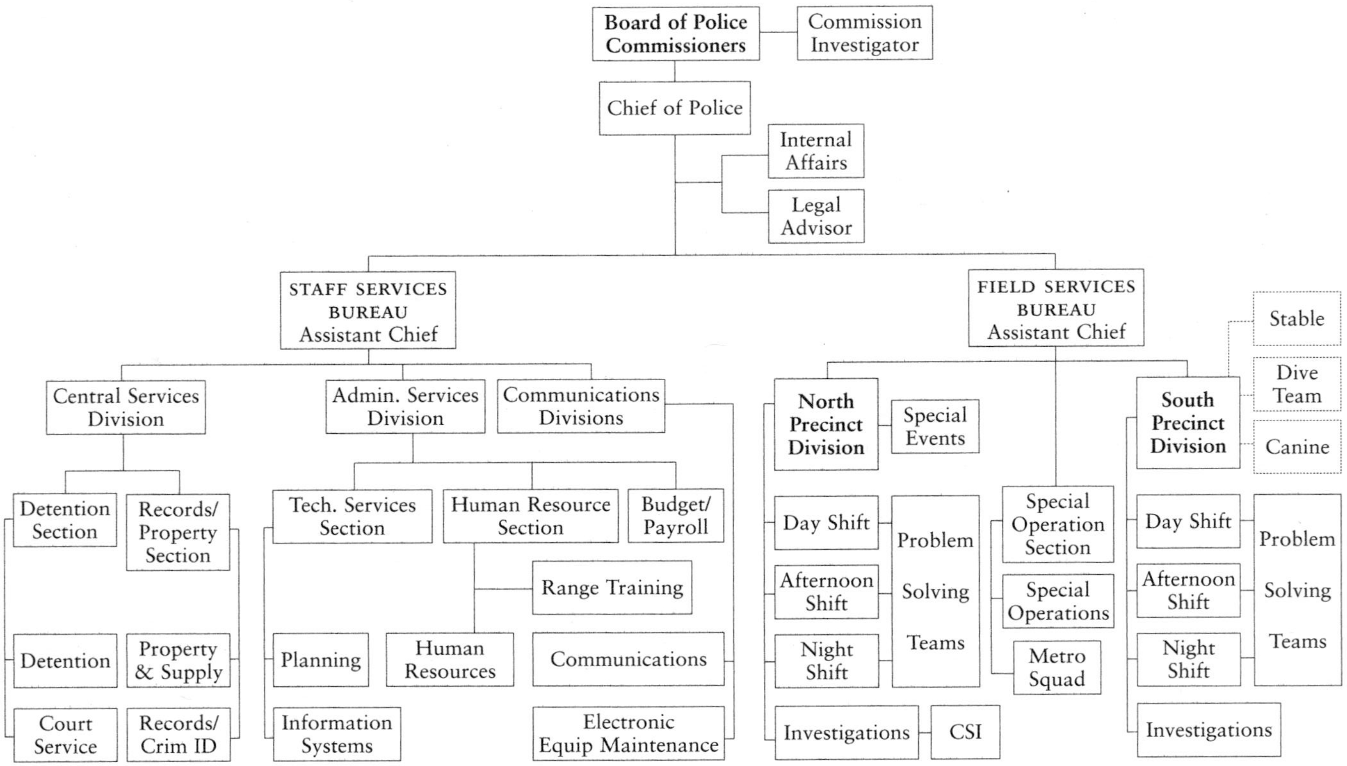

Fig. 5.1. Western Police Department organizational chart, October 5, 2000.

previous two chiefs supported crime analysis and crime mapping, but little police work resulted from their efforts. The organizational chart as of 2002 is shown in figure 5.1.

## Key Players and Political Networks

The dynamics of change in Western were driven by the field of events in the city, especially relations with minorities, changes in the key personnel, and their increased power in setting resource allocation. Although the changes were labeled as an aspect of the transition to community policing, they were also a part of the dance of new technologies and rationalizing more generally. This section and the next five are the dimensions along which the three cases are to be discussed. These materials are summarized at the end of the chapter.

## The First Step

According to interviews with command staff at that time Chief A, when appointed in 1991, had a shaky position, both internally in the department and externally in terms of political support, and he began very soon a reorganization campaign to reshape the department. The vision of Chief A was quite striking, but like many police leaders, he was not a persuasive people manager—was terse and unwilling to explicate "philosophical" underpinnings or ideologies. This was in part a matter of his personality and disposition and in part a matter of his always-tenuous political position. His time in office produced many publicly problematic events. Chief A staged two massive reorganization efforts in his eight years in office.

Shortly after being named, Chief A began the process of reorganizing Western. An advocate of Trojanowicz-style community policing (Trojanowicz and Buqueroux 1994), he created a dedicated community-policing unit, established a network center, and targeted a few areas of the city for community-policing (nonevaluated) "experiments." The plans to decentralize command began with the opening of the new West Precinct building in the spring of 1996. To set in motion his reforms, Chief A had first appointed a study group of officers of several ranks in 1991. He followed with an implementation group (mostly higher command officers) charged with carrying out the changes recommended by the study group. Several training sessions (one–two days long) introduced the concept of community policing to officers. These were cursory, delivered in lecture format, and considered by several officers interviewed to be "useless."

Being a pragmatist, Chief A reorganized the change process, labeling it community-policing operation and adding a mission statement and a stated concern for community relations. This was in response to the urgings of the mayor (a former high school teacher and local Democratic party activist). In his first innovation effort in 1992, he established a small community-policing unit with separate hours, flex time, territorial obligations, and a sergeant as supervisor. The unit was immediately stereotyped as composed of "do-gooders" and was seen as "not carrying the load." It was disliked within the department and well liked in the community and by the media. The chief emphasized the service-based aspects of his program, using the media to develop this angle, and the journalist associated with the professor wrote op-ed pieces, as well as laudatory stories in the local and regional newspapers, and kept the fax machines busy in the local college. The one active community police sergeant was widely featured in the national news, appeared on *Sixty Minutes,* and created both a positive aura for community policing and envy among his colleagues in the department. In due course, in the next two years, he retired, the center he worked in was closed, and the unit in which he worked was amalgamated into the patrol division (see below).

In 1991–92, some of the pressures on the chief to reorganize the department were financial. Thirty-five officers had been lost through retirement or resignation in the previous few years. More officers were expected to retire in the next few years. There was (and is) a long-standing conflict between designated community officers and "road" or patrol officers, based on the beliefs that community-patrol officers shirked work, went to amusement parks with kids while on duty, attended neighborhood meetings and ate cookies and drank punch, and were not doing crime-oriented work. They were seen as very autonomous, and with no workload. The workload of course was not subject to precise accounting, as were calls for service, calls cleared, or reports written. The CP officers were seen also as a political force, a clique who had the attention and approval of the chief. One minority CP officer, a Hispanic, sued the department for harassment (he lost). They were also sponsored within the department by a core of dedicated ranking officers, several with master's degrees. The wife of the lieutenant who later became chief was a very talented CP officer. The "road officers" saw themselves as the backbone of the department, as overworked and underrewarded, and as the thin and thinning front line of crime control. Patrol officers thought that not only was the work of the CP officers counterproductive and irrelevant socially, but their absence from the patrol rota also meant additional work for the present patrol.

## The Second Step

Responding in part to the criticism of patrol officers, Chief A created a second reorganization beginning in 1995. He first held a series of strategy meetings with his inner core of supporters to gather ideas and to formalize them. The resultant plans were to be put in place by another committee or implementation team. This reorganization was predicated on team policing and the formation of territorially based teams of specialized units and patrol officers nominally assigned to a sector or service unit within a district. Decentralized command centers, east and west, were purchased and renovated. Chief A introduced several programs, including a truant-tracking program and a social survey to measure citizen satisfaction (it was suspiciously high and invariant across questions and measures) and encouraged neighborhood watch and DARE (Drug Awareness Resistance Education). In part at the urging of the mayor, he also moved to add citizens to advisory boards in the precincts and supported the mayor's Community Relations Advisory Board (mostly an intermediary group seeking liaison between citizens and the police). Between 1992 and 2002, some forty-six neighborhood associations were formed in the city, advisory boards to both precincts were named, and 122 neighborhood-watch groups were assembled. Most were nonfunctional and acted in name only. His final move, to establish a full-service community center, was never realized, although representatives of several agencies and the police were assembled in a former state office building for a time. Let us review the process further.

Chief A made further changes. Patrol officers, approximately ninety, covering twenty districts, were to work four days on in ten-hour shifts. This change to ten/four with ninety officers contrasted with the previous pattern of 110–120 officers (or more) working fourteen districts in eight-hour shifts. The community-policing unit and the title "CP" (officers were called "CP officers") were removed from the organizational charts. Key loyalists, community-police advocates with the rank of sergeant and lieutenant, were promoted. During this period, Chief A developed a changed concept of community policing based on teams. The team concept (area based) became the community-policing vehicle in the spring of 1996. The chief remained committed to the community-policing approach as modified by his experience. In Western, team policing became the delivery modality, the public face of a strategy of decentralized, citizen-guided, service-oriented policing. The new plan, both the changes and the unchanged factors, played a role in the resultant drama. This was a façade, as the workload, modes of patrolling, territorial obligation, and contact with detectives (they worked out of downtown headquarters and did not frequent the two precinct headquarters), contact with citizens, actual problem solving, and team meetings were rare, and policing in the city remained unchanged.

The core idea of Chief A's second scheme was to develop area-based teams. Notional teams, some of which never met and none of which ere active, were to be assigned to areas within each precinct. Each precinct (two, east and west, had some control over resources and decisions) had ten teams and was headed by a captain and two lieutenants. Teams, not shifts, were to become the working basis for local policing. Ten teams of officers were formed in each precinct. Each precinct issued lists that were printed on colored paper and distributed. They listed officers by team and shift with voice mail numbers, while sergeants could use voice mail to send group messages to a team, for example, or an entire shift. A "hot line" and a media-information line were updated daily to include information on criminal incidents, community meetings, and current police issues. Lists of officers in teams and neighborhoods were printed and distributed, but the lists led to complaints because of reassignments of officers and foul-ups in the voice-mail system. In spite of uneven performance of the voice mail in the West Precinct ("It's never worked," said the captain in charge), it did increase sergeants' workloads. The phone menu that eventually allowed one to leave a message with the chief led one through four or five menus and ended with a tiny, tinny voice asking the caller to leave a message.

The East Precinct was located at this time in the headquarters building adjoining City Hall, and was scheduled for a move to a separate facility for three years. (In December 1999, renovations were completed.) A deal was made with a land developer and the city to rent and remodel an abandoned warehouse, waive a city ordinance to allow a new paved entrance to a major city artery to be constructed, and move most of the staff from headquarters to the East Precinct building. Officers assigned to West Precinct enjoyed a remodeled, light and airy former school with a basketball court, offices, meeting and conference rooms, and computer facilities. It was usually empty except for officers.

The most important core functions were now designated to be carried out by teams rather than patrol shifts. The twenty problem-solving teams included officers formerly assigned to the community-policing unit, traffic, K-9 duties, the Detective Bureau, and patrol. The formerly designated community police officers retained the CPO title. In the East Precinct, six teams had at least one CPO, one had two, and three had none. In the West Precinct, two teams had two, one had one, and five had none. These latent identities, based on past assignments, continued to be a basis for reference and interaction. One sergeant headed each team but did not serve on the same shift as all team members. For example, the designated head of the team, a sergeant, might be on "days" and have only one "teammate" officer on the same shift since the other team members could be on afternoons or nights. Sergeants were expected to hold team meetings at least once a month, and officers were paid overtime to attend if off-duty at the time. This in practice was not done, and the overtime was variously used for rewards by the sergeants. Some simply divided it equally as overtime pay, some did not disburse it at all, and some used it to pay officers for team meetings.

Some further reorganization of the officers was attempted. Detectives were designated as precinct based, and assigned nominally to teams, but they retained considerable independence. They never worked with the teams, nor spent much time in the precincts. As is the case in every community-policing experiment, detectives held out and maintained their traditional ways, records, secrets, and tactics of investigation. The Special Operations Division (SOD), the Criminal Sexual Assault unit, and the Crimes Against Persons unit remained in headquarters, as well as K-9, the regional ("Metro") drug squad, the administrative component (records, personnel, the jail, the chief's office, and Internal Affairs), and the traffic unit. The SOD retained prestige and considerable independence, remained outside the team-based structure, and symbolized active crime control, raids, warrant service, surveillance, and dramatic interventions (see the organizational chart). Special ad hoc squads, composed of officers who were rotated through, under acronyms such as "COPS," still exercised extraterritorial authority, operating across the city, carrying out raids, serving warrants, making arrests, and conducting investigations. The traffic division was particularly resilient to being disbanded as it had ceremonial and control functions as a result of the proximity of the state capital building and grounds. These specialized units worked at their own agendas, at their own speed, place, and time, with no coordination with the CP teams.

In summary, the "team policing" idea was operational only among patrol officers, and there were no formal means for coordinating investigations, SOD operations, warrant serving, raids, or detective work generally with the teams. Again, like many community-policing experiments, the necessary secrecy of the drug squad and warrant-serving, SOD-type units meant that their actions in areas ostensibly policed by teams of community-oriented officers were unannounced and often violated tacit agreements made with community members or were a surprise and embarrassment to territorially based officers in teams.

### Consequences of the CP-Based Changes

The program instituted by Chief A was based on a philosophy of decentralized, locally oriented, community-service-oriented policing. The chief had developed at least two complete plans with strategies (developed neighborhood associations, team policing, local territorial base, integrated detective work, decentralized authority in the two precincts, flexible hours and tasks, reduced specialized units) and tactics (team meetings, foot patrol in public housing areas, rewards such as overtime pay for team meetings), and he had developed a presentational rhetoric to convince the community, it politicians, and especially the minority community of its sensitivity to community needs and concerns. Little training was given; the patrol officers neither understood nor liked the idea of CP, and it had little of value to them. They were aware of command expectations that they should engage in proactive problem solving and team activities. There were no community meetings attended by officers. Insofar as CM/CA had any meaning at all, it had to do with tracking warrants and the occasional mention of using databases to define problem areas and crimes. Let us consider the reorganization as a prelude to the protean program of CM/CA that later emerged under Chief Streets.

Patrol officers felt an increased burden of work as a result of the reorganization and reduction in the number of road officers due to reassignment and retirement. In effect, since the team concept was overlaid on unmodified random, patrol-based areas (defined initially by work-loads), and with equivalent or less support from specialized units, team-based problem solving created additional obligations, contingencies, and unrewarded responsibilities for those officers. Conversely, CP was believed to result in the withdrawal of some officers from "the road." As Chief A noted dryly, "There is a perception of overwork out there." Fewer officers were routinely on the road as a result of attrition, reorganization, and reassignment. All officers were expected to answer calls and service uneven citizen demand. Officers continued to expect each other to carry their load, to cover for each other, to cover for them when they were out of service, and to range widely within the city to pick up work if and when needed. Research also suggested that officers rarely stayed within their assigned areas or even precincts and ranged widely, especially as "back-ups" on potentially difficult calls.

Little training in community policing was given, and that which was given provided no basis for systematic problem solving, organizing, or meeting with neighborhood associations. The training for community policing was a few days and was given in the academy for new officers. Suffice it to say that although the top command had a one-day session on problem solving in the fall of 1998, and three officers attended crime mapping sessions at the Police Foundation that same fall, the training in problem solving was wholly inadequate. This in turn led sergeants to say (in focus groups in December 1996) about community policing, "Order me to do something and I will" and "I have no way to supervise my officers in community policing because I have no clue what it is and neither do they." It is clear, also, that although one or two offices could articulate the mission of the department during its transformation, most could not. Those at the sergeant level and below were unclear about its merits, and just got on with the job as they defined and construed it. This meant a verbal commitment to "crime control" but, more practically, it meant attending to the obligations of the shift, clearing calls, backing up others, remaining reliable to colleagues, and staying out of trouble. As one retired captain said, the rules of patrol are "don't break the law and come to work early."

"Problem solving," using a SARA (scanning, analysis, response, and assessment) model or equivalent, "joint policing" or "team policing," and "crime prevention" were ambiguous or misleading terms the officers reported they had heard or read.[4] They found little (of what they imagine to be) teamwork that was consistent with their (ideological)

| | |
|---|---|
| Reorganize | Divide City of Western into 2 Precincts Directed by 2 Captains<br>Divide Each Precinct into 9 Teams<br>Assign 1 Sergeant and 7 Officers to Each Team<br>Reassign 27 Desk Officers' Positions to Problem-Solving Teams<br>Provide Problem-Solving (SARA Model) Training to Team Members |
| Identify Problems | Develop WPD Crime-Mapping Program Utilizing ESRI ArcView<br>Develop WPD Webpage "On Your Street" to Allow Citizens to<br>Report Problems |
| Record &<br>Disseminate<br>Information | Develop CAP (Community Awareness Program) Database to Track<br>Problems<br>Train Team Members on Using Crime Mapping, CAP, Webpage, Etc.<br>Allow Officers to Take Crime Maps to Neighborhood Meetings<br>Develop Internet-Based Crime Mapping for Citizens Utilizing ESRI<br>MapObjects<br>Install Laptops in Patrol Cars for Access to Information and<br>Offenses Reports |
| Get in Touch with<br>Greater Western | Develop Internet-Based Information & Referral Database for all<br>Human Service Providers in Order to Identify Services and Needs<br>(TIIAP Grant) |

Fig. 5.2. Western Police Department problem-solving strategies.

construction of police work. The imagery of police work was the "professional model" in Western, an imagery shared by most of the patrol officers and sergeants, and some of the command officers, including the deputy chief. The deputy chief (Deputy Chief A), frequently in silent in disagreement with Chief A, was an appointee of a chief who preceded Chief A. The chief created a format that was never used (figure 5.2). The second organization, the team-policing idea, caused reflection in focus groups on traditional approaches to patrol—"push things around, move 'em out of your turf, clean up the work at the end of the shift." Problems were place-specific—one could push problems into another precinct, across the river, to a nearby township, or to another district or beat. This pattern of "isolate and control" worked in Western because a freeway and a river divide the city (they are boundaries between the east and west precincts); because the police had two radio channels; and because of demographic differences, e.g., the percent of owner-occupied housing was much higher in West Precinct. A senior patrol officer, now retired, disagreed with this territorial strategy and claimed he did not want to "work for Atlas" (i.e., moving crime, people, and problems around); he wanted to "work for Orkin" (the bug exterminator). He saw the job as crime control. Of course, the "Atlas Van Lines" approach he attributed to team policing is consistent with the old notions of narrow responsibilities to maintain one's own turf and ignore displaced crime, or problems that transcend several districts. Crime prevention, or community cooperation, was not discussed in focus groups, although the department had targeted several areas in the city for concentrated efforts—harassing prostitutes and drug dealers and placing barriers to block access to streets in order to reduce traffic flow. These "crime-fighting" efforts and projects (usually targeting "crack houses") of the "COPS" program (consisting of special task forces engaged in community-oriented projects) were governed by traditional tactics.

Throughout these reorganizations, requirements for reform were absent, and these absences bore on the efforts of Chief Streets to develop a CM/CA capacity in Western in his first years in office. No rewards were granted to officers who excelled at CP, nor were they differentially assessed. The 911 system of allocating calls was unmodified so that as fewer officers were patrolling routinely, their workload increased. They attributed this in the first reorganization to community police officers being "withdrawn from service." In any case, with no additional "protected" time or time allocated to do "community policing," an officer who did such policing was seen as "out of service," as not carrying his or her part of the workload, and as not being a team player. There were no mechanisms to insure that team members attended community meetings regularly. (This was the key to the success of community policing in Chicago: officers were assigned to and did attend community meetings; see Skogan, et al. 1999.)

Let us now consider where the WPD sits in the larger network of communication in which it operates. This network is, as with most police departments in America, inconsistent, fragmented, uncoordinated, overlapping, and fraught with the potential for error and misadventure.[5] This network includes the 911 systems, the radio systems with the department and those of other public agencies, and the internal capacities of the hardware and software of the department.

The Nature of the Information Processing System

The Western police maintained a regional 911 center that was connected to one (out of the three adjoining counties and one nearby county) county sheriff's force, five local police and fire departments, four regional fire departments, and Western City's fire department. In this state, counties with elected sheriffs who were quite powerful in local affairs, cities, townships, and villages mounted police forces that shared responsibilities with the state, large cities nearby, county patrols, and private security organizations that patrolled malls, gated communities, and semipublic areas such as large parks and playgrounds. The city straddles three counties and includes a "township" embedded within its borders. The small township force had a chief, while the counties were headed by an elected sheriff. Two of the three refused to be a part of the regional 911 system and maintained separate, nonlinked databases and dispatch centers. The regional 911 system was fragmented and had been a continued source of political conflict for over twenty years. Some thirteen separate "emergency numbers" were listed in the Western City telephone book. These included the county 911 systems and the several seven-digit numbers to the police department, as well as the general numbers for assistance staffed by the local telephone company. Emergency medical care was available through the Western 911 system since fire departments served the emergency medical needs. Those fire departments served by the Western 911 also coordinated emergency medical services (EMS). The Western Fire Department had long resisted any integration with the Western 911 and therefore dispatched independently, and there was no mutual notification of calls of mutual interest. Occasionally, a state agency or the state police used the WPD 911 system. Western City funded the police communications center and controlled the police budget. Recall that patrol cars and task forces from the three abutting counties patrolled the city, the embedded township, and Western's small metropolitan "netherlands." While the state police in theory patrolled the highways running through the city, they were generally only seen on football Saturdays to supervise traffic and parking. In general, there were few tensions between the cities and the one county of the three adjoining it that were served by the Western communications center.

### Sources of Demand

The communications center of the department received and processed as requests for service 371,301 calls in 2001 (figure 5.3). Note

*Telephone Calls Answered*

| | |
|---|---|
| 911 Emergency | 71,490 |
| Cellular 911 | 80,014 |
| Emergency Option | 15,227 |
| Telco Operator Emergency | 6 |
| LPD Non-Emergency | 173,528 |
| Ingham County Sheriff Non-Emergency | 14,774 |
| Western Township Police Non-Emergency | 6,308 |
| Leslie Police Non-Emergency | 1,574 |
| Mason Police Non-Emergency | 4,451 |
| Williamston Police Non-Emergency | 3,836 |
| Hearing Impaired TDD Non-Emergency | 93 |
| TOTAL REQUESTS FOR SERVICE | 371,301 |

*Dispatches*

| | |
|---|---|
| LPD Emergency Dispatches | 42,823 |
| LPD Non-Emergency Dispatches | 50,105 |
| Client Emergency Dispatches | 43,129 |
| Client Non-Emergency Dispatches | 19,134 |
| TOTAL DISPATCHES | 155,191 |

*Telephone Reports Taken*

| | |
|---|---|
| Initiated and Finalized | 787 |
| Referred to Investigators | 921 |
| Referred to Precincts | 166 |
| TOTAL REPORTS TAKEN | 1,874 |

Fig. 5.3a. Western Police Department annual 2001 statistics.

| Year | Dispatches | Telephone Calls | Percentage of Calls Leading to Dispatches |
|---|---|---|---|
| 2001 | 155,191 | 371,301 | 42 |
| 2000 | 154,342 | 358,838 | 43 |
| 1999 | 137,243 | 312,660 | 44 |
| 1998 | 130,020 | 296,668 | 44 |

Fig. 5.3b. Annual comparison table of dispatches and telephone calls in the Western County 911 center, 1998 through 2001.

that almost half of the emergency calls (80,014) were from cell phones, and that the Western Police Department distinguished emergency from nonemergency calls within the 911 system, as well as calls from one nearby county police department and four local departments. Of the 371,301 received, some 155,191 (about 42 percent) were dispatched.

| Type | 1997 | 1998 | 1999 | 2000 | 2001 | % Change |
|---|---|---|---|---|---|---|
| Murder/Manslaughter | 16 | 10 | 11 | 15 | 8 | −50.0 |
| CSC/1 & 3 | 154 | 125 | 102 | 108 | 186 | 28.0 |
| Robbery | 265 | 280 | 255 | 170 | 226 | 36.1 |
| Felonious Assault | 1,086 | 885 | 818 | 784 | 936 | 5.7 |
| Burglary | 1,698 | 1,606 | 1,271 | 1,095 | 987 | −9.6 |
| Larceny | 5,858 | 4,982 | 4,734 | 4,074 | 4,376 | 9.6 |
| UDAA | 506 | 507 | 446 | 376 | 421 | 29.5 |
| Arson | 59 | 67 | 73 | 73 | 68 | −4.2 |
| TOTAL PART ONE | 9,642 | 8,462 | 7,264 | 6,710 | 7,213 | 7.5 |
| TOTAL PART TWO | — | — | — | 13,698 | 13,377 | −2.3 |
| TOTAL ALL CRIMES | — | — | — | 24,207 | 24,362 | 0.6 |

Fig. 5.4. Western Police Department five-year comparisons: crimes citywide.

The actual disposition of these dispatches, whether they resulted in a police action and what sort, was never reported, or that information was lost in the process of assignment to officers—how they dealt with the assignment. Like most departments, Western accepted phone reports and assigned some to investigators (primarily those concerning vice and drugs) and some to precincts.

Another source of demand for service was events that were reported to the police, considered valid, and investigated. These were typically presented within the Uniform Crime Reports (UCR) format as shown for Western in figure 5.4. Note that in Western, as with the national scene in the nineties, official reported and processed crime in Western decreased precipitously between 1997 and 2001, including a 50 percent drop in homicide. Part I crime (more serious crimes) dropped from 1997 (there were 9,642) to 2001 (7,213) and rose again between 2000 and 2001. These years were the combined years of Chief B and Chief C. Although Chief C was publicly seen as a traditional crime-control person, his period in office was too brief to have had much effect. Other than more officers being put on the road in 1997, there were no public or private changes in the relative importance of crime in the department or in the city governance.

The crime-mapping system, a third source of demand and management, was in fact only a server with the capacity to convert CAD (computer-assisted dispatching) data to mapping files. It was put in place in 2001 and at the time of the study had been in place barely a year. It is still being developed and is marginal to the day-to-day police work in the Western City Police Department. The interface between the system of analysis and the craft of policing is undeveloped.

Changes in the communications system began in earnest in 1996 when, through the initiative of a captain now retired, Western acquired a small grant from the COPS agency for (some forty) "laptops." These were to be installed in patrol vehicles (essentially, these are mobile digital terminals). This plan was realized for only a few cars because of the expense and the inability to link the digital transmission to an inexpensive network (the state police would have charged an excessive fee). The project was dead in the water when the first captain retired and his successor, who was a computer illiterate and was quoted as saying, "I hate computers," abandoned the project. The lieutenant in charge after 1999, Lieutenant Babbage, was imaginative in deploying IT resources.

The computer system was reorganized by Lieutenant Babbage between 2001 and 2004. He is a self-taught computer expert. I interviewed him several times. He clarified my understanding during the interviews and our trips around the communications center. During his time, the system was expanded and the main frame replaced with a number of servers. The police system was totally independent of the city's facilities, and only GIS (geographic information system) data and e-mail were shared with the city. All the software was Microsoft. They used Compaq and Dell servers and quad processors in the center for records and the jail census. There were dual servers for the mapping and mobile communications systems. About twenty servers carried out various functions, e.g., running records, storing information, doing backups of other records and functions, and connecting from time to time with other systems outside the department. The center had two switches that "talked" to the state and to the mobile data terminal (MDTs) in the cars. The several servers had independent functions (dispatch, files, records management). The communications center at the time of the study did not have mapping and on-screen visualization of the Western area, but displayed the cars in service and their current assignments with a number and name, e.g., "loud party" or "traffic accident," with time dispatched and accepted. All units were linked by radio, and all had MDTs functioning as laptops. These functions were carried out in completely dedicated form within the police department, so were not affected by demand from the city or county, uneven serving, and dependence on other agencies for servicing, repair, and budgeting.

Western had four 911 call-taking "cubes" for processing calls for service, and two were always staffed. The workload and the number of staff working varied with shifts and day of the week. The staff was entirely civilian and the center was headed by a civilian director. The desktop computers used in the center were stripped of all software to avoid viruses except the Printrak CAD and LEIN (law enforcement information network, a national database holding data on outstanding warrants, wanted suspects, etc.). The call takers had to leave the center and use another computer on breaks to access e-mail or the services available on the internet. In the department at large, in the old headquarters building near City Hall, and in the east and west precincts, the lieutenant controlled and serviced forty Dell laptops and one hundred Dell desktop computers. They were all compatible and used Windows 2000 operating system. According to the lieutenant, they ran the same common software (MS Office, LRMS, IIQ [a records search engine software], and Novell [Groupwise e-mail]).

## Databases

In 2004, WPD became part of a pilot system called "Services" that allows officers and command on the road to access LEIN, the departmental records, all jail and criminal records of a very large nearby county in the west of the state containing one of the largest cities in the state, a very large county in the east of the state, and the state department of corrections' and prosecutors' databases. The most often used and trusted are LEIN and SOS, followed by access to local records, including mug shots. According to Lieutenant Babbage, they are used by officers making field or traffic stops to check records, identification, criminal histories, outstanding warrants, and "MOs" that help point to suspects. All are linked by a Google search engine. Lieutenant Babbage noted in his response to my question about sharing data, "We all determine [personally] just how much information to share at the server level. Some of us share a lot, some just share names." In other words, there is no centralized database for noncrime data.

The complete transition to laptops in each car has been made. Babbage assured me that there are now "Panasonic Tuff books in every police car and command car. Officers use them to IM each other and receive calls for service. We still give calls via the radio however for all priority calls."

The radio is still the preferred mode of communicating. Patrol cars do not have cell phones, nor are command staff provided them by the department. Officers carry their personal cell phones with them while working, and the department has no rules about their being carried or used except that police are not to use them while driving. Of course, holding the radio-microphone while driving, a common practice, is not seen by the public as so provocative.

The point of this descriptive material on the capacities and nature of the channels of communication in such an organization is to highlight the question, What is happening on the ground? The communications system of the department, meaning the allocating and prioritizing of calls for service, was unchanged during the several reforms discussed here. Dispatching practices, informal understandings, and priorities were unaltered. Supervisors did not provide dedicated time for community-policing projects, nor did they provide relief from calls for individual officers so that they could develop problem-solving strategies. Some change in the overall workload may have occurred. Some other technological innovations are in progress. Criminal records are available in several locations via terminals, and motorists can make accident reports in either precinct.

## The Nature of Links between Databases

There was a records unit that maintained records on accidents, citations, warnings, and appearances in court. These were entered into LEMS (Law Enforcement Management System—see below). The list of subpoenas served was kept separately. A criminal identification unit kept records using AFIS (Automated Fingerprint System) and paper files on hand gun purchases and licenses (accepted and denied). These were not linked to CAD, criminal records, NCIC (National Crime Information Center), or other national databases except those shared through AFIS (Automated Fingerprint System) .

## How Were the Databases Accessed?

Other than those noted above, the databases maintained in Western were disconnected. As in most police departments, there were a very large number of independent or quasi-independent databases that could not be interfaced or had not been. In Western, mapping data covered only the past year, making any sort of trend analysis dubious. The several databases of calls to the police, fire, and EMS, as well as criminal records and jail populations in surrounding political entities (townships, unincorporated areas, counties, and small towns), which were interwoven within the city's boundaries in a peculiar fashion, were inaccessible from Western's Police Communications Center. Detective files on ongoing investigations, as is typical in all police departments, were not linked to the ongoing CAD or arrest files. The digital terminals in the cars could access LEIN data, crime records, and motor vehicle–secretary of state records and could communicate car to car. The data were available only for the previous year, although plans were being made for including records from past years to permit crime-trend analysis.

The data maintained for use in mapping and analysis in Western were entered laboriously, were not on-line, and were reprocessed by three sets of software. This system was obviously vulnerable to crashes and data loss in the transformation process. The data had not been systematically disaggregated in any useful way, e.g., by producing crime packages, or clusters of crimes, for broader attention within the force. Aside from adjusting crime-attack approaches as aspects of "problem solving," Western had not linked problem solving, prevention, community policing, and any aspect of crime mapping. It had no analytic role. These material and ecological limitations were necessary, but not sufficient, to make possible the use and application of crime maps. In spite of the chief's rhetoric concerning the use of crime analysis, in an October 1999 interview, he recommended tracking hot spots, using the arrest statistics as performance indicators, debriefing those arrested, and combining probation officers with officers on patrol (initiated July 1999 in the West Precinct). The crime analyst in 1999, a few months before his retirement, was anticipating entering data into a city police website that could be accessed by citizens. (This was funded by a U.S. Department of Commerce grant to the city and did appear in 2000.)

## Secondary Key Players and Infrastructure

Although the planning unit had some crime-mapping potential before Chief B was appointed, he supported development of the plan before he resigned. His hope was to use the system for identifying hot spots and using CM tactically. The crime-mapping project was coordinated by a captain and funded by two partnership COPS grants (12 and 130K) given in 1996 and one grant from the U.S. Department of Commerce (400K) in 1998. The aim was to produce a crime-mapping and statistics capacity and to fund the creation of a website with information on police and crime and other social services. The staff of the crime-mapping program (two "civilians") in Research and Planning was directed by a lieutenant. The server for the crime-mapping process hummed in the office of one staff member while one other staff member, a "crime analyst," sat in an adjoining room. He entered warrants served and arrests made and put them on e-mail. This was craft work. Two Ph.D. students, located in a precinct, were on a short-term contract to undertake some trend analyses and add to the databases (possibly from the 1990 U.S. Census). The members of the planning unit were isolated physically and geographically from detectives and patrol officers who worked from the two precincts.

The system for distributing mapping and crime-analysis information was decentralized, with some eighteen terminals and printers in the headquarters and the two precinct buildings. The original aim was to make it accessible and "cop-proof" (a pun on "idiot-proof," I was told by the civilian in charge of mapping). Data and maps could be displayed and printed easily. The chief, deputy chief, and other administrative offices had nine terminals; nine others were in offices (two captains', two lieutenants', two sergeants', and three in the two precinct-based detective bureaux). Each week, data were downloaded from the central main-frame database, LEMS, which was a dedicated Western database. Data on offenses, CAD, sex offenders, parolees, accidents, and filed contact cards were downloaded to a Dataflex program. Information on suspected drug houses was supposed to be entered by investigators (this was not being done regularly, according to the head of the planning unit). These data were then exported by text files to ArcView (geo-coded onto SHAPE files). The ArcView files were then copied to the planning unit's NT server and then could be used to create maps (accessed by the C drives of the eighteen terminals or mapping stations).

The overall process was imagined as shown in figure 5.5 in planning documents. (This system was not in place in July 2002 but came on-line in the next year.) The plan for expanding the current crime-analysis capacity is detailed in figure 5.6. Three databases (arrests, offenses, and calls for service) were merged weekly. The system was not on-line and was not designed to be. It was in effect a resource. The databases were

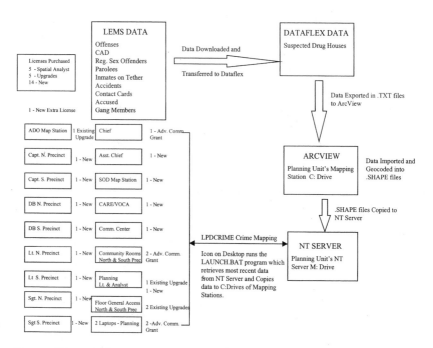

Fig. 5.5. Western Police Department crime-mapping data flow.

processed four times before being available. The ArcView software could create tables and graphs with a database that included roughly the preceding year of information. The maps (see figure 5.7) showed suppressible crimes (breaking and entering, residential and business; alcohol; obstructing; traffic offenses; juvenile crime; and multicrime locations). The planning unit put selected crimes and information on social services on a website in late 2000, and elaborated the databases and access.

### Data Users and Clientele

There was little infrastructure in place to encourage use of crime mapping, and minimal training was done. Officers were given a handout and a day's lecture (not hands-on experience) on crime mapping. The crime analyst's duties (see above) did not include preparing "packages," analyzing crime patterns or trends, or receiving feedback on operations other than arrests. Although addresses of "suspected crack houses" were supposed to be entered routinely into the database, they were not, nor did the system store data on sex offenders, parolees, or those on electronic tethers. The system was unused by investigators (detectives, and the task force on drug enforcement). The crime-mapping network was not part of the laptop database that permitted car-to-car communications and access to LEMS (the local police database) on-line. There was no intelligence unit within the department, perhaps a function of its size. Crime analysis-mapping was not a part of strategic planning, there were no "compstatlike" meetings, although there were bimonthly crime meetings headed by the present chief, and the head of the crime-mapping project said in an interview, "I don't think any one cares about it [crime mapping]. . . . GIS can't stand alone, [you] need to change the philosophy of the organization." He continued,

| Map Types (introduced) | Phase I Spot Maps | Phase II Thematic Maps | Phase III Internet Mapping |
|---|---|---|---|
| Crime Layers | Robbery Fel. Assaults Domestic Abuse Burglary (Res., Non) MDOP Stolen Vehicle Police-Initiated "Arrests": Narcotics, Disorderly, Obstructing, Juvenile, Alcohol, Weapons | Selected Calls for Service: Prowling, Loud Party, etc. Vehicle Recovery Locations Contact Cards Home Addresses: Parolees, Inmate on Tether, Confirmed Gang Member, Accused (Burglars, Car Thieves) | Robbery Fel. Assaults Domestic Abuse Burglary (Res., Non) MDOP Stolen Vehicle Larceny fm. Vehicle (SQL Programming to Allow Direct Access from GIS to Databases) |
| Map Features | Streets Rivers Schools Boundaries for Teams, Reporting Areas, and Precinct | Rental Properties Financial Institutions Apartment Complexes Liquor Establishments Census Data | Rental Properties Financial Institutions Apartment Complexes Liquor Establishments Census Data |
| Queries | Date Reported Teams and Precincts | Scene Types Daylight/Darkness Shift (possibly) | ArcView Internet Mapping will allow citizens/neighborhood assoc./other city depts. access to mapping via the internet/WAN. |
| Time Frame | June 1998 | Fall 1998 | 1999 |

Fig. 5.6. Western Police Department crime-mapping phases.

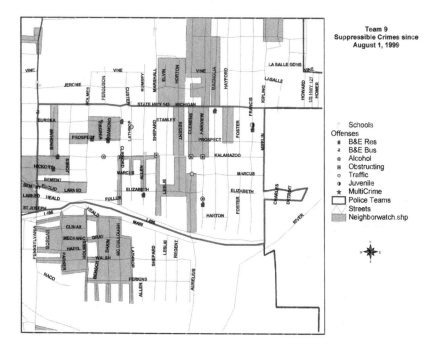

Fig. 5.7a. Map showing suppressible crimes in Western (breaking and entering, residential and business; alcohol; obstructing; traffic offenses; juvenile crime; and multicrime locations) since August 1, 1999.

"Support for the system [crime mapping and problem solving] begins at the top, it won't go anywhere without that . . . but support is less as you go down [the ranks]. But without support from the top, nothing will be tried."

The difficulties of use were in part a function of the ambiguities initiated by the community-policing reorganization(s). The questions that remain are as follows: What is the responsibility of officers—to their sergeants, a lieutenant, their area, a shift, or a "beat"? Are they to do some, any, or no community problem solving? (In general, they are doing none, according to observations.) Are these duties to be added onto or performed at the cost of their current responsibilities, or are they to be done during a specificied time? The patrol officers did not do community policing as a systematic activity, nor did they use or request maps. Chief A, when asked if anyone (officers) was doing problem solving, said, "I think I could name one. . . ."

**DESCRIPTION GROUP  ALCOHOL VIOL          COUNT    4**

| TEAM | DESCRIP | ADDRESS | SCENE | EARLY DATE | AVTIME | LIGHT | OFFNUM |
|------|---------|---------|-------|------------|--------|-------|--------|
| 9 | ALCOHOL VIOL | 627 S FAIRVIEW AV | STREET | AUG 08 1999 | 205 | DARK | 9914036 |
| 9 | ALCOHOL VIOL | 1321 E KALAMAZOO ST | OTHER | AUG 19 1999 | 2142 | UNK | 9914775 |
| 9 | ALCOHOL VIOL | CLIFFORD ST & KALAMAZOO ST | OTHER | AUG 21 1999 | 2219 | UNK | 9914927 |
| 9 | ALCOHOL VIOL | 1400  PROSPECT ST | OTHER | SEP 09 1999 | 2033 | UNK | 9916276 |

**DESCRIPTION GROUP  B&E BUS          COUNT    1**

| TEAM | DESCRIP | ADDRESS | SCENE | EARLY DATE | AVTIME | LIGHT | OFFNUM |
|------|---------|---------|-------|------------|--------|-------|--------|
| 9 | B&E BUS | 125 S PENNSYLVANIA AV | OTHER | SEP 01 1999 | 303 | DARK | 9915621 |

**DESCRIPTION GROUP  HOME INV 1ST          COUNT    1**

| TEAM | DESCRIP | ADDRESS | SCENE | EARLY DATE | AVTIME | LIGHT | OFFNUM |
|------|---------|---------|-------|------------|--------|-------|--------|
| 9 | HOME INV 1ST | 1115  HICKORY ST | SINGLE FAMILY | AUG 31 1999 | 515 | DARK | 9915574 |

**DESCRIPTION GROUP  HOME INV 2ND          COUNT    8**

| TEAM | DESCRIP | ADDRESS | SCENE | EARLY DATE | AVTIME | LIGHT | OFFNUM |
|------|---------|---------|-------|------------|--------|-------|--------|
| 9 | HOME INV 2ND | 610  ALLEN ST | SINGLE FAMILY | JUL 20 1999 | 1630 | UNK | 9914096 |
| 9 | HOME INV 2ND | 1314  PROSPECT ST | SINGLE FAMILY | AUG 19 1999 | 1010 | DAY | 9914768 |
| 9 | HOME INV 2ND | 1124 E KALAMAZOO ST | SINGLE FAMILY | AUG 18 1999 | 1200 | DARK | 9914827 |
| 9 | HOME INV 2ND | 200  CLIFFORD ST | APARTMENT | AUG 07 1999 | 800 | UNK | 9915146 |
| 9 | HOME INV 2ND | 230 S FRANCIS AV | SINGLE FAMILY | AUG 27 1999 | 2130 | DARK | 9915388 |
| 9 | HOME INV 2ND | 239 S FRANCIS AV | SINGLE FAMILY | SEP 04 1999 | 1430 | DARK | 9915943 |
| 9 | HOME INV 2ND | 122 S MAGNOLIA AV | SINGLE FAMILY | SEP 13 1999 | 640 | DAY | 9916560 |
| 9 | HOME INV 2ND | 605 S FAIRVIEW AV | SINGLE FAMILY | SEP 21 1999 | 1930 | DARK | 9917195 |

**DESCRIPTION GROUP  NARCOTICS          COUNT    1**

| TEAM | DESCRIP | ADDRESS | SCENE | EARLY DATE | AVTIME | LIGHT | OFFNUM |
|------|---------|---------|-------|------------|--------|-------|--------|
| 9 | NARCOTICS | 1400  PROSPECT ST | YARD/LAWN | SEP 09 1999 | 2010 | DARK | 9916281 |

**DESCRIPTION GROUP  OBSTRUCTING          COUNT    3**

| TEAM | DESCRIP | ADDRESS | SCENE | EARLY DATE | AVTIME | LIGHT | OFFNUM |
|------|---------|---------|-------|------------|--------|-------|--------|
| 9 | OBSTRUCTING | FAIRVIEW AV & KALAMAZOO ST | OTHER | AUG 11 1999 | 40 | UNK | 9914180 |
| 9 | OBSTRUCTING | KALAMAZOO ST & SHEPARD ST | STREET | AUG 20 1999 | 2355 | DARK | 9914868 |
| 9 | OBSTRUCTING | CLEMENS AV & KALAMAZOO ST | STREET | SEP 22 1999 | 1500 | DAY | 9917199 |

**DESCRIPTION GROUP  TRAFFIC          COUNT    3**

| TEAM | DESCRIP | ADDRESS | SCENE | EARLY DATE | AVTIME | LIGHT | OFFNUM |
|------|---------|---------|-------|------------|--------|-------|--------|
| 9 | TRAFFIC | CLIFFORD ST & KALAMAZOO ST | OTHER | AUG 21 1999 | 2129 | UNK | 9914923 |
| 9 | TRAFFIC | 222  LATHROP ST | STREET | SEP 24 1999 | 1557 | DAY | 9917358 |
| 12 | TRAFFIC | CLEMENS AV & MAIN ST | OTHER | SEP 06 1999 | 2229 | UNK | 9916059 |

**DESCRIPTION GROUP  TRUANCY          COUNT    1**

| TEAM | DESCRIP | ADDRESS | SCENE | EARLY DATE | AVTIME | LIGHT | OFFNUM |
|------|---------|---------|-------|------------|--------|-------|--------|
| 9 | TRUANCY | 123 S FRANCIS AV | SINGLE FAMILY | SEP 22 1999 | 845 | DAY | 9917174 |

**Grand Total: 22**

Fig. 5.7b. Offenses detailed report for Western, September 28, 1999.

The Ecology of Information Distribution

Two people worked in the mapping office isolated in the second floor of the headquarters (as if 2002, empty of day-to-day police-patrol functions). Some detectives worked out of headquarters, and the reactive nature of patrol work put them "on the road." The lack of supervision and evaluation of "problem solving" meant officers had little interest in mapping, little contact with the office, and little reason to use it. The crime-mapping function was isolated physically in headquarters in the planning unit, and the staff had irregular face-to-face contact with detectives or patrol officers. The links to external organizations were being created consistent with developing a community-accessible web page.

While crime trends, mappings, and distributions of crime by time, area, and even modus operandi could be produced in Western centrally and at each precinct for about a year, the maps were used (when they were used) merely as tactical representations of distributions, incidents that could be suppressed through crime-attack tactics. Investigative officers did not use the system, nor did they routinely enter data into the database. Since detectives worked on a case-based activity, they had no reference to trends or patterns unless they appeared recently, e.g., a series of unsolved house breakings in a particular neighborhood over the previous few days or weeks.

By design, the Western system was ecologically and functionally decentralized, and this was the stated aim of Chief A in his reorganization plans. It was perhaps also a function of the size of the organization and its history. The various components that constituted the criminal-intelligence complex were isolated from each other physically and functionally. The Research and Planning unit had no contact with patrol officers. I asked one of the staff, "What counts [what is seen as a basis for good performance] from a patrol officers' perspective?" and "What are they expected to produce?" He answered, "I have no clue."

Patrol officers did not have access to the mapping system on-line in their vehicles, nor did they use the map-printing terminals. This was consistent with their view of needed knowledge, their job, and the aesthetics of control on the streets. The Research and Planning division made a decision to decentralize and not to make the mapping data available on-line because they did not see it as contributing to the patrol function. One captain interviewed reported that perhaps 1 percent (of the patrol officers) used it. Sergeants did not use the information to evaluate their officers. The absence of training in the use of the terminals and mapping was doubtless a factor. Moreover, maps were rarely produced and even less commonly used. Since the crime information that was distributed was after the fact—e.g., information on warrants served and arrests made—it had marginal utility for patrol officers and could not guide or alter their activities. Maps were not distributed to neighborhood groups or used to register and monitor officers' behavior or evaluate their performance, except by the one captain.

## Mapping in Practice in Western

The command personnel of the department at the time of the study period were divided on the value of the mapping system.[6] One captain, now retired (in late 1999) but formerly precinct head, refused to use computers (he had been head of the laptop project a few years previously). Chief C, as a captain, attended a crime-mapping seminar at Harvard's Kennedy School, and actively used maps to guide and query officers. He printed out crime maps showing recent clusters of crime and urged officers to investigate, problem solve, and "do something" about the crime. He prepared a detailed memo (written in summer 1999) comparing drug arrests by team and precinct and arguing for a change in targeting by the drug squad. Chief B, when interviewed, doubted the value of the current system because the various databases were not linked (pawn shops' licenses, property room holdings, stolen cars found and location thereof), and because none of the information is on-line (it was approximately one week old). The maps were not used by command staff for strategic planning, aligning resources in either investigation or patrol, evaluation, or tactical movements of resources, although they were discussed in command staff meetings.

When maps were used in Western for crime-focused work (even with citizen access to social services on the department's web page), it should be noted that the broader questions of the interconnection of crime, disorder, and disarray were not noted or taken on board. What was tried in Western was severely limited, a range of interventions from on-the-spot negotiations to arrests. As used by one captain in Western, crime mapping identified current, short-term trends or clusters. IT did not make visible alternative approaches to the apparent problem, options such as crime-prevention efforts, problem solving, coproduction with local groups, or noninterventionist approaches.

The level of abstraction required of officers was increasing as a result of the introduction of software such as crime-mapping software, expert systems for detective work, and administrative devices like the NYPD's compstat process and meeting. To develop a broader use, the maps and the data "behind" them had to be viewed as more than mere collections of colorful icons, or as electronic pin maps. This view did not emerge in Western. Crime maps (and other analytic models), while often colorful, fascinating, and provocative, had no intrinsic actionable meaning and were abstractions. A picture does not speak for itself; it may in fact require a thousand words to explain it. Maps combine diverse types of information, bearing on many aspects of social organization, often with complex linkages, and use dramatic size, color, and dynamics to command attention. The map is not the territory or the thing represented; it is only a representation that must be interpreted.

Western's officers, even those with college degrees, like officers in other police departments, had no generalized conception of the nature of crime, its causes, dynamics, or meaning. This may not be needed to patrol the streets, answer calls for service, and make arrests when needed. It is, however, essential to any long-term alignment of efforts to problem solve or prevent crime. When asked about the causes of crime, officers either provided individualistic motives (greed, money, sex, pleasure); "ready-to-wear sociology" (broken families, lack of values and moral standards); and the inevitable explanation, that society is declining in principle and morality in general is low. They saw a deterioration of social bonds (a general police belief) as inevitable. Anecdotes served as evidence of these anodyne remarks. None of these "explanations" had value in acting to prevent or intervene in crime. They were useful shorthand recipes for managing in the here and now the crime and disorder that police encountered daily. There were no rewards or perks for being competent with this data.

The consequences of these transitions within the WPD were several (Manning, 2001a). They raised questions of loyalty (to what and to whom) across the ranks; of responsibility (to where and to whom—and if to "the community," to what groups and people within it?); of morale; and of the foci of policing in the city. These questions resonated with the already-present political divisions within the uniformed patrol group and the top command concerning the direction and mission of the department. The events in the city resonated with the changes in the police department, including its move toward crime-analysis capacity.

## Comment

This first case study describes a middle-sized police department in a middle-sized city in which the pressure for crime control and intervention was modest, or at least periodic. It surveyed and built on public trust through a rather staggering ten-year array of command changes and reorganization. The department remained unstable and problems remained, including the absence of problem-solving role definition, training, or an infrastructure for crime analysis (despite the chief's support of ideas such as CM/CA); the lack of organization of personnel within the teams (shift differences); and unresolved differential attachment to the philosophy of CP by some sergeants and command officers. These all added additional uncertainties. Uncertainty, of course, is a product as well as a cause of organizational change.

While police organizations do not easily change, it is important to note that the size and complexity of an organization shapes its information needs and analytic priorities. The WPD did not plan to become a mini-compstat-based organization, in part because the size of the organization permitted direct supervision of captains and lieutenants in charge of precinct-level decisions. WPD did not present the governing issues that a police department in a city the size of Chicago, Los Angeles, or New York does. "Compstatlike" meetings and other such modes of rationalizing are management tools designed for rewarding and controlling the higher level of management, and perhaps down to the sergeant level. Compstat and its clones, like all police innovations, are as much about controlling the patrol officers as controlling or managing crime and disorder. It is clear from recent research (Weisburd, et al. 2003) that the appeal of the compstat approach comes from several of its features: it is a direct, "street-relevant" tool; it can be tied to the ideology of crime control and crime reduction; it is fashionable; and it holds out hope that the command cadre can direct operations. It does not require reorganization, a great deal of money, or a shift in resources. Staging the meetings does not mean they have an impact on the environment. Whether the consequences of compstatlike meetings are all positive for the departments and communities remains an open question (Moore 2003).

The compstatlike process has various appeals depending on its fit with the conventional wisdom of the patrol segment (this ideology is reflected and supported verbally up and down the ranks of the police organization). Previous ethnographic research demonstrates further the sources of police resistance and/or acceptance of IT: police response is based on time and manner of introduction of the IT, officers' rank, officers' specialized function, and the level of information to which officers have access and that they must use. These instrumental matters are complemented by local policing practices and traditions that are symbolic (Manning 1992, 2003). The perceived utility of a given "tool"— e.g., cellular phones, mobile digital terminals, computerized databases for crime mapping, and other analytic software—interacts with these variables. However, immediate responses to inquiries, accessible databases, and rapid processing of data in preformatted records are universally trusted and welcomed.

It is characteristic of police organizations that they recruit and train their own specialists for a wide variety of tasks—vehicle maintenance, photography and evidence processing, management and research, computer-based data processing—and these niches are much valued by those who hold them. These niche positions are an elaboration on the basic occupational-organizational culture based on function, rank, and orientation to the job. The rank structure blurs the differentiation of activity of patrol officers in particular, or those below the rank of sergeant, but other evidence based on time and motion studies suggests that the tasks of officers below top command are so similar that one cannot in good conscience differentially reward them, nor reduce radically the number of ranks on the basis of skill. The position, the skills required to carry it out, and the skills of the individual role occupant are inconsistent in all bureaucracies (Thompson 1962: 138–51). The broad base of lower participants (those below the rank of sergeant) in policing requires that rewards flow to them directly or indirectly in order to sustain morale.[7] The technical support staff in Western was limited, and most of those who worked managing and maintaining the IT system were self-taught.

The crime-mapping system in Western was incomplete. It was awash in the ripples and tides of larger organizational movements. It was an idea being developed from a small room near the chief's office and with his blessings. It was staffed in the late nineties by one person with a master's degree in criminal justice and some flair for computer work, who spent his time checking his investments on MSN, checking his e-mail, and looking forward to retirement, and one civilian clerk who has since retired. The other clerks in the room carried out a few minimal tasks—basically supplying a set of figures, crime reports, a few maps, and the odd warrant. One project was mounted by Chief C when he served as captain. He compared the number and location of arrests for drug offenses in one precinct with the other. He then urged the officers in the East Precinct to increase their activity and arrests.

The databases were unlinked except that the LEMS (offenses) and arrests were merged weekly (after the study period, information on sex offenders, parolees, accidents, and field contact cards was to be added). Information on suspected drug houses was to be entered by investigators. These texts could be exported into SHAPE files and then copied to the planning unit's computer/server. These could be used to create maps that could be printed in one of eighteen terminals or mapping stations. No ad hoc requests for analysis or planning were reported by the head of the planning unit, nor were there any projects of this nature ongoing within the planning unit itself.

The problem-solving facilities were not linked to the community-policing program, which was itself a superficial and hollow exercise manipulated and eroded by the sergeants and most road officers (Manning 2001a). Very little, if any, problem solving was being done in any case, and none of it was recorded officially or acted upon continuously. Crime analysis was not analysis. The crime analyst kept information on warrants and crime-stoppers tips and did some information gathering (Western, Annual Report, 2001: 39). The capacity was entirely reactive.

The key players within the police department were at least tacitly supportive of crime mapping and crime analysis but were untrained and unfamiliar with its logic or merit. They were devoted to the ideology of CP. The connections between the two were not drawn. The mayor and other members of city council were supportive but unaware of the crime-mapping projects, although the mayor's office and his executive were keen on checking the progress of the commerce-funded website. Crime analysis/mapping had no media coverage, nor was it featured in any any media-amplified event that became a kind of "big theater," and there was no public concern—i.e., moral panic—about crime events, violence, or police veniality in the city. While there was a COPS-funded grant for statistical analysis, this "partnership" did not produce any noticeable results in connection with crime mapping or crime analysis.

The infrastructure of support and the capacity of the computer system were never issues. The system was untested, in part because it was not intended to be "on-line" but rather a weekly update, in part because the demands of the structure and format of data production were modest.

It is all too easy to attribute lack of rationalization in the form of crime mapping within police departments and in Western in particular to resistance arising from the "occupational culture," in this case meaning the uniformed, patrol culture, not the complex set of occupations and segments within the organizations based on rank, attitude, and interests. The craft notion, or what constitutes "good police work"—reactive response and crime management—remains powerful in spite of thirty years of development of complex, interlinked databases; management systems for storing, retrieving, and aggregating data; geo-coding (tiger files); and software (since the 1990s) for analyzing crime patterns by space, time, victim, offender, and offense, etc., as well as intellectual movements urging a rethinking of policing (Goldstein 1990). What is accepted most easily "on the ground" is what is seen by patrol officers to work—to save time and effort and symbolically contribute to their safety or their crime-control capacity. This perspective may lead to innovation and create resistance to conventional approaches. Significant matters patterning the use of new IT are structural and historical. The appearance of new technologies brings out the play and ways of technologies—how they fit in, slide around, and are adapted to context and organization. Organizations shape and embed technologies and may alter the routines.

Clearly, the patrol officers in WPD, where the interface of policing and the public existed vividly, were opposed to any sort of direction that deflected in their view from the crime-control mission. This mission they sought to maximize as a mini-ideology (a "canteen culture" describing "real police work" as crime fighting; see Waddington 1999). They were also in conflict with top management. Their unclear mission, low morale (in part the result of organizational changes, leadership fluctuation, retirements, and resignations), and ambiguous accountability (to a territory, a precinct, a beat, a shift, a partner, a sergeant, neighborhood associations, political "pressure groups," or the public) remained.

Other problems were conflict regarding the crime-control mission with the specialized units who did not connect with patrol regularly; lack of training for patrol in problem solving; poor or absent supervision under the team system; and variations in workload that the organizational changes produced (including the ten-hour shift system). All of these had an impact, and the crime-analysis project was one small step in the dance of organizational transformation.

The Western Police Department during the study period had an infrastructure of databases and servers, graphics capacity, and some limited expertise. It was supported by the top command and grants from COPS. The progressive leadership of the department fully intended to expand the use and general utility of the crime-mapping system, but the capacity for problem solving and actual use remained undeveloped. The few examples of use were tactical. The predominant rationality was one that emphasized the pragmatic, here-and-now, short-term-results approach to policing based on controlling known incidents after they take place.

# 6

# Metropolitan Washington and Police

## Introduction

In the Western department, there was a will at the top among the ruling cadre to make changes in the dance, to try out new steps, but this did not take place. The infrastructure was lacking as well as the necessary administrative staff. The demand from the perspective of call, workload, and size and scope of the department did not call for a compstat-like meeting, and the mapping capacities were used on an ad hoc basis and were not used by sergeants or officers. The community policing reorganizations were sufficiently taxing that effort to put in place a CM/CA capacity failed. The following case study based in Washington, D.C., using the same comparative dimensions, focuses on a project (COPSAC—Community-Oriented Problem Solving Analysis Center). The project was intended to integrate data gathering, data analysis, and spatial display through maps and feedback to precinct commanders and staff, officers, and the public, showing the delimited and defined territorial obligations of officers and the areas of neighborhood associations. As we shall see, not only was the information-processing network complex and almost impossible to overhaul on a piecemeal basis but also political infighting among the inner cabal, the conservative "old boy" network, and the change-oriented clique of people surrounding the chief was a source of resistance as well part of the field and surround of the District. The politics of the department were linked to those of the city government, in part because of the fiscal crisis of the District. The department was also being reformed from within by a group of consultant experts with the backing of the chief and his head of Research and Development. The political situation or field was highly charged because of the essentially bankrupt status of the city during the time of the study, and the surround was volatile as a result of the terrorist attack of

2001 and the earlier, still-unsolved celebrity death of a congressional intern, Ms. Chandra Levy. The combination of a new chief, the power of his core of loyalists (brought as a condition of his being hired), the financial status of the city and the department, and the very volatile surround meant that any innovation was faced with resistance from several sources both in and out of the department. The command, interviews revealed, was so preoccupied with maintaining a semblance of control (they did not know how many officers were employed by the District, according to an interview with Mr. Smith[1] in August 1999), given the numerous little theaters, or dramatic events involving the police, that arose, that internal innovations of modest immediate impact had little chance of command support and active resource allocation.

## The City of Washington, D.C.

The District of Columbia is a beautiful, violent, and hot city described by John F. Kennedy as a southern city with northern charm. It is a window into American government and policing for millions of people. It is distinctive in America not only because it is the national capital and a thriving and massive tourist center but also because it is one of the three or four predominantly African American cities (others are Detroit, Miami, and Philadelphia) in this country. Here, people of color are the substantial majority, the middle classes of color have a long history, and the elected officials are almost entirely people of color. The District is governed as a kind of plantation society with federal funding and oversight, even more so in the last few years, with periodic crises emanating from the Capitol and its politics. A fetid racist atmosphere of blame and shame abides in the city and arises from the sharp splits between the black citizenry and elected politicians and the white, highly educated middle- and upper-middle-class people who work in federal government and related service industries in and around the District. In many ways, the District is a microcosm of America in which wealthy white citizens "running the show" stand on the shoulders of the people of color who do the work of the city, especially its essential, tough, dirty, dangerous, and messy tasks.[2] The politics of the city revolves around race and the federal/District split, which replicates the racial divisions within the city. Its racially de facto segregated areas and divided school system, with most whites attending private schools and people of color in the public system, make crime a sharply divisive racial issue, especially when the victims are white (Chambliss 1994).[3] Attitudes toward the police, their capacity and trustworthiness, vary by the racial composition of the areas of city (Weitzer 2000; Weitzer and Tuch 2006).

The District is a square set on one point, nestled between Virginia and Maryland on the mouth of the Potomac. It was established in 1791, was named after George Washington, and was originally composed of two villages, Georgetown and Alexandria (the latter being across the river—it was ceded back to Virginia in 1846). According to the 2000 Census, 572,059 people lived there, 60 percent African American, 31 percent white, 8.9 percent Hispanic-Latino and the rest, "other" or more than one "race."

The city is highly stratified, racially segregated, and striking in the contrasts between the area west of the Rock Creek Parkway, almost exclusively white; the upper reaches of the central area of the city, a mixture of peoples and cultures; and the area to the south of the Capitol esplanade itself, which is almost entirely African American. The white, lower-northwest section of the city, called Georgetown, sits in the place of the original settlement and is the home of Georgetown University, fine restaurants and hotels, and lovely, very expensive brick row houses occupied by old families and high-status public servants. The seven police districts (shown below) were drawn to reflect workload and the sociocultural and economic stratification of the city. They are further subdivided into smaller beatlike service areas that were intended to be used for community-policing allocations but are not. The distribution of official reported crime and calls for service across the seven districts reflects these ecological divisions (crime and calls for service are highest in the southeast, in District 1). Unlike most large American cities, D.C. is not a city of immigrants but a city of migrants, from the South and elsewhere. The average income is $41,000, while unemployment is low, because about one in thirteen people living in the District is employed by the federal government. The District is surrounded by middle- to upper-class cities and commuter suburbs that are predominantly white. Forty-two percent of the adults over twenty-five have at least a bachelor's degree, making the District second only to the Silicon Valley region of northern California in educational attainment.

Several sociocultural features shape policing in the District, often subtly and sometimes directly. These features include its high-profile role as the national capital and the associated vast number (estimates of the numbers vary) of federal agencies and agents policing the city. Even the FBI has its own police, the FBI Police, which patrol the area around the D.C. office of the FBI. There are federal police subject to the control of the judiciary, to the legislature, and to the executive branch of government. The metropolitan police share jurisdiction with these organizations and most closely coordinate with the U.S. Park Service Police, who have responsibilities for the national monument and grounds. This overlay of responsibilities for patrolling, investigating, and managing buildings and grounds leads to unpredictable responses to incidents, negotiated authority in events, communications problems with the several channels and different megaherz radio systems, and virtual lack of shared databases and systematic data links within and between federal and district agencies. National events, such as presidential inaugurations, summit meetings, and demonstrations at the White House and Capitol, are handled well as a result of long-standing tacit conventions about planning, deployment, response priorities, and obligations. Even the several sewer and water-storage installations are routinely watched and patrolled during these events. The District is governed by two sets of courts since the federal law applies as well as local law, and police have the option of seeking prosecution in either court system.

These sociocultural features have daily consequences for governing the police department. If, for example, an outbreak of robberies occurs at a Metro stop, a rash of stolen cars appears in an area of the city, or a series of murders (more than two) makes the news, these occurrences are magnified by media attention and lead to further scrutiny of the chief and the department. When this occurs, the chief's office is occupied almost totally with damage control, media relations, and meetings concerning the incident.

The department is subject also to informal as well as formal scrutiny by Congress, the elected city council, the mayor, and, through 2005, ad hoc supervisory groups (a control board and a city financial officer) designed to enhance fiduciary responsibility. It has the highest density of officers per capita of any United States city. Its role as a "showcase" for many federal programs and research projects makes it a constant target for evaluation, although it is subject to periodic scandals, reform, and renewal in city agencies, as in any large city. In other respects, it is a typical large city with uneven rates of crime and disorder across its area (61.5 miles).

After 9/11 the department had only modest security screening at the main doors off Indiana Avenue. In 2000, an enraged man being questioned by officers in the department pulled a gun and shot an officer. Security, in the form of guards, searches, and magnetometers, increased over the year and half of my research.

These features of the District play into the high politics of crime and justice, as opposed to the high and low politics played out within the organization. High politics and media concern are not driven by statistical thinking, averages, rates, or comparisons of various sources of data (victim surveys, past trends, UCR [Uniform Crime Reports] from other cities, social surveys of citizens) but rather by "news" and the resultant "spectacle politics" (the politics of entertainment and media hype). Unrealistic, short-term, media-based episodes and their amplification detract from long-term organizational change, even when planning is required to more effectively control or prevent crime and disorder.

The District, as of 2002, was also unique for its governance plan. The mayor at that time, Mr. Anthony Williams, had formerly been the chief financial officer under Mayor Barry, and took office in January 1999. Prior to his election, there had been a major reorganization in the District. A control board had been created to oversee the human services and police. This board set performance standards, monitored agency budgets, and assured compliance with D.C. law. This control board reported to the city council, which in turn reported to the House of Representatives with respect to budget. The chief financial officer of the city oversaw financial officers in each major agency, including the police. These structures magnified the attention of external evaluators on the police. There were in effect two budget controllers operating for any budget request, and related paperwork. An atmosphere of "transparency" and a highly political atmosphere were both significant and abiding factors in the D.C. department. It was scrutinized by the media, the control board, the city council, the mayor, the courts, legislative committees, and, to a lesser extent, the public of the District in the form of neighborhood associations and advisory boards. The license plate for the District reads, "No taxation without representation."

## The MPDC Department

The District first was patrolled by an auxiliary watch until the formation of the Metropolitan Police Department in 1861. Since the early seventies, when President Nixon boosted its number to over four thousand officers, the District police department has maintained the highest density per capita in the United States—about eight officers per thousand residents, not counting the more than five thousand federal and regional forces in the some seventy-four police agencies working in the District (Kappeler, Sluder, and Alpert 1998: 192). Its crime rates do not reflect the results of this high level of police presence. It has been almost consistently rocked by corruption scandals for the last thirty-plus years (Kappeler, Sluder, and Alpert 1998), and mismanagement of personnel resources has been notable, including mismanagement of overtime and placement of far too many people in desk jobs (40+ percent). The department has also seen misuse of confidential information ("leaks") and corruption (Kappeler, Sluder, and Alpert 1998: 192 ff.).

## The Department: Districts and Police Service Areas (PSAs)

At the time of the study, the department was composed of approximately thirty-six hundred officers and six hundred civilians (15 percent), it employed about 25 percent female officers, and over 22 percent of the officers in the department were people of color. The city was divided into seven patrol districts for administrative purposes. Each district had a website and listed the commander's letter, staff, the smaller units, and those assigned to them (PSAs). For example, District 4 had fourteen PSAs numbered from 401 to 414, and the lieutenant and sergeants(s) in charge were also listed. The website also included the shift desk sergeants, their e-mail addresses, and their phone numbers. Also listed were the fax number and the specialized units housed in that police district. These seven districts were overlaid by three regional operations commands (ROCs), and they contained smaller units, eighty-three police service areas (reduced to forty-four in May 2004). These were created by Booz Allen, a consultant firm, some ten years previously. No one knew what the basis for these divisions is or was (see below). According to the District website in 2002, the outlines of the PSAs "follow neighborhood and natural boundaries." A given PSA was headed by a lieutenant and sergeants, and some officers. It was described on the website as follows: "The police service area (PSA team) is supported by the Focused Mission Teams, the detectives, the Mobile Crime Unit, Major Narcotics Branch, the Office of Youth Violence, the Special

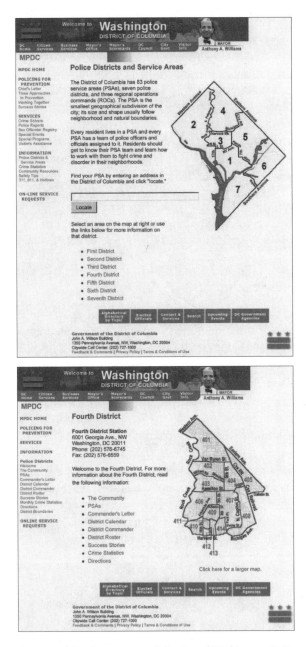

Fig. 6.1a & b. The seven patrol districts of Washington, D.C., and a detail of district four. See http://mpdc.dc.gov/info/districts/districts.shtm.

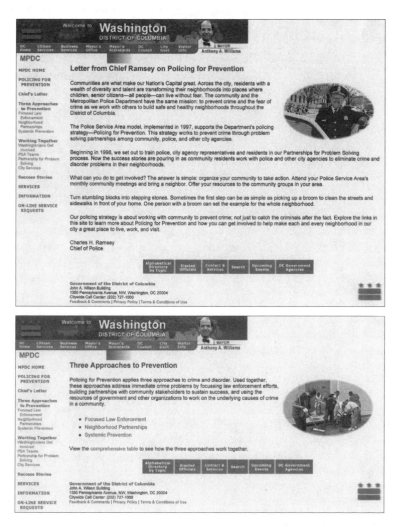

Fig. 6.2a & b. Police Chief Ramsey's letter on policing and his "Three Approaches to Prevention: Focused Law Enforcement, Neighborhood Partnerships, and Systemic Prevention" from the Metropolitan Police of the District of Columbia website.

Investigations Division, and other critical departmental resources." My fieldwork interviews did not contain any references to or use of the PSAs in any operational sense. The website also described the "Policing for Prevention Philosophy" that each team was responsible for carrying out on the basis of what was spelled out in the "Role of the PSAs Handbook." According to the website, this handbook was a "how-to" guide for team members so they could implement Policing for Prevention. Meetings were held in each PSA. This pattern of territorial responsibility, partnerships, and prevention echoed the idea that community policing is a tactical matter, with the addition of the fundamental thrust of crime prevention. This network of local groups was to be incorporated in the community-policing plan described below.

The chief at the time of my research, Charles Ramsey, came to the MDCPD from the Chicago department in April 1999, bringing with him a number of key people in computing, human resources, and management. His experience as deputy commissioner in Chicago was highlighted by his heading the Chicago Alternative Policing Strategy (CAPS) community-policing program. It was by all indications a very successful and well-funded program (Skogan and Harnett 1997). Chief Ramsey developed and publicized the three-part program described in figure 6.2.

His program emphasized, as the outline shows, focused law enforcement, neighborhood partnerships, and crime prevention. It was clear, logical, and comprehensive, and consistent with the conventional wisdom of policing. It was an impressive plan, and his team was headed by outstanding and experienced people. In large part, the attention of his period in office was on the law enforcement side of this program, in addition to the costs and time entailed in reorganizing.

His period in office was punctuated, as with many big-city chiefs, by very dramatic and nationally publicized events—the disappearance of Chandra Levy, the related salience of Congressman Condit, the finding of Levy's body after the study period and her presumed murder, the crash by terrorists of a plane into the Pentagon on September 11, 2001, and the related anthrax attack via the U.S. mails centering on the Capitol and its buildings. The murder of Chandra Levy was still a public concern, as was the fear of additional terrorist attacks. The anthrax attacks had not been solved, and the Capitol resounded and shuddered at each new terrorist alert, or clearance of the Capitol building (as occurred during the funeral of former president Reagan in July 2004 and twice in 2005 because of stray small airplanes).

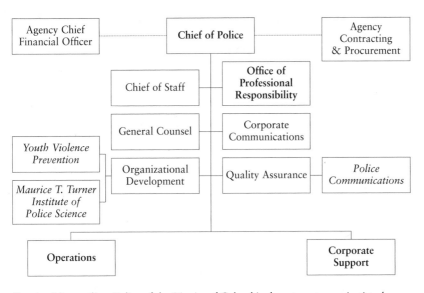

Fig. 6.3. Metropolitan Police of the District of Columbia department organizational chart.

The top command of the department was composed of the chief, three deputy chiefs, and the three regional commanders. The organization, featuring the investigative, patrol, and administrative arms as central, was a familiar one. Note that the human resources and development and research component within which the COPSAC project was housed was large and included a variety of functions. Note also that the Office of Efficiency and Organizational Oversight (OEOO) headed by a civilian with wide police management experience, Mr. O'Toole, is the central mover in rationalizing the force. In effect, Mr. O'Toole's role is to co-opt and coordinate the many hired contracted experts, consultants, wise men and academics enlisted in the reform efforts. While it is in many ways organized and structured like any large American police department, the MPDC department is unique as noted above.

In many respects, like all police departments, the MPDC and its subunits from time to time run in a crisis mode. Data and analyses are demanded immediately, sometimes by a phone call or unannounced walk-in, and these demands were given priority. These crises ranged from minor to large-scale impediments—they were called "refrigerators" because they displaced everything else on the desk—that interrupted and altered staff work. In fact, routine work was perhaps the exception

| Crime | 1993 | 1994 | 1995 | 1996 | 1997 | 1998 | 1999 | 2000 | 2001 | 2002 | 2003 | 2004 | 2005 |
|---|---|---|---|---|---|---|---|---|---|---|---|---|---|
| Homicide | 454 | 399 | 361 | 397 | 301 | 260 | 241 | 242 | 232 | 262 | 248 | 198 | 196 |
| Forcible Rape | 324 | 249 | 292 | 260 | 218 | 190 | 248 | 251 | 181 | 262 | 273 | 218 | 165 |
| Robbery | 7,107 | 6,311 | 6,864 | 6,444 | 4,499 | 3,606 | 3,344 | 3,553 | 3,777 | 3,731 | 3,836 | 3,057 | 3,502 |
| Aggravated Assault | 9,003 | 8,218 | 7,228 | 6,310 | 5,688 | 4,932 | 4,615 | 4,582 | 5,003 | 4,854 | 4,482 | 3,863 | 3,854 |
| Burglary | 11,532 | 10,037 | 10,184 | 9,828 | 6,963 | 6,361 | 5,067 | 4,745 | 4,947 | 5,167 | 4,670 | 3,943 | 3,571 |
| Larceny/Theft | 31,466 | 29,673 | 32,281 | 31,343 | 26,748 | 24,321 | 21,673 | 21,637 | 22,274 | 20,903 | 17,362 | 13,756 | 14,162 |
| Stolen Auto | 8,060 | 8,257 | 10,192 | 9,975 | 7,569 | 6,501 | 6,652 | 6,600 | 7,970 | 9,168 | 9,549 | 8,136 | 7,467 |
| Arson | 200 | 206 | 209 | 162 | 150 | 119 | 105 | 108 | 104 | 109 | 126 | 81 | 61 |
| TOTAL | 68,146 | 63,350 | 67,611 | 64,719 | 52,136 | 46,290 | 41,945 | 41,718 | 44,488 | 44,456 | 40,546 | 33,252 | 32,978 |
| % Change, Previous Year | N/A | −7.00 | 6.70 | −4.30 | −19.20 | −11.20 | −9.40 | −0.50 | 6.60 | −0.10 | −8.80 | −18.00 | −0.8 |

These statistics reflect official Index crime totals as reported to the FBI's Uniform Crime Reporting program. These totals may differ from the preliminary monthly statistics presented elsewhere on this website for a variety of reasons, including late reporting, reclassification of some offenses, and discovery that some offenses were unfounded.

Fig. 6.4. Citywide crime statistics, annual totals, 1993–2005.

rather than the rule in the Research and Development Unit (RDDU) unit because it served other units within the department, especially the chief's office and the head of RRDU. Crime and the official UCR figures are political statements and always of concern in this police department. The district's reported crime figures for 1993–2000 are shown in figure 6.4. They reveal that crime in general decreased after 1997. Homicides were at 454 in 1993 and dropped to 242 in 2000.

## The Rationale for the COPSAC Grant

A grant to the Metropolitan Police of the District of Columbia from the federal COPS Agency was intended to establish a Community-Oriented Problem Solving Analysis Center (COPSAC) using link analysis and crime mapping. This grant money organized and focused efforts to bring crime mapping and crime analysis into place in the MPDC. It enabled the hiring of several people on short-term "soft-money" contracts to institutionalize the program. It was the framework within which the discussion of crime analysis flowed. As we shall see below, the theory of the COPSAC grant was to build up databases that would permit the flow of information among the public, neighborhood associations, and PSA teams. These materials, ideally, would be accessible to the public and the PSA teams and would include information in addition to crime statistics for the districts.

The argument presented in the successful grant application was that since policing in general is demand driven—organized to respond to calls, investigate crimes, and clear them—and is often heavily tasked and deals with uneven demand, it is rarely able to plan, to develop analytic capacities, and to integrate patrol and crime-prevention and -control plans. The aim of the center, as stated, was to enhance problem-solving capacity in the department, as well as to increase interagency cooperation. This project was an effort by the MPDC to strengthen its community-policing program by training crime analysts with access to relational databases and crime mapping in analytically based problem solving. This grant was viewed by the department and members of the RRDU as a creative and ground-breaking effort to link information technology, analysis, and problem solving.

The original idea was to have an integrated information-analytic

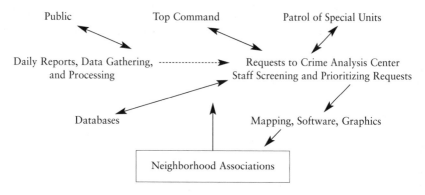

Areas of Concern: Quality of Life, Crime Prevention, Crime

Fig. 6.5. Community-Oriented Problem Solving Analysis Center (COPSAC) information flow chart.

services design, as shown in figure 6.5. This would include preparing routine reports, such as the daily report, as well as responding to requests for maps, trends, tables, crime analysis, or assistance with problem solving. In time, there would be channels for obtaining feedback and using crime-data and trend analysis to pattern deployment both routinely and in response to issues arising, such as a series of robberies, rapes, appearances of open-air drug markets, and auto thefts. The key people in this enterprise would be two people, an advanced doctoral student with government-grant-processing experience (Mr. Smith) and an M.A. with skills in math, software programming, and computer science (Mr. Jones). They would be supported by an executive assistant and the staff of the Central Crime Analysis Unit (CCAU). The CCAU was at this time three sworn officers. The center would be linked to the Research and Resource Development Unit on the one hand and operations and patrol units on the other.

The project team, when first interviewed, recognized that preconditions were essential to the success of COPSAC and related rationalizing moves. They were first working on determining the quality of the data input, assessing the problems and prospects for linking the extant databases, reorganizing crime-based information for analysis and response within the department, establishing the unit itself, and developing a clientele of users. Even more hopeful was the plan to link these data processes to neighborhood associations in the PSAs, and to respond to problems and issues arising within these groups and associations. The COP-SAC project was part of a larger transformation and rationalization of the MPD. It was also linked to reorganization by a chief appointed from outside the MPD. The implementation process faced a series of problems, including technical ones such as integrating the databases, articulating soft- and hardware, managing organizational and political issues, and still others emerging during the time of the study. These changes were also linked to external changes in the polity. The political process in which COPSAC was embedded extended outside the department. Planning, meetings, and negotiations, which began in 1998, were underway to bring together the databases, skills, office space, and personnel involved in IT in the department as a whole. There were a number of high-level committees on IT, including outside consultants and internal functionaries. The Office of Professional Integrity coordinated these. The COPSAC project was part of a larger strategic plan to reshape the overall structure of IT in the department. Some of the issues in this change inevitably overlapped with the COPSAC project. Assessing and evaluating the capacity of the COPSAC project to explicate interrelationships between crime analysis and community dynamics, and their capacity to augment MPDC's problem-solving efforts, was twinned with this large reorganization effort.

Let us now consider the six dimensions along which CM/CA efforts are analyzed.

## The Move to Crime Mapping and Crime Analysis

### Key Players and Their Political Networks

Systematic data have never been valued as a basis for running the department, according to an interview with the district commander. Such data have historically been absent, incomplete, or wrong. But control of data as a basis for power was of interest. Especially since this was a new chief, the power issues were salient and the struggles were characterized as conflicts between the old guard and the new people (in this case, "Chicago people"). Several important groups had an interest in data and data management both inside and outside the department. These networks altered the political processes of the department, from budgeting to promotions and reassignments. First, there was an inner core.

People mentioned that there were those (high-ranking officers) in the department with strong and direct political ties to the mayor or city council members. Second, there were internally based networks that of course extended outward into the city and federal politics, but these ties were unofficial, although very influential from time to time.

The external forces and players who shaped indirectly policing in the District were members of the mayor's office and the mayor himself (a former city treasurer), who had links to top command officers. Elected members of the city council had continuing interest in service to their electoral districts and the way they mapped onto the PSAs. Federal politicians and agencies had interest in the police since they funded the District formally, and also supported a wide range of grants and contracts to research groups, universities, and District agencies. The elected U.S. representative from the District, Ms. Norton, was very often in the news and commented on police performance. In addition, the committee in the U.S. House of Representatives that approved the District's budget was a constant concern to top command. As is true in most large cities, the local and national media, especially the national networks, daily newspapers, and television stations, were both feared and courted. These groups surfaced in importance in times of apparent crisis that evolved out of issues such as a horrendous crime, a series of robberies, a celebrity or high-status white victim, violence by the police against citizens, or a corruption scandal. The complex relationship between and within the many police departments functioning in the District made any coordination, advance planning, mutually shared facts, or analysis problematic. The one exception to this generalization was the presidential inauguration parade and ceremony, which had in the past functioned with apparent mutual aid and respect among the some seventy-four agencies policing the District.

Inside the department, three groups having power relevance or power bases were linked to the chief and were loyal to him and his programs. These might be called the *cliques* (Burns 1953) within the department. The first of these was the "Chicago Group," a group of approximately twenty people who were brought by the present chief as part of the conditions of his employment. They held key positions in Human Resources, data management, and technical support, and served as formal and informal advisors to the chief.

The second supportive and powerful group consisted of the many research-based consultants, who were both in and out of the organization. These researchers were advising on computerization and a series of other projects, and were paid on very large projects as well as being hired for short-term work. They maintained offices in the department and were there on a scheduled and an ad hoc basis for meetings. This group included contractors and consultants from present and past contracts and grants (because their influences were still seen in everyday operations in the MPDC), as well as employees of the Urban Institute, the Institute of Law and Justice, and private research organizations in the Washington region. They came in on selected days and were given desks in a large office on the fourth floor of the headquarters, not far from the RRDU offices.[4]

The third supportive group was a loosely associated group of "inner consultants" working directly with the Office of Efficiency and Organizational Oversight (OEOO). These were researchers with connections to the Police Foundation, the Police Executive Research Forum, federal agencies such as the National Institute of Justice (NIJ), and the Community-Oriented Police Services (COPS) Office, and who served in state and local government in Research and Development units in police agencies. This inner core spoke the language of social reform heard in the professional meetings of the key associations such as the American Society of Criminology, the American Criminal Justice Society, and public administration societies. They had read much of the latest research on policing and could cite it and quote key parts effectively and persuasively.[5] This articulate miming of research made the research interviewing somewhat a reflective and reflexive task. (It was like listening to myself.) Those interviewed would quote the latest research on community policing, on reform of police, and on managerial transparency and data management. When I asked if they thought the reform of the department would be a success, for example, they would quote studies funded by the NIJ, the Police Foundation, and COPS on the success of research projects. They represented the intellectual core of people offering advice to the chief.

These were the three chief cliques that supported the chief, and they overlapped in fact and exchanged ideas and advice formally and informally.

On the other hand, there were conservative groups that I call "cabals." The most important cabal was the "inner circle," or old guard, who had held power in previous regimes and under different chiefs. These officers had been shifted around and reassigned to reduce their power, but because some were linked to politicians in the District, they continued to have latent power. One of these officers, who had been shunted to a project and given a suite of offices behind closed doors, used to walk around the department out of uniform in short sleeves and with no tie, greeting people and gossiping in the hallways. He was especially popular when he dropped by to visit with the women in the communications center of the department. I interviewed him in his well-furnished office, and he told me in general terms that he was working on the juvenile delinquency problem in the District. The second group was the uniform patrol division itself. Officers on the ground in the districts viewed political change at the headquarters as a remote and futile exercise in self-promotion at best and a destructive waste of time and resources at worst. This cabal group included most of the district commanders although the three regional operational commanders were supportive of the chief.

The relationships between the cliques and cabals and between the internal and external groups were dynamic, and their alliances were issue dependent, uneven, unpredictable, and episodic. They are best described as "loosely coupled" with each other. That is, the demands made, one upon the other, and the content of the responses, varied widely from day to day, week to week, and month to month. It was something of a loose network of exchange relations.

It is always difficult to assess power, which is important even when it is not used. The most powerful internal network regarding data and information contained the chief and his people, or "the Chicago people," as they were referred to (even though some were not from Chicago): the deputy chief and people in the human resources-management, development area; Ms. Waite and her assistant, Mr. Green; Mr. O'Toole and his consultants; the head of research, Hercules Nonpareil; Mr. Smith and Mr. Jones (mentioned above); and Ms. Ulysses (a trained researcher). The most important member of this network in the data-management area was Mr. Aregato, an officer who joined the MWPD as an associate of Mr. Ramsey and who had developed a rather primitive crime-mapping capacity in Chicago and was trying (unsuccessfully during the research period) to refine and apply it in the District. Aregato had no contract with Research and Development or with the COPSAC project and worked with the chief's blessing. Members of the Technical Assistance Unit were also allies of the chief and were modifying the IRMA system of mapping developed in Chicago to be used in the MPDC. The department's chief information officer was also closely allied with Chief Ramsey. Members of this network or clique were not of equal power, and the social distance between a given person and the chief was the primary gauge of power. This is the essence of feudal loyalty. A set of past associations connected some members of an external network in government, private foundations, and research corporations to an internal network, a powerful clique. These experiences and associations included working in and for the NIJ, the Police Foundation, and the COPS agency, writing, obtaining, and monitoring federal grants; acting as consultants to the same organizations; publishing with major figures in criminology and criminal justice; participating in Harvard's Kennedy School seminars and minicourses; and in every way being linked into the conventional wisdom of the field.

Another internal network was constituted by deputy chiefs, the regional commanders, and the seven district commanders. Operations and corporate support stood far beneath the chief on the organizational chart. The deputy chiefs commanded three groups of districts: Central, North, and East. The usual divisions of power, authority, and resources were reflected in the organization when one examined the networks connecting CID; the SOD (Special Operations Division—basically a dynamic-entry, warrant-serving, and SWAT-team unit); the vice and narcotics officers; the street-level officers in the PSAs; and civilians. Each had stakes and interests in controlling and using data as it then existed. There were other groups within the department who had held power under the previous chief and awaited the fall of Mr. Ramsey. They were not linked tightly to the mayor at the time, but the former mayor, Marion Berry, and his supporters on the city council were allies of these groups. They were not so much active resisters as they were part of a retrograde cabal that avoided change. A final, rather marginal group consisted of all those associated with the community partnerships, restorative justice, crime prevention, and community organization.

These networks had consequences for decision making, as did the data-management groups (see below), in an indirect fashion. They were often shadow boxing in the dark rather than directly dealing with or meeting with each other. The simple flow of influence appeared to be from the chief's office through the consultants and the members of the Chicago group outward into the top- and middle-management level in headquarters and indirectly to the top- and middle-level managers in the seven districts. Much of the resistance was not direct, but passive. It was more likely to be agreement to act, combined with passive resistance and failure to act, e.g., to collaborate to combine databases. As mentioned above, resistance need not be self-interested narrowly, but may be unit premised or functionally based, as was the case with the CCAU and the Communications Center. The connections and actions of these cliques and networks did not always work in the same direction.

The vested interests in the TSU and CCAU were in many respects in controlling their data domains, and to a lesser extent in controlling others'. The resistance to centralized data analysis and to integrated databases was on the one hand based on a wish to develop and use a particular mapping system adopted from Chicago, and on the other hand based on a wish to control servers and software and to maintain present routines, servers, and software. The strong support and resources given the TSU meant that it could operate largely autonomously without cooperation with other units. The former head of the CCAU, Sgt. A, who was displaced for a time (see below) and then reemerged, had investment in his own cobbled-together version of a well-known office software ill-suited to sophisticated data analysis or to his servers, staff, database, and skills. During the study period, the duties of the unit were to provide daily crime reports and create and print out the occasional map. The center was routinized around these functions. Its autonomy was threatened by new software introduced more than a year previously (ArcView); changes in servers and their location; changes in the use and flow of crime analysis; and the new power of the TSU. Physical changes in the work space of Sgt. A and in employee functions took place in the late spring of 2001, as did some retraining . Placing the unit at the center of crime analysis as a community-policing–problem-solving function was a major change in duties, expectations, tasks, and status.

## The Nature of the Information-Processing System

In very large departments, such as the Washington, D.C., department, the aging computers, lack of modern wiring (fiber-optic cables that increase bandwidth and communications speed), and overloaded and slow circuits were major impediments to information-based change. The twelve computers in place at the time lacked the memory, speed, and storage capacity to support major data-based innovations. This problem was compounded by the tendency for federally funded software, such as applied expert systems for detectives, to be abandoned when federal funding vanished (Jacoby and Ratledge 1989). This in turn meant that the oral culture and institutional memory soon faded and officers no longer knew how to access the system or how to use it, and even the operating manuals were lost, misplaced, or dated. While there were many recommendations to restructure the information network of the department, it was always resisted by the District's budget office and oversight committee. All modifications were premised on the main frame and perhaps additional servers as needed.

1. There were some ten computer-based and -maintained databases of a major sort in the MPD.[6]

- LEGIS: contains arrest records for the District
- WALES: a regional system that contains access to NCIC (National Crime Information Center) and warrants
- PRECIS: lists stolen property
- TASIS: contains personnel information
- T-CAP: contains crime analysis and data on major crimes for UCR
- MUG shots
- Fingerprints (not digitalized or automated)
- Criminal Intelligence
- CAD (computer-assisted dispatching): contains dispatch data from Communications Center
- WACIIS: contains case management information

2. The primary aim of the period of 2000–2001 was to integrate the investigative databases with the criminal records. This was not accomplished during that time.

3. Some of the key softwares in use were Harvard Graphics, Microsoft Word, Windows, ArcView, IBase, Oracle, and UNIX. The mapping capacity of the crime-analysis unit was impressive, and maps of great size (four feet square and larger) and detail could be produced easily and cheaply.

4. There were in addition a number of non-computer-based files, such as those on current and past cases kept in the Special Operation Division, the Modus Operandi Office, the Juvenile Department, CID, Internal Affairs, and previous versions of the above-listed now-computer-based systems. These hard-copy paper files could only be used and merged by hand. The vast bulk of records

were on paper, filed and handled by civilian clerks and housed in the central headquarters in central Washington, D.C.

## Links between Databases

These databases represented a sort of archaeology of systems, lying on top of each other yet not linked. They represented historical innovations, impositions of new systems, and political decisions about what data would or would not be made available, and were at best full of out-dated information, whatever their capacity at the time. In large part they were used to track current decisions rather than to plan, anticipate, prevent, or control the "external environment" of crime and disorder. They were often not current, or out of date, from hours to many weeks. Basically, the core systems of data, those relating to crime and dispatch rather than investigative work per se, did not "speak" to each other, and they were not linked to exchange information freely. The data were entered in diverse formats. Some data sets, such as those used to create the daily crime report, were not formatted, or varied by district.

There were at least six centers of data processing that bore on crime analysis and crime mapping. They require description at some length.

The first was the CAD center, which contained about twenty people a shift, twenty-four hours a day. These civilian, mostly black females, answered some fifteen lines: calls to a seven-digit number, a 311 number intended to channel nonemergency calls, and the regional 911 number. The CAD system, revised in December 1999 when a decision was made that it was too expensive to replace the present system and main frame, permitted event description in the screen used by the operators to enter the details of the call in the box and was tightly formatted, but it was not linked to the current crime database (T-CAP). All call takers answered calls in order and thus each call taker might answer a call to 911, 311, and the department's seven-digit nonemergency number. This lack of triage made unlikely any subsequent division of labor among patrol or other units, or efficiencies that were to be expected as a result of the addition of the 311 number.[7] The call takers were oriented to the basic questions of who, what, when, and where, in no particular order, and might put important matters into the "comment" box at the bottom of the screen's menu. These comments providing context were not saved to a file when the incident was sent for dispatching. The operators functioned as pass-through agents rather than as information shapers.

While all police claim that the heart of the work is responding to calls for service, in the MPD and most departments, these data were used neither as on-line materials to monitor demand, check clearance of jobs, workload, or problems, or deploy officers, nor to make everyday decisions. The processing role of the call takers was fully consistent with this flat and empty ritual of fact mongering.

The calls to whatever number were answered by the same people sitting in a hot, dense, closed, and bleak room. The clerks were wired with headsets. The noise was constant and distracting. The clerks had to rise from their chairs, still connected to their phones by long wires, to use the crime WALES database at a separate terminal sitting at the front of the center just on the supervisor's raised dais. This meant that people got up with their headsets on or disconnected and used the database and then walked back to their terminals. The operators were dressed in a variety of nonuniform outfits (although there was a dress code, it was not enforced) and slumped and scowled at their desks. People wandered in and out, and the operators walked around talking, drinking soft drinks and coffee, and chatting to each other when they were not on the phones. Greasy, abandoned hamburger wrappers decorated the small desks, and Styrofoam cups sat everywhere. There was an air of anxiety that rested heavily in the room. A sergeant sat in a small office and could view the operations of the center, while the director of communications had an inside office near the center and next to the sergeant's office. Neither of these officers had any special training, education, background, or experience in communications management, information systems, or human resources. They reported that morale was low and performance poor, but had no suggestions about how to change those matters.

The second data-processing center was the crime-analysis unit that prepared the daily crime report. This unit has been described above and is discussed in detail below.

The third "data-processing unit" was the RRDU. Its staff processed grant information such as violence in schools and the UCR reports and prepared miscellaneous internal reports as requested.

In time, at the end of the formal research period, a fourth data-processing unit emerged. This was designed to deal with the forthcoming inauguration in 2002, as well as being a response to the attack on the Pentagon, the anthrax attack, and the possible planned and foiled attack on the White House. It was called the Synchronous Command

Center. It was housed in a large, windowed, oblong office with chairs and computers arrayed around a long black table. It was something of an "operations center" to be staffed in the case of an emergency of national proportions. It did no data analysis at the time of the research. The crime analysts in the districts and in the ROCs were the fifth group. They merely totaled the number of reported crimes daily, called or faxed them in to headquarters, and produced monthly and annual reports for the districts. They did no analysis.

A sixth group, officers in the intelligence and internal affairs units, gathered and handled data in secret or for limited purposes. People who worked in these six groups and with access to these databases had interests, often unacknowledged, in maintaining the status quo ante, if not in resisting actively any changes. Most of them did data processing, not analysis of any kind.

## Secondary Players and Infrastructure

A number of data minders with control and responsibility for central data collection were part of a fragmented records-management system (Abt Associates 2000) with a number of discrete databases and related software programs. The power networks based on these matters and related dynamics shaped the development and implementation of the rationalizing forces in the department.

Eight groups either manipulated, controlled, or used the major databases, software, and hardware within the department. These included the following.

- Current data "keepers." These were the managers of the (nine-plus) disparate databases within the department. These included, as I outline below, WASII, TCAP, CAD, and WALES, among others.
- Technical development people or the technical development unit. They interfaced with the data keepers and the users, and were writing software to establish a mapping database brought from Chicago that could be accessed using Oracle.
- The information services people (those who distributed, repaired, installed, and moved the computers in the department).
- RRDU members. They were at the time the number one user group, and most reliant on current operational data. They were

eager to have data for day-to-day use as well as for tactical, strategic, and policy planning. Their interests included crime analysis as well as other types of management information. They were often asked to process or find information from various sources, create brief summaries of crime trends, or characterize organizational units such as the contours of the present eighty-three service areas or PSAs.

- Officers and command staff in Operations (patrol). They could look to the RRDU for a research and planning base, but it is not clear that they did so.
- The chief's office and his immediate personal staff.
- Consultants hired on short-term (a year or less) contracts of various lengths.
- Crime analysts in districts who primarily did daily crime reports. The three regional command areas had crime analysts with slightly larger responsibilities but no formal training.

These eight groups did not meet, share data, or share concerns. They were linked as and when a situation arose that required some cooperation.

## Data Users and Clients

The primary clients for systematic data from the crime-analysis unit, other than the CAD data used from time to time by Internal Affairs, were the chief's office and to a secondary degree the Research and Development office.

The daily crime reports produced by the CAU were a set of tables produced daily without narrative for each category of major crime in each of the seven districts. The reports were created between 4:00 A.M. and 6:00 A.M. by the night-shift clerks in the districts and then transmitted by fax to the central headquarters unit. While the night clerks were called crime analysts, they were not trained; many could not read a table, i.e., add columns and rows, according to an interview with the sergeant in the CAU in August 2002. They were called "crime analysts," but they did not analyze; they counted and reported. The personnel entered the data and created the tables for the UCR crimes for the day, the month, and the year for each district. They printed them up, presented them to the chief's office by the 8:00 A.M. deadline, and prepared other copies for display. The tables, on 8 × 11 paper, were hung on a clipboards for each district in the CAU. This constituted the workload of the CAU for 95 percent of the time, as observed during the study period. After 8:00 A.M., the clerks, who were all sworn officers, tried to look busy, making phone calls, surfing the internet, leaving for long periods of time, and otherwise sitting and wandering around looking sullen and bored. They did not have the education, training, or skill to do other than very routine clerical work.

The chief's office was acutely sensitive to variations in the publicly known official crime rate as gathered by the crime-analysis unit. The most feared and carefully watched was the figure on homicides. Special care was taken to communicate indirectly and directly with the media. The sergeant who was head of the unit in the summer of 2001 prepared a bimonthly report to the newspapers on homicides, carefully edited to omit names of victims, witnesses, and suspects (if any). These were sent electronically (two- to three-line e-mails) to the newspapers, who then followed up with questions to homicide or to Sgt. A himself via phone. These were brief descriptive notes of three to seven lines of text, describing the scene as reported in the initial investigators' reports. They contained no comment, analysis, observations, or implications. The facts were to speak for themselves, and were edited to a level of triviality intended to protect citizens and the department from lawsuits or embarrassments.

The chief's office, often on short notice (twenty-four hours), also called for maps or tables. It responded to the city council's legislation that it evaluate the effectiveness and efficiency of the eighty-three service areas. They did not replicate the political districts of the city so that city councilors could not locate their responsibilities in connection to the PSAs. Information on trends in crime were requested, but usually in reference to the preceding two weeks. These were "refrigerators" dropped on the desk of the COPSAC-funded staff. Data demand also arose from district commanders, especially one, who maintained interest in systematic data collection and use. One district commander maintained a crime analyst on his staff. Her duties at the time were to assemble the daily report figures. Another source of demand was the odd officer who decided he or she wanted to check on some "hunch," e.g., that more dogs on patrol would reduce armed street robberies, and wanted to gather data for a month or two to "test" the idea. Maps were produced after two months, but they were disappointing. The results were not impressive. Three other groups in theory were to be clients: patrol officers, detectives within the department, and neighborhood groups, associations, and interested citizens. No requests from any of these groups were received by the CAU during the study period, although responding to citizens' concerns and providing feedback to them was a key element in the COPSAC plan.

## The Ecology of Information Distribution

The MPDC is a huge, confusing building of six stories, two sets of elevators, four sets of stairs, some of which do not go to all floors, and unnamed, unlettered doors that encircle the curious visitor. The halls are dim and barely lit. The name plates at the sides of doors in the halls are not present for some offices, and most do not have the accurate name for the offices inside. Some rooms that are public are left unlabeled. Some are mislabeled to conceal activities and units that require secrecy. There is no list of rooms, functions, or persons in the main lobby or on any floor. It is almost impossible to find a room unless one knows where it is and who occupies it. The building, like the Pentagon and the FBI headquarters, is designed to confuse and mislead any casual visitor, even one with an appointment, a purpose, and an office location. Anyone who ventures to find an office usually calls ahead or knows where he or she is going. The ground floor at the rear of the building and the first floor are full of public offices such as the drug-testing unit, probation, acupuncture office for drug treatment, and the District's registry of vehicles. The placement of services, offices, and units has long become a victim of circumstance, movement, and politics.

During the study period, computers and their service components were scattered. This included the main frame of the department and various servers and routers. The databases were supported by different servers in three different locations within the building (sixth floor, basement, and fifth floor). The sixth floor housed the communication center. The various locales for data storage varied as well, since they were partially in servers and computers and partially in paper files. Because the larger scheme for distribution of crime analysis and maps was not realized, at the end of the study the three access points for systematic data and/or analysis were in the crime-analysis center (as redesigned and reconfigured) in headquarters; in the offices of crime analysts in the districts; and in the district commanders' offices.

## *Mapping in Practice in Washington*

While there was considerable support at the top for the idea of integrated data use, especially with respect to plotting changes in calls for service and reported crime, community liaison, and problem solving, the support throughout the department was uneven. As I noted above, the flow of influence was from the chief's office through the members of the consultants and the Chicago group to the top- and middle-management level in headquarters. From there, it passed orally or indirectly to the top- and middle-level managers in the ROCS and districts. The resistance was not so much explicit in respect to this process but part of a broader political conflict about current command. The extent to which patrol officers were influenced by these changes was not known in detail, according to my informants, but the influence seemed to be very little if any.

Aside from the inability of the department to mobilize the COPSAC scheme, a number of clear points emerged. According to interviews I conducted in the Research and Development unit, there was a general feeling that the political environment of the city and the department made change very difficult. The unit was hampered not only by budgeting and bureaucratic inefficacy but also by the several oversight committees that reviewed requests and budgets. There was little interest in the department at the higher levels of administration in use and distribution of data. One regional commander said, "We never believed in data as a base for decisions, in part because we never had it, and now we are having trouble recognizing what might be there to use."

The administration, research officers, and change agents, all the key secondary players, were sophisticated and well-educated researchers and former police managers who had been at the heart of police reform for many years. They knew the research, the jargon, the names, and the buzz words. They were skilled interviewees.

There were no general crime meetings, no general crime analysis being done, and no links between the prevention thrust and the actual data and infrastructure to obtain and process it.

What can be summarized at this point is the status of the crime-analysis center, as it was envisioned by the COPSAC grant, at the end of the study period. The major players in the emergent strategic crime-analysis center at that time were Smith and Jones. The CCAU, as noted above, was a table-making unit and was headed for many years by Sgt. A, who had invented and modified the software used to collect and process the data. This patchwork system had developed over a number of years. Control over the software, the staff, and the production of needed numbers was his power base. Sgt. A had considerable investment in his patchwork of software, servers, staff, database, and modest skills. He maintained the system by almost daily adjustments in the miniprograms he had written. His autonomy was threatened by new software introduced more than a year before the end of the study period (ArcView); changes in servers and their location; changes in the use and flow of crime analysis; and the new power of the idea of an actual functioning crime-analysis unit.

In the summer of 2000, physical changes in his workspace and employee functions were carried out, along with retraining. Smith and Jones moved upstairs into these offices, rearranged the furniture, computers, and desks, and created a little Windows enclave at the rear of the room. They literally carried this out on their own. The sergeant heading the unit went on vacation, was deposed, and then was reassigned to a new unit called the Synchronous Command Center. Sgt. A, however, had the support of the cabal and one of the deputy chiefs. The deputy chief was well liked, and was an opponent of Chief Ramsey. This deputy chief was involved nominally in a "major project," had himself been vanquished for political reasons, and kept a small, secret, two-room office to which he retired to work on this major project.

In the spring of 2001, Jones supervised the staff of three sworn officers, and Smith headed the unit (Smith has since left the department). At that point, the duties of the unit were to provide daily crime reports and the occasional map. The center continued to produce the daily report based on information provided by district clerks. The center produced maps on request, and did a handful of reports on crime trends in PSAs. These were simple tables showing percent change by police district for the part I UCR (reported) crimes. No explanation, analysis, or comment was attached. In many respects, the unit functioned as a data-processing unit designed to obtain, via faxes and electronic files, data necessary to produce promptly the daily report on major crimes. The center was routinized around these functions. It was not linked to other databases such as those containing CAD data, crime-offense (UCR) data, or criminal records.

Attempting to place the unit at the center of crime analysis as a community-policing–problem-solving function required a major change in duties, expectations, tasks, and status. There was only a small change in the music, perhaps, but a new dance had to be learned and performed. At the end of the study period, the unit was doing an analysis of robbery trends requested by an officer. It was producing the daily reports with a new format and software. Most of the projects undertaken required the skilled staff to undergo training, teach themselves the software, and iron out the data as they tried to use it. As each new person was hired (two during the summer of 2002), she was given painful, daily tutorials by one of the other staff members in the office. The fate of the integrated program was unclear, but the grant money had ended.

## A Preliminary Assessment

Unlike the case of the Western department, where each of the necessary features of the six needed to produce a CM/CA capacity were missing except the server-based capacity, software, and graphics components, the Washington department had the potential and some of the infrastructure necessary to develop a crime-mapping-and-analysis capacity. It had a small but capable staff who had written plans, an idea about the direction of the center, and the motivation to accomplish the work. They had imagined the future, but it had not come to pass.

The needed six elements are highly interrelated. The presence of one connotes the others and their potential. If we consider the steps in the logic of development, this department had some funds and some skilled key players, but the project was insufficiently important to merit immediate, direct, and visible political support. While the project of the COP-SAC group was approved of by the consultants' group, their priorities were elsewhere, and major revamping of the information system had been decided against. There were far too many other issues arising that called for attention and resources.

In addition, there were other limitations upon this effort to change the dance. The data-gathering and data-entering processes throughout the department were flawed, uneven, and rarely validated by cross-checking (the UCR data were an exception). Missing data were so frequent as to make questionable generalizations from any sample about trends, patterns, or even synchronous reports from districts. Even daily reports had columns that did not add up. Major databases were being cleaned, formatted consistently, and validated in the interest of linking them, for example, linking CAD data and crime trends. In 2002, the count of homicides kept by the department in its paper files differed from that of the FBI, and civilian analysts spent most of the summer trying to find the files, correct the records, and match the figures. The major databases were not connected so that tables, graphs, and narratives could be constructed after the data files were merged, and many data-gathering functions were carried out in many ways. It was a main-frame-plus-a-multiserver environment. As noted, the ecology of the servers, computers, offices, and officers created problems in communication. The data-gathering units, places where databases were kept, places where servers were located, and the specific rooms allocated to these staffing functions were spread throughout the department from the sixth floor to the basement. In addition, the district crime analysts, clerks gathering daily crime reports from officers in the districts and passing them on, had no role in the larger analysis of crime. The diverse ecology meant that the users of various databases, servers, terminals, printers, and programs did not communicate electronically. Information did not flow in, become transformed, and flow out efficiently. While it appeared only secondary, an infrastructure of technical and repair support seemed lacking. This included coordinating the purchase, maintenance, and installation of technology with the data managers, technical people, and RDD people who were the primary data analysts (of crime or other data). Even the responsibility for budgeting and acquiring new equipment was unclear because of the several loci of fiduciary responsibility constraining expenditure in the department, in the city, and in the oversight committee. The groups working on data analysis were varied and uncoordinated. These were people with diverse skills, including both civilians and sworn officers, and they ranged from computer-repair people to high-level programmers, data managers, and people with Ph.D. degrees. There was little training provided for analysis, although this was in progress for several officers and civilian clerks during the study period. Clearly, the mandate and mission of the unit were never clear, nor were they distinguished from other functions or protected by top command. Finally, the links to other clientele—district commanders, crime analysts in the districts, patrol officers and detectives, and, eventually, the public in the form of the neighborhood associations and groups —were undeveloped. The politics of the department and its vulnerability to the crises attendant to policing a national capital were always imminent. These were ever-present new "refrigerators on the desk."

The struggle over control of databases and their uses led to the demise of the initiatives of the COPSAC grant, and the money ran out. For the last month or two of the grant, it was not clear whether Smith, Jones, and the administrative assistant would be paid. Nevertheless, in the period observed, from summer 2000 to summer 2001, changes of the CCAU are revealing. The CCAU and TSU, when first observed, were quite autonomous. At that time, the interests of these two units were in controlling their data domains and, to a lesser extent, controlling other databases. This led to a low-level resistance to any approach to integrated data processing and analysis. This was in part based on their knowledge of the data, in part on the modified software they possessed, and in part on their long-term power or their support within the MPDC at the time. This remained the case at the end of the study period. The crime-analysis unit was still perceived as a report-processing, map-creating, and printing center, not an analytic unit. This low morale, absence of training, and disinterest in the work were compounded by the shifting mission of the center and by efforts to be responsive to requests for analysis of short-term current trends, e.g., robberies, auto thefts, etc. The overall scheme was approved but never realized, although parts of it became part of the operations of the department, e.g., some short-term analyses were being done in the Synchronous Command Center.

Other forces prevented the realization of the integrated-service notion and the rationalizing initiative. They were important forces shaping the transformation process. Most importantly, the data needed were not available to middle management or patrol officers. The project had no effect whatsoever on detective work. Precise geo-coded materials, workload data, and reported-crime data were not sufficiently standardized across units reporting and officers entering the data to give consistent totals even of such crucial matters as reported homicides. The computers and the software were of uneven reliability. The computers were often out of service: for example, only three of the twelve were functioning on April 5–6, 2001. According to my interviews, this was a constant problem. The previous software was not reliable and "crashed" twice in the first few months after Sgt. A left the unit. Jones had to reprogram it and create new formats for entering data for the daily report. There was a slow but steady accrual of training for staff in ArcView and crime-analysis processes, but it remained primitive. Ms. Ulysses, Mr. Smith, Mr. Jones, and two sworn officers were trained on

ArcView in the spring of 2001 but were not using it, as they were engaged in other "fire-fighting–problem-solving" activities within the unit and department. The vague mission of the unit was not clear and was still seen as a matter of processing the daily report. It was being asked to handle and respond to a variety of requests of various origins and dimensions and had no set properties or workable system for prioritizing, refusing requests, making assignment, or reviewing those assignments. This was the subject of one general order that did not "work" and a drafted memo on priorities and review of "demand" that resulted in no changes in practice. In part because rank is power, the unit often had requests for information from the hierarchy as those "lower" got word about the current concerns of top command. This captured the issue of defining the mission and the nature and focus of the requests for service. These requests were invariably stimulated by recent upward trends in crime rather than long-term analyses, trends, predictions, or problem-solving concerns.

This problem reflects on the issue of demand production as well as, those interviewed said, on the lack of understanding in the department of the nature and role of crime analysis. There was little understanding of its strengths and/or weaknesses and its role in planning allocation or evaluation of policing. This perception of the uses of the data meant that current crises must be responded to rather than developing longer-term projects or refining the database or software. This meant a very immediate, short-term focus for the dialogue between the center and its users. Some requests came directly from the city council or council members and were mandated with precise deadlines that moved aside other work because they were given priority.

This vulnerability indicates the pragmatic, here-and-now rationality that dominated the department from top to bottom. The crackdown, hot-spots ideology of crime smashing and reduction of crime by misdemeanor arrests of the weak and powerless had no credibility in this department, and compstat was neither talked about nor mentioned as a model of approaching crime control. A few of the top command and consultants supported the need to introduce new steps and new music, but they were few and clung to the emergent rationality hope—that as data supplied results, more people would adopt the position. This view of rationality was shared by some within the dominant coalition but not all, and it was opposed by the chief information officer of the department, who was the most powerful of the data gurus, and the sergeant who became the chief data minder in the Synchronous Command Center (the new planning and incident command center described above). The most erosive sort of rationality, responding to the media, doing damage control, and seeking short-term quiet, was the position of the chief and the deputy chief, who made the television appearances in connections with the matters that reached wide public attention (the Chandra Levy case, the pornographic-racist e-mails, the work to make the city more secure after 9/11). These faces of rationality were in conflict with respect to resources, personnel allocation, and energy devoted to tomorrow's tasks.

## Comment

The attempt to alter information processing in the department was politicized and problematic. This was a result of the commitments of the information-power-based cliques and networks within and outside the department, and the fact that the data managers were invested personally in control and manipulation of their information, guarded access to it, and did not feel it was a departmental matter that should be widely, quickly, and easily disseminated. Here, I include the technical unit and the Crime Analysis Unit. There was little inclination of anyone below the management-staff level to use crime-and-disorder-based information in any systematic fashion. A few officers did request maps, but they were not routinely and generally distributed or made available in districts through terminals.

The period between Chief Ramsey's accession and the end of 2001 created a climate of change and a new direction within the department, as well as the development of a tentative infrastructure for analytic services. Features of the organization, its power and dynamics, meant that a long-term rationalizing process was embedded in a series of political-power issues within the city and the department. These included most saliently the politics of organizational change and organized resistance that is characteristic of police organizations and was complemented, unfortunately, by the uneven skills and training in the analytic tools needed for crime analysis. This placed a heavy work demand on the skilled people who could and did undertake requisite tasks. The high politics of the District also contributed to slow progress. These political centers of the District, including the mayor, "watchdog" committees, the city council, and committees of the U.S. House of Representatives, intervened from time to time to make their presence felt. Internal struggles were reflected also in conflicts between data managers or keepers of the current data and their staffs; technical and infrastructure inadequacies; problems of level of staff skill; and changes in software, configuration, and mirroring of databases. The lack of infrastructure for repairing, moving, installing, and buying new computers was often both frustrating and crippling. A grounded network in the neighborhoods for police purposes that might channel information in and out of the police department to the neighborhood districts, users, and monitors (as we might call the neighborhood associations) was absent in 2001. Hope for linking neighborhood associations and their priorities to crime analysis and mapping as tools for community problem solving was present but fading.

The efforts of those implementing the rationalizing process were felled by the sword of politics. In a sense, the dance stopped. This was in part also due to the expiration of the grant and the exit of Smith to a university position. The pressure of demand management, the pressure of the here and now, the rationales provided for what was done, the chief responding to crises, and the bureaucratic infighting kept databases, software, and clientele well apart. The arenas in which power struggles were played out showed that those in power had no interest in fully developing the crime-analysis capacity

Any attempt to reorient policing to information-based or evidence-based operations implicitly challenges many assumptions about how policing ought to work. The assumptions of CM/CA—because it argues for an analytic approach using various databases, techniques, and software to make long-term trend analyses, solve problems, or respond to problems that require facts not found in CAD data—challenge the incident cynosure notion of the police culture. The implicit questioning is directed to the occupational culture that narrows the job to crime control or visible presence, the organization of police personnel deployment that is geared to very short-term trends, and failure to integrate community concerns and problems with everyday decision making. Thus the CAD system is the symbolic center of the organization's information system because it provides here-and-now, present information that officers consider the essence of their work.

# 7

# Boston and Police

## Introduction

In the two previous case studies, the music shaped the dance, and the organizations did not produce a viable and realized crime-mapping/crime-analysis capacity. Technology has played an important role in the transformative movements in these and other large urban American police departments, but technology is insufficient to alter the basic routines and practices of any police department. Each of the three cities studied was in the midst of change, although the effects of field and surround in Washington, D.C., were dramatic and more extensive since the city was essentially in a receivership. The salience of the political field meant that crime analysis and mapping had a certain cachet in Western and a looming importance in D.C., but in each case the potential was not realized during the study period. It is clear that the police organization is embedded in a field of forces, and that the external political structures, or the surround, can be penetrated by police actions as well as police actions being shaped by the high politics of a city. External politics are reflected in and reflect upon internal processes and reorganization. Technology moves within these constraints.

This chapter and the next two feature the Boston CAMs (crime-analysis meetings) because they make visible the ways in which the technological capacity of the Boston department is embedded in its traditional practices.[1] The meetings show the subtle interconnections of format, structure, and content and the nuances of sense making in collective arenas. After discussing the city and the department using the six dimensions, I provide a sketch of a selected meeting. The chapter ends with reflections on the complex interplay of IT and organized collective police action. Chapter 8 explores the way this complex sense making is accomplished.

## The City of Boston

The city of Boston is one of the oldest in America (founded in 1630), and it arguably has one of the oldest police departments in the country as well, according to its website (http://www.cityofboston.gov/police). The city had a population of 589,141 resident population as of 2000 and covers some 48.9 square miles. The city's general budget was $1.8 billion in 2003. Boston is perched on a peninsula and lies on a 45 degree angle from northeast to southwest, is surrounded by water, and has a large harbor at the confluence of several rivers. Islands dot the shoreline, stretching both north toward Maine and New Hampshire and south toward Cape Cod. The city is bounded on the north by Cambridge and Chelsea and to the west by old, affluent suburbs such as Brookline, Newton, Lexington, and Concord.

The city has a long and complicated history that conjoins its early role as the center of the American Revolution and civic culture with its later role as a technological and educational center. It has had one consistent theme over the last century—it is an immigrant city, nearly 30 percent of the city, according to the 2000 Census, having been born abroad, about the same as after World War I. However, as McRoberts (2003: 25–29) points out, there has been a small and significant number of African Americans in the city since the seventeenth century. Unlike other northern cities such as Chicago and Detroit, it did not have a huge influx after World War II. The most significant facts about resident people of color are the enduring concentration of Massachusetts-born in the city; the recent post-1970 influx of blacks from the South (the Carolinas and Virginia); the recent migration of blacks from the Caribbean, especially the West Indies and Cape Verde; and, finally, the shifting ecological concentration of blacks from near Beacon Hill to the South End and thence, by 1950, to the Dorchester-Roxbury neighborhoods in south-central Boston. The patchwork of small, ethnically based areas and neighborhoods such as South Boston, the North End, and Roxbury remain vibrant and a part of the landscape and politics of the city. Some areas, such as East Boston, Roxbury, and Dorchester, have remained as symbolic markers even as their demographics reflect the influence of new migrants from Haiti, the Dominican Republic, Cape Verde, and Somalia. The spatial concentration of blacks is the most extreme in the United States (Massey and Denton 1983), but the cultural differentiation within this segment of the population is very complex (McRoberts 2003: 43).

Like London, the city is in fact a concatenation of villages that in time were to become a part of greater Boston. The metropolitan region is called locally "The Hub." As of the 1990 Census, the city was composed of 59 percent white, non-Hispanic, 24 percent non-Hispanic black, 11 percent Hispanic, and 5 percent Asian-Pacific Islander. The unemployment rate in the city was 8.3 percent in 1990, while Dorchester (11.5 percent) and Roxbury (14.3 percent) had the highest rates within the city. Boston has a history of low violent crime when compared with other major U.S. cities, and has had a recent history of quite remarkably low rates of youth violence (McDevitt, et al. 2004). Violence, when it occurs—often in spurts, such as in 1992 and again in 2004—is responded to variously by the police and other politicians, and is not seen as a matter of eradication or suppression but to some degree as a matter requiring social intervention and prevention.

Many events shape the low politics and high politics of a city. These are sociocultural and are based on the ecology and the pattern of consistent ethnic/racial conflict within the city. Boston is a small city, a peninsula surrounded by water, a city with a relatively small school system, a very high proportion of Catholics, and a tightly integrated political machine. As Banfield (1965: 39) observed in an early and perceptive overview of Boston and its politics, the strength of the party system in local government (and the Irish and Italian control of the Democratic party) is the power it gives to the mayor to appoint people to city positions, including the commissioner of police, and to city jobs.

Boston is characterized by a high degree of ethnic concentration/segregation in residence. While it prides itself on being an ethnic city because of the long history of Irish and Italian immigration and assimilation into the politics and business of the city, race (really a surrogate for color when combined with ethnicity) is an "unmentionable" in the city. It is the axis of crime, of law enforcement, of the conflicts within the city between rising and falling social groups. The city defines itself as democratic, civilized, and nonracist. It has a long history in this regard of impressive achievement by people of color in the professions, and this is celebrated in the city. It prides itself on its connection to the abolitionist movement, the antislavery efforts, and the Underground Railroad. Yet, it also suffered one of the most painful, violent, and continuing race-based conflicts in this country during the 1974 court-ruled "forced busing" process (Macdonald 1999). The fact that it is a "liberal" city with a highly educated population, hosting over forty colleges and universities, is another reason why race is an unmentionable in political rhetoric and in policing.

The city is governed by a historically strong Democratic machine, based on deep roots in the Italian and Irish sections of the city and the city's highly educated population. The links between City Hall and the police department are historic, powerful, and continuing. All hirings, firings, promotions, and appointments to top command are approved by the mayor unofficially. (This was previously done officially.) The mayor still appoints the police commissioner, who serves at his pleasure. Boston is also a strong union city, and this influence is felt in the police department as well. Boston is a crowded urban area surrounded by the sea and rivers and has very high housing prices, as there is very little expansion in the city proper. Boston is a historic city with some very narrow streets and areas that have been preserved. This is important for the very rich visual texture of the city and its moral topography, but for policing, the city's aesthetic complexity is a burdensome reality, as time and space cannot be collapsed and it is impossible to skirt above or around the city easily on freeways, even north to south. (The suppression of the north-south interstate road, called locally "the Big Dig," declared finished in 2003, 2004, 2005, and 2006, is intended to change this.) Response time by the police means little in this city, with its heavy traffic, winding and narrow roads, large parks, harbors, rivers, and large, irregular Commons.

## The Boston Police Department

Although semiofficial policing patrols were begun as early as 1635, in 1838, day patrols and a night watch were established. The website claims, "The Boston Police Department was the first paid, professional public safety department in the country." The official date for the establishment of the department is 1854 (as shown on the official coffee mug), and the first department telephones were installed in 1878. The police officers wear a shoulder patch that includes the date 1630— the nominal beginning date for the establishment of the city of Boston —and this same shield is displayed over the doorway of police headquarters.

The Boston Police Department, in July 2004, had some 2,044 sworn officers, of whom about 67.3 percent were operational and 32.7 percent occupied "desk jobs" (or served in support staff capacities such as in the photo unit or ballistics). This yielded a figure of about 3.5 officers per thousand inhabitants. This ratio put the BPD toward the lower end of large cities, closer to the Los Angeles Police Department than to the Washington, D.C., MPDC (see chapter 5).[2] The daytime population exceeded two million (BPD 2003 Annual Report: 2). There were 796 civilians employed, about 39 percent of the departmental total. This was probably the highest proportion of civilian employees in any large American department. The department iin 2005 employed about 36 percent minorities, and women comprised about 14 percent of the total. In 2002, only 116 officers had been hired in the previous four years, and some two hundred had retired or resigned from the force. The most unusual aspect of the Boston department, other than the strong patrol officers' union and the support for higher education that is a result of the Quinn Bill,[3] was the prevalence of "details."[4] These, along with regular overtime payments, yielded some amazing salary figures (always published in the *Boston Globe*) for uniformed officers. The budget of the BPD for 2003 was $211 million.

The BPD is an old-fashioned department in some ways, with the strong influences of unions, ethnicity (especially Irish and Italian), the Democratic party, and the state Civil Service Commission, which reviews disciplinary decisions and firings. In many respects, the key players inside and outside the department were linked to the internal politics of the department and the constant issues of succession—the issues of who had "juice" as a result of being in the inner clique supporting the current commissioner, of who formed the cabals, of who sought power, of who resisted the current networks of power, and of who were direct enemies of the top command. The drag of incompetence, work avoidance, and promotion on the basis of political clout rather than ability remained as shadow factors in Boston, as they do in all police departments.

The internal politics of the BPD are important in fashioning any change, but they were particularly salient in the change being studied here for several reasons. The commissioner has overall responsibility for governing the department and is directly accountable to the mayor. The commissioner appoints, with informal mayoral approval, all the top positions in the department: the superintendents, of which one is normally termed the "superintendent-in-chief" or "chief," and the deputy superintendents. This number can vary at the pleasure of the commissioner, who can alter the organization chart to elevate jobs such as administrative services to the level of superintendent or not. At the time of the study, there was a superintendent-in-chief and five deputies; as of September 2005, there was no "chief." It was an open position. There were two superintendents, heading investigative services and patrol, who stood in effect just under the commissioner. There were three deputies in charge of the support services associated with patrol and the uniform division. These top posts were positions that could be held regardless of rank. The commissioner in effect could elevate an officer of any rank to fit an organizational leadership need. Achieving this level of political power was a function of political connections, favors, sponsorship, and support of officers inside the BPD, as well as political connections in the city and in the Democratic and Republican parties. The rank of officers in charge of special operations, the police academy, and so on were variable, and people could be appointed or achieve their position via rank promotion. In that case, a movement was both a position change and a rank change, but this might not be the case. The officers in charge of the police districts in Boston were captains and had achieved their rank via the usual series of exams and interviews, combined with political sensitivities and longevity. This combination of appointments and civil-service and union ranks meant a constant tension among years in rank, experience, and seniority, on the one hand, and networks of power relations within the department, on the other. It also created a tension common in bureaux between people of talent, skill, expertise, and training (or perhaps education in some cases as a surrogate measure of competence) and the positions they held. Some observers have called this the tension between skill and position (V. Thompson 1962) or between the professional model and the bureaucratic model of functioning (Wilson 1968). In effect, not only were there two different models of organization, a political one and a civil-service-union one, but there were also two different sorts of careers that arose in the organization: a "political career" and a "rank-based career." When political shakeups occurred because of the appointment of a new commissioner, "political" appointees could be returned to their achieved rank, laterally transferred, or forced to retire.

The consequences of this dual model of careers and advancement were several. It tended to make the top officers more likely to be politically accountable, as they could be forced to resign the position, request a transfer, be transferred, or, in some cases, retire as a result of a mistake, major public disaster, killing, beating, or failure to carry out an assignment. It gave some stability to members of the lower ranks who were not oriented to rank or position promotion or to promotion to a niche or "soft spot." Their rewards lay in time off, overtime, detail-based pay, and perhaps an organizational-skill-based niche somewhere in the organization. When transition in leadership occurred with the naming of a new commissioner, the top positions were invariably filled by new appointees of the commissioner, and former position holders were transferred, demoted, or reassigned (keeping the same rank), or they retired (by choice or not).

The BPD had both mission and values statements that were publicly displayed. The values of the department as stated in the Annual Report were to guarantee the constitutional rights of all citizens; maintain the highest standards of honesty and integrity; promote the professionalism of the Boston Police Department and the neighborhoods; enhance the working relationships between the department and the neighborhoods; and improve the quality of life in the neighborhoods. The mission statement was flashed constantly above the high desk occupied by a sergeant that faced the security-enclosed headquarters front door: "We dedicate ourselves to work in partnership with the community to fight crime, reduce fear and improve the quality of life in our neighborhoods."[5] How these were connected to everyday policing was not immediately discernible.

Boston had a commissioner-chief system of organization. Figure 7.1 shows the organizational structure as of 2003, with the top command superintendents and deputy superintendents reporting to the superintendent-in-chief and the "chief," as the latter person was called locally, reporting to the commissioner. Note that there were five coequal bureaux and no superintendent-in-chief; during the time of the study, two superintendents had served in that position, one as an acting chief and one as a result of an appointment by Commissioner Evans. The department was organized into five districts (A–E) and each was subdivided into two subdistricts, except E, which had three subdistricts (see figure 7.2). A precinct commander with the rank of captain headed each district and had a small staff (each captain's statement and staff were listed at the website, http://www.cityofboston.gov/police). Each of the districts was subdivided further into precincts and beat areas, patrolled by one-officer vehicles.

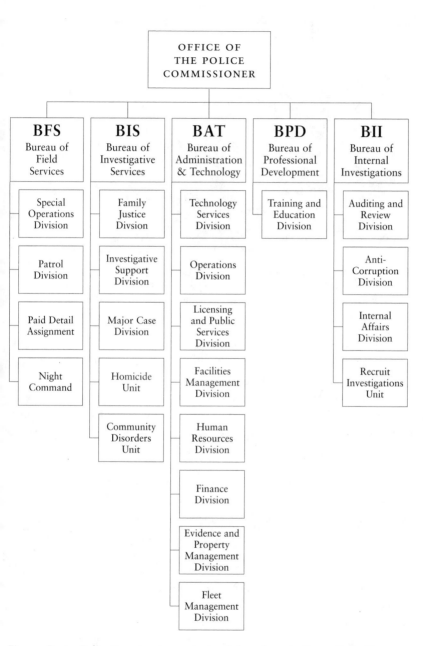

Fig. 7.1. Boston Police Department organizational chart, from the Boston Police Department, Annual Report, 2003.

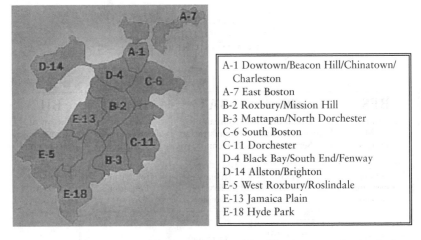

A-1 Dowtown/Beacon Hill/Chinatown/ Charleston
A-7 East Boston
B-2 Roxbury/Mission Hill
B-3 Mattapan/North Dorchester
C-6 South Boston
C-11 Dorchester
D-4 Black Bay/South End/Fenway
D-14 Allston/Brighton
E-5 West Roxbury/Roslindale
E-13 Jamaica Plain
E-18 Hyde Park

Fig. 7.2. Map of Boston's neighborhood district stations. The department is organized into five districts (A–E), and each is subdivided in two subdistricts, except district E, which has three subdistricts. See http://www.cityofboston.gov/police/district.asp.

The "same-cop–same-neighborhood" scheme was described on the website as the working principle for the way officers should spend their patrol time. The same officers were assigned to a beat and were to "spend no less than 60% of their shift in that designated beat." It was unlikely that this actually occurred, and there was no way to determine whether the standard was met because no one monitored the pattern of movements of officers, whether on horseback, on bicycle, on foot, or in motorized vehicles. The department website further stated that the department had reconfigured police districts and sectors, held educational sessions with supervisory personnel, identified potential road blocks and how to avoid them by middle managers, and carried on an ongoing dialogue with the Boston Management Consortium. The theme of the website was the familiar claim that these measures build partnerships, shared ownership of problems, and "greater familiarity of officers with the areas they work in." It was also "a useful tool in helping to bring the City of Boston to its lowest level in overall crime in 29 years" (posted as of August 8, 2004). The department had an active media relations office, a civilian spokesperson who responded and commented on public events affecting the department, and a website with links to city government, help lines, and FACs; postings of newspaper articles involving the police; and a link entitled "press releases (of the department)." The department also issued a fairly standard, up-beat, and positive annual report. The BPD website also had links to a number of federal agencies.

The thirteen districts had specialized staff assigned to them, including crime analysts. These officers were listed by name in the description of each district's activities in the BPD Annual Report.

Let us now consider the information technology in the Boston department.

## Key Players and Political Networks

Boston is a political city, and it regards politics as a high art, not the sham it is regarded as elsewhere. In some ways, it is not a cynical city but one that prides itself on its civilized, highly educated population, which coexists with a large recent immigrant population. It sees itself as "not New York" in all relevant matters cultural, political, and sporting. The key players within the city/police ambit revolve around the traditional Democratic political machine of the city, the city council, and the supporters of the commissioner within the department. The idea of a network is that people are linked together by relationships that vary in intensity, duration, and content, and that not all the parties in the network are linked to each other. They are all at the dance, and depending on the number and issue, they may dance with each other, but not with all attending and in the network.

The city police, ranking with New York and Philadelphia as the oldest departments in the United States (Lane 1967; Reppetto 1977), have suffered cycles of popularity and success and wild spirals of failure and public denunciation by the media. At the time of the study, and for the previous six years or so, it was highly regarded as a successful police department. This had not always been true. The BPD had experienced important changes in the preceding twenty-five years. Some *six landmarks* punctuated the history of the police from 1991 to 2003, at which time the study was ended. Its ending date coincided with the resignation of Commissioner Paul Evans in December 2003.

The first landmark event was a brutal murder and its subsequent investigation. The city police department, in 1992, was seen to be in disarray, a perception brought on by several events surrounding the Stuart murder (Charles Stuart, it would appear, killed his wife, named an unknown black assailant, and in due course committed suicide): the savaging of the predominantly African American Mission Hill neighborhood in the search for the killer; evidence planting in connection with the investigation; and the reaction of the African American community to events. The mayor at that time, Raymond Flynn, then appointed a commission headed by Boston lawyer James St. Clair to investigate the department and make recommendations.

The second event was the issuing of the St. Clair Report in January 1992. This was a turning point in reforming the police department. As a result of its acceptance by the mayor, the police commissioner (Mr. M. Roach) was forced to resign, and a new commissioner, William Bratton, was appointed. The recommendations for substantial change in major areas were taken on board. These included increasing supervision (lowering the sergeant-to-officer ratio), developing leadership, improving training, developing written policy and the mission, improving information technologies, and institutionalizing more systematic citizen-complaint procedures. The department was criticized in virtually every area of the report.[6] Perhaps the most salient aspect of the St. Clair Report was the finding that the police department had no written goals, missions, performance standards, or evaluative processes, and that they typically announced with fanfare plans that in fact came to nothing or were never even mounted. It was, in short, an old-fashioned police department run on personal ties and face-to-face relationships, trust, ethnic cliques, and networks inside and outside the department, and it was basically oriented to traditional policing.

It is important to note the impact and importance of the succession of commissioners at this point. Mr. William Bratton, formerly with the Boston Police Department, was named as the new commissioner in 1993, but left abruptly to become commissioner in New York City. Paul Evans was then appointed commissioner, a position he held until December 2003. Evans was a career officer, a former Marine, and had a law degree he earned while serving with the Boston department. At about this time, changes were undertaken: the building of a new headquarters and a move from the center of the city to an area bordering Dorchester, the institutionalization of research, and the installation of new informational technologies (Nesbary 1994). Superintendent-in-Chief ("Chief") Hussey served under the commissioner (until he resigned and retired in February 2004). Mr. Evans's brother was a captain who once had headed a BPD district. During his time in office, Mr. Evans was associated with a move to community policing, a decentralization of authority, including the dispersal of detectives to the districts, and high-tech innovations. These positioned the BPD in the forefront of information-technology-based advances in this country.

The third major event was in part an extension of the previous concern with the department's practices and a spike in publicly noted youth violence. All city agencies, especially the police, vary in their attention to and concern about gangs and youth violence. "Gang violence" is an elastic, flexible label for all manner of disorder perpetrated by those between twelve and twenty-four years of age (the cohort definitions are also elastic) and does not require a definition of "gang" or "violence" to raise public concern. While the underlying dynamics leading to crime by the young are well known, concern varies in large part as a result of media amplification of key events that, through dramatization, they convert actively into a larger issue.[7]

A number of other media-amplified incidents focused national attention on efforts in Boston to reduce youth. One of these was the previously mentioned murder of Carol Stuart and the massive search and saturation of the African American area of Mission Hill. Later, in 1995, a prosecutor who was known to be focused on prosecuting gangs, Paul McLaughlin, was assassinated. The punctuating event that moved concern from little theater to big theater was the shooting and stabbings at Morning Star Baptist Church in May 1992. These events were touched off by the funeral of a murdered gang member, and gang members' wish for retaliation and revenge. These events transpired in the long-standing shadow of the horrendous conflict in Boston in the seventies over busing of children into and out of South Boston.

A fourth event was in fact a series of related issues arising from concerted attempts to control youth violence. Responses to homicides in particular had been a tense and frequent part of the high politics of Boston in the preceding ten years. Homicides highlight and dramatize the focus of this book because the youth-violence-control projects and efforts of many organizations, including the police, were moves toward a kind of rationality. In many ways, the reported success of the program described below shaped policies in the department afterward.

A program designed to reduce youth violence was developed, including discussing and maintaining dialogue to define a problem (gang violence, gun use, and related youth homicide); deploying resources; and gathering data that enabled evaluation of their impact. A series of multi-agency-based programs and police operations was mounted beginning around mid-1995. (The police like to call concentrated activities "operations" and to give them provocative names following the military model of forceful, effective, violent, and tenacious attack.) Agencies were pulled together to work cooperatively. They used group problem solving and mapping and targeting to sharpen the focus of the project. The Harvard researchers most directly involved called these interrelated projects the "Boston Gun Project," but the activity described involved a number of agencies, missions, and tactics (Braga, et al. 2001). The named projects included "Operation Night Light" (teaming probation officers, street workers, and police); "Operation Scrap Iron" (to cut off the flow of illegal guns into the city) and "Operation Ceasefire" (to mobilize interventions with youth, especially gang members). When a violent incident occurred (according to McDevitt, et al. 2004), probation officers, police, ministers, and gang workers saturated the area to communicate, threaten more arrests, and note the dire consequences of gang violence. The projects included the involvement of the AFT and the U.S. Attorney's office to prosecute illegal gun possession and use. Particular gangs involved were first threatened and then the pressure was widened (McDevitt, et al. 2004: 63). Known offenders were told they were being targeted and watched; notices to this effect were posted; and meetings were held with people on probation where they were warned of the consequences of gang violence. This was a result of increased joint (many agencies were involved; McDevitt, et al. 2003) efforts and meetings to further define the problem, lay out strategies and tactics, and use crime mapping of known gangs, their numbers, and their territories (Braga, et al. 2001). The heart of the project was communicating directly with known gang member; targeting them and their areas and associates; and keeping up the pressure of surveillance, advising, and forums as well as threatening to use federal gun laws to prosecute gang members in federal courts and send them to sentencing in distant federal prisons. Federal law and federal courts and prisons were used.

One of the most celebrated efforts in this host of operations and projects was one that came to be called the Ten Point Coalition (TPC). It was organized and headed by three African American ministers: Eugene Rivers, III, Ray Hammond, and Jeffery Brown. It included some forty churches (Winship and Berrien 1999: 59). The organization was touched off by the shooting and stabbing at Morning Star Baptist during the funeral of a gang member in 1992 (see below). A fight ensued in the sanctuary. The TPC group, focused primarily on youth violence, held forums, observed police practices, responded positively to policing they perceived as fair, and consulted frequently with the police under the then commissioner, Paul Evans. The driving ideas or principles were several:

- Inner-city violence should be dealt with as a crime problem rather than as a symptom of other social effects and forces (broken homes, unemployment, and so on).
- Only a small percentage of youth cause the vast majority of crime problems.
- The community should have a say in the disposition of some offenders (first offenders, those with mitigating circumstances).
- If the police behave badly, they are to be held accountable.

According to Berrien, McRoberts, and Winship (2000), the ministry proved effective in targeting youth who were serious offenders while providing services in diversion, counseling youth, and presenting opportunities; they added a spiritual quality to the advice and consulting they did with youth and the police. This, according to the three authors, granted the Ten Point Coalition credibility and gave the police an "umbrella of legitimacy."[8] The argument of Berrien, McRoberts, and Winship is that by working closely with youths, counseling, adjudicating informally various delicts, and working with the police to ensure fairness, the Ten Point Coalition was the primary cause of the drop in homicide and, notably and dramatically, teenage murders.[9]

Some systematic evidence of the impact of this series of programs and operations, mounted in 1995 and continued with waning intensity throughout the study period, has been adduced by the research of Braga, et al. 2001, by Winship and Berrien (1999) on the basis of a senior thesis written by Berrien for the Harvard Department of Sociology, and McRoberts's published dissertation (2003). Both groups argued that the drop in youth homicides, the lengthy period of twenty-eight months without a single youth homicide, was correlated with the 1995–96 interventions following the death of Paul McLaughlin and the beginning of Operation Ceasefire. The drop in youth homicides became known as a national success story or, more vulgarly, as "The Boston Miracle."[10]

The aim of the projects was broad, but the most dramatic data were shown by the official police homicide figures. Homicides in Boston in the period 1990–96 dropped 61.2 percent, from 152 to 59. In 1997, forty-three were recorded, and in 1998, thirty-five. This was a total decline of 72 percent from 1990 to 1998 . The most commonly cited figure to support success was that from midyear 1995 until January 1998, there were no teenage homicide victims (Winship and Berrien 1999: 56). The period after 2002 showed a small rise in homicides and youth homicides and continued media attention to the rare police shooting or gang-related youth homicide. There were sixty-four homicides and four youth homicides in 2001 (Berrien and Winship 2001: 223); and thirty-eight total and twenty-two youth homicides (through August 6, 2004, according to the *Boston Globe*) (see figure 7.3). The rate of homicide per one hundred thousand on average in Boston has been 17.2 (or about ninety a year) since 1965.[11]

Braga, et al. (2001) argue, on the basis of the correlation of Operation Ceasefire with a 63 percent decrease in youth homicides per month, a 32 percent decrease in gunshots calls to police per month, a 25 percent decrease in gun assaults per month, and a 44 percent decrease in gun assaults in a targeted area (Roxbury), that it is likely that Operation Ceasefire in 1996–97 affected youth violence. Other programs were also noted (see Braga, et al. 2001: 60–62). These findings remained, they argued, even when other social factors that might affect the numbers were controlled statistically (Braga, et al. 2001). Braga, et al. observed that other cities absent this set of interventions saw drops in the homicide rate, but not as substantial a drop as in Boston.[12]

Several value questions should be examined along with the pragmatic claims that this worked or "this works." The program and the widely publicized results had an important effect in raising police prestige and legitimacy. However, since the ostensible aim of all the activity was reducing youth violence using youth homicide as a surrogate, the consequences of these programs on violence of all kinds, and the corollary effects on community relations, family relations, or future offending (Rose and Clear 1998) were not mentioned. The narrow definition of a project's purpose based on a criminal-sanction notion of "success"—arrests, incarceration, drop in official homicides, or calls for service concerning gunshots—does not suffice to tell us whether the "gang problem" or youth violence was successfully reduced in fact. Gang activity includes far more than homicides, drive-by shootings, and revenge cycles among gangs. The Winship-Braga et al. studies were a product of interviews with elite members of the minority community, the ministers who were the core of the Ten Point Coalition group, police gang experts, city-employed gang workers, and meetings and operations described in publications of those deeply involved in the projects, as well as Harvard academics. As McRoberts (2003: 100–121) points out, this effort was not a community effort in the broad sense, because the parishioners did not live in the area targeted, and only two churches of those listed in the coalition were "activist" in secular terms—eager to change society rather than to convert people to Christianity, save their souls, or give them hope of a heavenly journey. No interviews were reported with gang members, community members, family and friends of gang members, or victims, and their perspectives were not presented or represented. It is impossible to sort out the impact of the ministers, primarily the Ten Point Coalition, threat, fear, deterrence, arrests, and lengthy federal jail sentences for known juvenile offenders. Finally, the periodicity of violence, gang violence, and homicides has been well known since the nineteenth century, and the inability of research to sort out and control the several factors that contribute to the drop, which might be attributable to other interventions (e.g., gun laws and the effects of gun ownership on homicide) is well known.

A fifth turning point was the continuing focus on guided and rational change within the Boston department. The department continued to innovate, focusing on community policing. They had a policy that officers would spend at least 60 percent of their patrol time in a given designated area or "neighborhood beat." (These beats were much like the PSAs in Washington, D.C., but unlike Washington's, Boston's data were actually available on-line down to the beat level.) They sought to maintain their reputation for success in reducing youth violence and crime in general. They received less media attention for this than the NYPD. They avowed civility and democratic policing. The department's video, shown repeatedly in the main lobby-reception area of the headquarters, showed the value position and mission statement of the department (see above) and emphasized its aims: problem solving, partnerships, and prevention. Informative screens showed phone numbers for domestic violence and other city services. The headquarters included a public cafeteria and a child care center and adjoined a park and children's playground. The recruitment posters for the department showed smiling, rainbow-hued officers on horses, walking. They emphasized community policing without providing details of its promises or accomplishments.

The sixth event in the period prior to December 2003 that changed the BPD department was the introduction of crime-analysis meetings.

The CAM is a modified version of the NYPD's "compstat" meeting, but like everything else in Boston, was seen as different and operated quite intentionally differently. On the other hand, the objectives of the CAMs, according to the CAM Booklet (see below figures 7.4, 7.5), were to those outlined in the compstat documents. These were listed under "Commissioner's Expectations": accurate and timely information; rapid and coordinated deployment of resources to address problems; utilization of effective strategies and tactics; and relentless followup and assessment. As will be seen, this list implicitly valorized information, a short time frame, effectiveness, and followup. The ways in which these exhortations were realized were revealing, for they were taken as a gloss on "good police work." The objectives of the CAM, however, were broader and more provocative, including, to paraphrase the CAM Booklet, urging informed decision making based on widely shared data, use of crime analysis, and innovative problem-solving techniques. The list also urged identifying problems, supporting creative problem-solving efforts, developing a shared pool of knowledge, information, and strategies, enhancing awareness of the identified problems and solutions at the district level, and sharing those problems and solutions in order to "increase the department's ability to prevent and reduce crime." The emphasis on information, problem solving, analysis, and sharing, as well as on distributing solutions, was new. It portended a shift in perspective or paradigm that was contradicted by the "bottom line," both literally and metaphorically, increasing the ability of the department to prevent and reduce crime. Crime is a massively powerful expression that points to and often blinds people to its own contradictions and anomalies.

It should be noted that this history of six events or changes after 1992 interwove in public events politics (who gets what when and where), ethnicity (primarily people of color, whether African American or of other origins), the media, and policing. Violent events, namely, homicides and police shootings or dramatic chases, almost always implicate or directly involve these factors. They call for the production of new forms of dramatizing order and showing who is "in charge." It can be inferred that any increase in police efficiency, targeting, surveillance, or interventions, with or without technological impetus, will be redolent with these same tensions. The rather ephemeral consequences of direct police interventions and crackdowns are clear, yet the lasting institutional tradition of such shows remains.[13]

Information Processing: Key Data Minders

At the time of the study, the Research and Development unit was well funded and was located just down the hall from the commissioner's office. It was staffed by a director (who was a civilian and lawyer by training), a deputy director (who became director in late 2003), and twenty staff people plus part-time student assistants. It defined its role broadly, not simply as a clerical function, for according to its website, it saw its audiences as the mayor's office, the media, various criminal-justice agencies, other police departments, and the public. It did data analysis of assistance to the department. It had also "undertaken innovative and comprehensive empirical research projects aimed at expanding the Department's knowledge and decision-making capacity on topics such as hate crimes, citizen police academies, violence against police officers, prostitution and community policing." It also gathered city-wide crime data and hired staff to support the CAMs.

The deputy director of OR&E (Office of Research and Evaluation) had previously been a key player in the innovations in information technology carried out under Chief Dennis Nowicki in Charlotte-Mecklenburg County, North Carolina. The deputy explained in an interview (August 13, 2002) that about six years earlier a few departments moved toward a sophisticated information-technology infrastructure, including laptops/mobile digital terminals and, most importantly, electronic in-the-car record-accessing facilities. Boston, Los Angeles, and Charlotte-Mecklenberg were among these departments, which were perhaps moving toward a fully paperless (in imagery at least) operation and exploring the next step: wireless communication systems that link large databases across agencies, regions, and states and include access to federal databases in such agencies as the Federal Emergency Relief Agency and those now combined in Homeland Security.

The OR&E housed and equipped the crime analysts assigned to the several districts and had ten working terminals in well-equipped work stations. Most of the analysts had advanced degrees in criminal justice or related fields. They organized the crime-analysis meetings, presented an overview of crime in the preceding two-week period at the beginning of the meeting, and also responded to ad hoc requests for maps, crime figures, and photographs. Seven crime analysts were assigned to prepare materials in each district. These analysts prepared crime figures and reports, did maps on request, and participated in the rehearsal of officers who were slated to present at the bimonthly crime-analysis meetings at headquarters. Unlike the pattern in the NYPD under Bratton, the districts expected to present were given abundant advance notice and were rehearsed, coached, and prepared. They also were present at district-level crime-analysis meetings, called "mini-CAMs." They prepared officers for these and consulted on the content with the captain and his (all are males) chosen mini-CAM advisory groups (usually a sergeant, a detective, and the captain). The crime analysts prepared data for district captains, responded to requests for data from captains, participated in mini-CAMs in the districts and at headquarters, and prepared the slides, photographs, figures, tables, and charts used in the mini-CAMs and the CAMs. The office also organized the PowerPoint presentations and briefing books that were essential to the visual displays that were the focus of the meetings. A special software, called "Crimeshow.1," was used to collate the materials for the Power Point shows. It could be used to display on-line data in the conference room of the OR&E. Great care was taken to gather and process the data and materials for these meetings, first in OR&E and then in the districts. Although the crime analysts were assigned to districts, they were housed and normally worked in the headquarters building.

The communications center in the new headquarters was located on the second floor and was staffed by approximately sixty people (one-half officers, one-half civilians with uniformed officers, led by a deputy superintendent, as supervisors). It was in transition to be staffed entirely by nonsworn employees. It received calls on a ten-digit number (all calls were by then preceded by the area code), and 911 calls. Some of these were sent to a "neighborhood interaction unit," a car that managed nonemergency calls. The communications center was linked to the Criminal Justice Information System (CJIS), the National Crime Information Center (NCIC), and other national databases (see chapter 2).

The BPD Annual Report (2003: 2) reported a total of 625,102 "calls recorded" and noted that slightly over 100,000 were from cell phones. On page 19, the call total is listed as 481,356. The emergency calls from 911 and cell phones were 425,281. The calls had been steadily declining since 1999, when the total was 555,171 (p. 19).[14] The BPD Annual Report does not include data on what percent of the calls received were dispatched, assigned, or disposed of. Through a unique software, the operators in the Communications Center were able to shift calls that clustered from a given address or location—e.g., the scene of an accident, a neighborhood where shots were heard, addresses near a bar as a bar fight broke out—to an automatic system that informed the callers that the information had been received and a unit had been dispatched. Emergency calls and all calls on police channels were taped and could be retrieved for investigation of complaints.

Crime figures, based on reported crime, had declined in recent years. In the summer of 2002, they reached a thirty-one-year low and remained there through the following year. In summary, in many respects the transition of the BPD building from the center-of-town location on Berkeley St. to a more centrally located area geographically (but distant from the Boston Common, the symbolic center of town) in the late fall of 1997 and early winter of 1998 altered the fundamental communicational capacities of the BPD. Unlike other police departments, it had a fully integrated fiber optic system built into the building, all vehicles equipped with mobile digital terminals, databases that were linked, and, as well shall see next, adequate server capacity, terminals, speed, and memory.

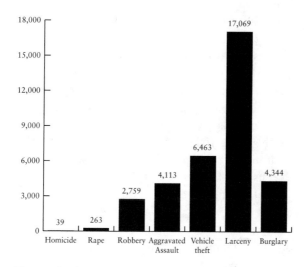

Fig. 7.3. On August 22, 2002, the *Boston Globe* reported the rise and fall of crimes committed in the first six months of each year from 1964 to 2002 as reported by the Boston Police. Property crime, such as burglary and vehicle theft, peaked at 32,784 in 1976 and dropped to 14,096 in 2002. Violent crime, such as homicide and aggravated assault, peaked in 1990 at 6,869 crimes and went down to 3,367 in 2002. This graph is a breakdown of crimes by type in 2003.

## Databases and Links

The BPD had ad hoc access to databases and surveillance capacities in the National Security Agency (NSA), which gathers information internationally via many satellite listening and imaging systems, and Immigration and Customs Enforcement (ICE), which monitors movements of persons in and out of the United States. It also had links to the Federal Emergency Management (FEMA) database. The BPD exchanges data with the FBI, which maintains the National Crime Information Center (NCIC, containing information on wanted and missing persons and stolen vehicles, firearms, and property); the National Incident Check System (NICS, listing those disqualified from owning firearms); an Automatic Fingerprint System (AFIS); Uniform Crime Reports (UCRs); and the National Incident Reporting System (NIRS) for recording serious crimes. The FBI is developing a national DNA index system. Massachusetts maintained a state file of criminal records and state vehicle and license registration, to which the BPD had access. The department also maintained electronic records on field stops, the jail population, outstanding warrants, "mug shots," and a management information system for basic operating records (payroll, attendance, etc.).

These databases could be accessed in headquarters, in the districts, and through the MDTs in the vehicles. The software and hardware capacity of the department was relatively standardized because the equipment was new since the department moved into its new headquarters. According to one informant in the headquarters, the former head of strategic planning, there was concern that the memory capacity of the servers and the main frame might soon become a problem, although funds had not been set aside for upgrading at that time (2003). In the Office of Research and Evaluation, all the standard graphic capacities and map-printing capacities were present, although requests from the districts were rare and no analyst reported receiving a request directly from an officer.

The Boston police maintained a civilian computer-maintenance staff, and many of the crime analysts were competent programmers and skillful at working out temporary problems.

## Secondary Key Players

If we consider the primary data users and players the OR&E, and the units that processed crime-and-calls data, as well as the crime analysts

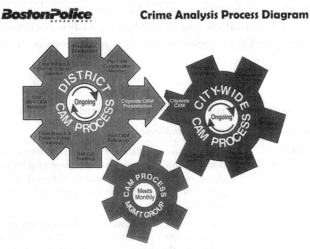

**BostonPolice** **Crime Analysis Process Diagram**

Fig. 7.4. Crime Analysis Process diagram from the Boston Police Department Crime Analysis Meeting (CAM) booklet. The largest cog is the ongoing District CAM Process, whose prongs include Host Mini-Cam Meetings; Crime Analysis and Effective Strategies Selection; Presentation Development; Pre-CAM Coordination Meeting; Crime Analysis and Problem-Solving Initiatives; Roll Call Briefings; and Post-CAM Follow-Up. These then lead through the Citywide CAM Presentation into the Citywide CAM Process cog. The Citywide Cam Process, which is also ongoing, contains Post-CAM Debriefing; CAM Process Management Meeting; Attend Mini-CAM Meetings; Review of Proposed CAM Presentation Topics; and Pre-CAM Briefing. These cogs spin together with the CAM Process Management Group, which meets monthly.

themselves, then the secondary players were members of the CAMs, captains and their staffs at precinct level, and, to a much lesser degree, officers on the beat. As the crime-analysis meetings showed, there was a widespread obligation to gather and use data, if not to understand it. The crime-analysis process was outlined and published as a booklet by the department. The booklet drew on focus groups and interviews about the process, its strengths and weaknesses. A committee was formed in 2002 to improve it in the short and long run. The process is shown in figure 7.4. The major secondary movers, to whom greatest responsibility was given, were the district captains. They were expected to supervise the mini-CAMs, carry out evaluation after the CAMs, distribute information at shift-based roll calls, meet with crime analysts to prepare for mini-CAMs and CAMs, and suggest major issues for discussion for the districts' presentations at CAMs. They were also expected to take the lead in education and in submitting ad hoc requests for data from OR&E. The CAM booklet states these obligations quite plainly, as described in figure 7.5.

| **New CAM Process — Department-wide Overview** | |
| --- | --- |
| *Activity/Frequency* | *Participants/Goals* |
| **Citywide CAM** (every 2nd & 4th Friday) | Senior Command staff will be "active listeners" as each district provides an overview of its emerging crime trends, the actions that are being taken to address them, and any particularly successful beat team and/or other effective strategies. |
| | Where necessary, they will question presenters and seek to engage other participants in an active dialogue on the techniques they have used, results they've achieved, resources used, etc., in order to highlight their good work, and to recommend any additional areas for further improvement, inquiry, partnership building, community involvement, etc. |
| | Where answers to these questions are not immediately available, Senior Command staff will request that further information be provided by a specified future date, and/or that additional followup activity, use of additional resources, etc., be undertaken prior to that district's next CAM presentation. |
| **Post-CAM Debriefing** (following each CAM) | Senior Command staff confer, then create and return written feedback to each presenting district. These appraisals will highlight both the perceived strengths and weaknesses of the presentations, as well as any specific items for further followup that were not (or could not yet be) addressed in the CAM presentation. |
| | The office of the BFS chief will provide these appraisals to the district commander along with comprehensive notes from the meeting generated by OR&E staff. OR&E staff will assist in the provision of any specific data, maps, etc., necessary for the required followup activity. |
| | Senior Command staff will identify the appropriate information from the presentations for larger distribution and use throughout the organization, and work with the relevant district, OR&E, and any necessary staff members to ensure its timely circulation and use. |

Fig. 7.5 (*above and opposite*). New CAM process: department-wide overview and CAM presentation format and guidelines.

# CAM Presentation Format and Guidelines

The following outline is intended as a reusable "agenda" or template for district CAM presentations:

| Personnel: | Presentation segment: |
|---|---|
| Commander/ District Captain | Introduction of all team members and presenters who will be participating |
| District Captain and any other relevant personnel | Followup from previous presentations, including new data, updates on the status of new initiatives, and answers to all questions asked during the district's most recent presentation |
| District Captain and/or Detective Supervisor | Crime Trend Overview—Description of current district-wide crime trends, their causes and effects, comparisons of data to previous months, years, etc. Both significant increases and decreases should be noted, along with explanations for these changes. |

District Captain and any other necessary personnel*

**Core Presentation on Selected Major Issue(s):**
1. **Primary Focus:**
   —What is the problem?
2. **Problem Definition:**
   —When and where is the problem occurring?
   —Is the problem primarily confined to a tour of duty, or a geographic area that can be shown visually?
3. **Assessment & Root Causes of the Problem:**
   —Who or what is impacted by problem?
   —What patterns or trends are shown through analysis of the data related to the problem? (i.e. how much, how many, how often—daytime vs. nighttime, day of the week etc.)
   —Who are the primary players involved? (names, photographs, modus operandi, drug houses, gang members, possible suspects, etc.)
   —What other information is available on the problem?
4. **Measures Taken to Address or Resolve the Problem:**
   —What measures have already been used to resolve the problem? (i.e. resources, initiatives, partnerships, etc.)
   —What quantifiable results have already been achieved (if any)?
   —What future actions will be taken? When? By whom?
5. **Evaluation and Followup Recommendations:**
   —Is the current strategy working?
   —Why or why not?
   —What other specialized resources are needed (if any)?
6. **Q & A, Items for Follow-up**

*Including, but not limited to, district personnel, BPD specialized units, other law enforcement agencies (i.e., DEA, MSP, MBTA, Boston University Police, etc.), community partners, etc.

<u>**All presentations will be limited to 45 minutes**</u>

Data Users and Clientele

The use of the data "on the ground" can only be inferred from this study, although the crime analysts did not see officers in the OR&E. The vehicles were all equipped with radios as well as MDTs. None was equipped with video or audio equipment, and it was unlikely, given union strength in the Boston department, that this would take place in the near future. All records of stops, arrests, and assignments were entered into the database electronically. Changes in the classification of an incident were required as well. That is, if an assignment was dispatched as "gunshots" and the officer discovered that it was a series of firecrackers, the call would be reclassified. These records were kept and permitted a more refined analysis of incidents than the calls-for-service record itself. The available software created in the department provided on-line access to the activities on the ground by supervisors. Data could be arrayed by incident category, date, time, place, and shift, on-line. The vehicles had access to the databases named above. The most frequently used were data on outstanding warrants and jail population, driving licenses, and vehicle registration licenses. Cell phones were used by officers informally, and all supervisors carried them.

The Ecology of Information Distribution

The primary data repository was the OR&E, which was the distribution center for requests. As they were located in the top floor of headquarters, there was little "walk-in traffic," and most of the data requests went out to district offices via computer. Maps could be printed in each of the districts, and each district had a small staff of people who looked after the computers and software. Buying and installation of computers was done by staff from headquarters. The capacity for rapid dissemination of simple maps and lists existed, and much could be conveyed to officers in districts if they requested it.

A few general remarks can be made in summary of the information processing systems of the BPD. The centralized information processing system in headquarters reproduced that in most large departments: ecological dispersal of officers with a great deal of independence, autonomy, and freedom in regard to their definition of information needs and relevance, and information and analytic ability concentrated in headquarters offices. The capacity to process information, including computer speed, memory, and function, quickly and efficiently did not translate into effective impact in the environment. Thus the vast increases in capacity had little consequence on the ground except to increase the number of ad hoc queries to databases. These queries, as has been long known, were incident based, not problem based. They had little to do with altering the social conditions or access to criminal opportunities or "crime prevention." Officers were loosely coupled (Weick 2000) to the information systems available, and were focused on the incident at hand, the current situation, returning to service and disposing of their portion of the workload over the course of their shift.

## A Glance: Crime Analysis Meeting

The purpose of this section of the chapter is to put some intersubjective realities into play. The music, the structure of the organization and some of its variants, may help us to see the dance more acutely. The arena for seeing and saying is the CAM.

### An Initial Visit to a CAM

My first visit was odd, for I now see that I missed many relevant details, such as the names on the place settings and the ecology.[15] I was introduced to the BPD by Jack McDevitt, a soon-to-be colleague, who made calls and prepared the way for my visit. I walked over from the university with Jack through Ruggles "T" station, across the bus street, and in the main entrance. (Later this was locked and passage was allowed only through the main door at the side of the building, which had metal detectors and an attendant sergeant as well as the supervising sergeant, who sat high behind a wooden desk, really a high podium, facing the door.) On my first visit I missed, did not note at all, the playgrounds with children's equipment, the cafeteria, the offices, and other amenities, including the child care room. Outside the main room, but inside a first door as we came in, was a table with coffee, stacks of uninviting Styrofoam cups, bagels, doughnuts, cream cheese, and juices in an ice bucket. This table was aligned against a wall, and a narrow hallway ran away from us on our left. People greeted Jack, and he smiled and waved to a number before we sat down and arranged ourselves. The room was a large one with a very big screen directly in front of the participants. A few feet back from the screen and running a third of the length of the room across was a set of portable folding fiberboard tables at which were seated, from left to right, the superintendent-in-chief and the commissioner. On their right were the two operators of the computers that processed the PowerPoint materials: maps, pictures, charts, tables, text, and cartoons. On the screen were to be projected two or more PowerPoint presentations from the computers humming on the desk and operated by young clerks, civilians from the Office of Research and Evaluation of the BPD. On their right were arrayed the rest of the top command: the seven bureau chiefs and the superintendent-in-chief, called "Chief." (They were required to attend, along with a named fifty-eight others, including legal counsel, technical service personnel, district captains, and people from major case, forensics, and media relations units.) Just in front of the screens to the left of the audience was a podium. On the far left, in a section that was about fifteen rows deep, sat the officers who would be presenting at the meeting that morning. Some were in uniform, some were in sports coats, all were without hats, and all were armed (I assumed). The largest part of the room was given over to seats for the nonparticipant audience, and some fifteen rows of chairs arrayed in a semicircle behind the front desk and facing the screen and the podium. The audience saw the backs of the main players: the commissioner, high-ranking officers, and civilian staff.

Before the meeting began, the room was quiet, but people were walking and greeting each other in a pleasant way. The atmosphere was relaxed, not charged or combative, and it remained so. "Good morning," the superintendent-in-chief said to the crowd. "Good morning," they replied, almost cheerfully. Guests were introduced and welcomed. The room was full at 7:45 A.M., and people walked around, weaving from one side of the room to other to get coffee and greet acquaintances quietly before the ceremony began and as breaks came in the programs. Two police districts were announced as those presenting, and they wandered forward. Each district featured a unique presentation, e.g., a drug unit had made a raid and was giving a special presentation for this district.

My presence was announced at the opening of the session by an officer who was running the meeting on behalf of the absent commissioner, Paul Evans. I was tired, slightly hungover, distracted, and uneasy. I was not sure what I wanted to write down or why. I took superficial notes. I listened and watched. The first district to present was called.

The presentation was introduced by the captain in charge of the district (this duty, I later discovered, could be assigned to another officer), and then a detective came forward to outline current cases and discuss investigative issues. Questions were asked in the course of the presentation at any time, asked very courteously, and answered courteously. What caliber was the gun used? Where is that corner or intersection? (A zoom was done to highlight the intersection using a map projected by PowerPoint.) A second district was called and presented in a very orderly fashion.

At the end of the meeting, two hours later, the CAM was adjourned, and people filed out, pausing to chat, make future appointments, ask questions of each other, and adjust their clothes and uniforms as they left the room.

## CAM: The Meeting and Some Observations

After my first visit, I returned repeatedly to the crime-analysis meetings, having gathered permission from the deputy chief, and worked my way formally and informally through the bureaucracy of the small, highly political departmental hierarchy (see appendix A for more details). The following remarks are based on these many visits.

### PREGAME PREPARATIONS AND PERORATIONS

The officers and staff in the districts planned ahead for and were rehearsed by staff from headquarters for their presentations at forthcoming CAMs. There was a fixed rota of districts called to appear, although the precise content of the meeting was not fixed. Prior to a scheduled appearance at a CAM, an advisory group met with the crime analyst assigned to the district, and they discussed the presentation's content, the figures needed, and any special topics or accomplishments they wished to highlight. These might be a major problematic facing the district, a successful program, a series of arrests—anything that might be of general interest to other districts. The OR&E unit of the police department prepared a mini-CAM district-based book for rehearsing the officers who were to present, and planning for the presentations was encouraged. The book contained data on the required areas (crime figures, etc., discussed below), and the data was put into a plastic ring-bound notebook into which papers and transparencies could be inserted or removed. The same book was used by the operators at the front table to project maps, zoom in on areas, and display other visuals used in the presentations. A locally developed software, Crimeshow.1, was used to present the materials and was designed to process data from the several databanks used in the department routinely: crime figures, CAD (computer-assisted dispatch) data, maps, and other indices of disorder or quality of life. All the records created by officers were entered electronically and were essentially on-line and useful, once submitted to the server. This meant that the tedious job of creating daily, weekly, and monthly written, circulated, official departmental crime reports that occupied the time of "crime analysts" in other departments was done in the BPD electronically. The format, topics, and headings remained fixed for each meeting. But special presentations could be scheduled or special areas of concern could be subject to a presentation, e.g., the 911 center, a particular issue, or a series of gunshots or shootings in a district could be highlighted.

### THE FORMAT

The format and related content of the cime-analysis meetings had evolved over time and in part had been developed to make sharp contrasts with the compstat meetings of the NYPD. That is, emphasis was placed on accountability, problem solving, identification of best practices, sharing of knowledge across districts, and maintenance of civil discourse (my addition to a characterization given me from the director of Research and Evaluation). As mentioned above, the order of appearance was set in advance, so that districts knew when they would be called and could rehearse the content and presenters who would appear. The meetings did not reveal the "shame and blame," confrontational style that characterized the Bratton-Maple-led meetings. The ritualized openings and closings and the sequencing based on hierarchy provided a tacit ordering that was overtly displayed by polite distance and question-and-answer sequences.

The meeting was opened by the senior person deputed by the commissioner if the commissioner was not present. Announcements were made of general importance (e.g., the death of an officer), but the focus was not "administrative" but on the process of information sharing. Any guests or visitors were announced (visiting police officers, academics, and other guests).

A crime analyst from the OR&E took the podium in front, facing the audience, and summarized the part I violent crimes and significant property crimes for the city for the preceding two weeks. Some comments or points were made to highlight or draw attention to some facts, e.g., trends up or down from the preceding two weeks or month or for the year. The most significant violent crimes of the preceding two weeks were discussed in more detail: the number of homicides, robberies, and assaults and how they were committed (weapon or not, domestic or public scene). A given rise, e.g., in auto thefts or shootings in the city, might be pointed out. Hot spots or clusters were identified and named as "resilient" or "emergent" depending on the length of their known persistence. Firearms calls were noted and compared to 2001 and 2000 calls, and firearms-related arrests were displayed. The figures were projected on the screen behind the presenter and another crime analyst operated the Crimeshow.1 software through a PowerPoint program in a laptop. The laptop screen was projected onto a large screen behind the presenter. The presenter could ask for screens to be changed, or moved. This required cooperation, as the presenter (whoever it was) did not carry a remote or "zapper" to change screens as he or she talked.

The opening presentation might or might not be accompanied by or stimulate questions. In general, it did not. The officers from the districts on the agenda shuffled forward and slumped in the chairs at the left of the podium. One person remained standing. The captain who headed the district was the default lead speaker but might delegate the task. The meeting unfolded as follows.

The presenter from the first district to perform introduced the other officers who would speak that morning. Violent crime within the district was reviewed by means of tables. A detective presented data on the violent crimes from his or her district—sex crimes, robberies, and aggravated assaults—and might comment on clearances. They were typically very low. Pictures of those arrested could be projected—usually "MUG" shots taken when they were booked. (Fingerprints were put into readily accessible electronic files.) Assaults were distinguished—domestic and others—and burglaries, commercial and other, were shown. Reviews were possible and could include trends from one to three years. These were available down to days if necessary. (In other words, all the aggravated assaults for a given day in that district, beat, or smaller unit could be pulled up and shown at the request of the presenter.) Any special events, such as a probation check using officers and probation officers, a drug raid, or a crime prevention program, could be presented as well. Calls for service were given a quick show. A special issue such as gang violence, a cluster of drug-dealing incidents, prostitution in public, or other matters of disorder might take up to ten minutes. These little minishows were sort of "dog and pony" rituals[16] designed to display innovations, show activity, alert top command to ongoing issues, or give experience to presenters.

A second district was set for an appearance after a brief coffee break. In general, the presentations followed the same order and emphasized similar crime-based topics. That the quality, style, and competence of the presenters was varied was commented upon by the top command and implied by their questions (they were quite polite but pointed). At the termination of each minitalk, the presenters thanked the audience and the audience mumbled, "Thank you." A similar exchange marked the closing of the meeting by the senior person who was chairing the meeting.

## Some Initial Reflections on the Crime Analysis Meeting

After some months of operation, in 2001 a group was assembled, including a consultant, to review the CAMs and present some suggestions. Material was gathered via interviews and focus groups, and was included in the CAM Booklet (cited above). The participants noted several points consistent with the stated objectives but added that from their point of view, additional advantages were the opportunity to learn from other districts, the timeliness and completeness of data, and the fact that districts were forced to better know the crime and related issues in their own districts. They also mentioned some weaknesses. While several were included, one was emphasized: the tendency of officers reporting to fill time with unsubstantial matters. Suggestions were made for improvement: better laptops with bigger memory, a force-wide intranet, and more crime analysts. In many respects, these comments addressed the fine tuning of the meetings and assumed that the meetings made sense and were useful in some fashion.

Some rather general conclusions can be gleaned from my observations of the CAMs and the uses of information technology displayed in them. Conversely, it is useful to consider what potential the technology has that is merely suggested but not revealed in practice.

- There was a very strong format effect (the order of topics focused discussion and limited the direction of attention). The set format drove and shaped the content that was presented week after week, and shaped expectations of audience, top command, and other participants.

- The format and the ritualization of presentations served as a kind of *aide memoire* in that reference could be made to previous presentations and data, and these could be recalled by means of the PowerPoint software.

- The crime analysts had great facility with the databases, and the PowerPoint presentations were slick, impressive, and virtually flawless. They did very little "analysis," but neither were they burdened with weekly and daily reports.

- All databases of relevance were linked and on-line. Other databases could be tapped, such as AFIS (Automated Fingerprint System) national crime information, Customs, FEMA, and emergency databases. Also available were the standard state-based agencies that retain information on motor vehicles, registration, lists of probationers, and sex offenders. This linkage made the visual displays and access dazzling at times.

- The format and menu were flexible enough, given the databases, to permit a wide variety of algorithms to emerge. For example, one could move by screen from a series of gang-related shootings to maps of gangs' "territory" to proximity to housing estates (public housing and their configurations) to pictures of key gang figures and then overlay the screens on maps of gang areas.

- Given a crime, or series of crimes, one could "drill down" to look at the ecology of a given street, to see the specific placement by address of a set of crimes, and then to connect them to their perpetrators (with stark, angry pictures of their resentful faces).

- The meetings were crime shaped, crime suffused, and crime was the trigger that set in motion questions, some problem-solving discussions, and suggestions or questions about possible immediate or tactical interventions.

- The meetings focused on the here and now of the preceding two weeks rather than on past problems solved or reports of previous efforts (failures or successes) and were designed to highlight the recent (the previous two weeks) and the largely successful (in the conventional terms of arrests and reductions in crime).

- Certain matters appeared to be omitted, whether by policy, practice, advice, or tact, I am not sure. Such matters included, for example, police shootings, fatal or extensive chases by officers of "fleeing felons," ongoing court case settlements, and so on. Some were matters that were in court, some were matters not discussed because they were deemed "administrative" or union-contract matters, and some matters were perhaps avoided in order to keep the media from seizing on the discussion to claim a serious uncontrolled problem at hand. (This is discussed below in more detail.)

- In many respects, the information technology was invisible because it worked so efficiently and well, and served every purpose put to it in the meetings observed.

- There were no questions concerning followup of previous plans or projects, and the problem solving that was done consisted of verbal, "top-of-the-head" observations and suggestions rather than structured sequences of formulating the problem and moving through to evaluation.

- In general, because civility was emphasized and rehearsals done, answers tended to be "standardized," almost scripted, and the presentations were done by the same representatives from the districts.

- The audience cooperated with the headline performers, not on the basis of rank or deference but as an audience: laughing at small miscues, embarrassing moments, and dis-ease at the podium, while also overlooking potentially disruptive cues. A working consensus emerged that was based on proximity, teamwork, and the veil of ignorance (Rawls 1970).

## Summary

The city of Boston and its police department are well organized and funded. The first look at the crime-analysis meetings in the BPD revealed that it had the most advanced version of crime mapping and crime analysis of the departments studied. The BPD had developed the infrastructure and the personnel and used these much more than the other two departments studied. The centerpiece, and the manifestation of the capacities, was the crime-analysis meetings that were held twice a month in the BPD. It would appear that the idea of a crime-analysis meeting of this type and the capacity to create it were stimulated by the success of the NYPD's compstat meetings. It was a comment upon the power of the commissioner at the time, Paul Evans, that he was able to create this new forum and that he helped to give it legitimacy. He put it into place as a possible source of new information for officers at the precinct level and below. Yet, as Crozier (1964: 142) wrote, "There are always weak spots, and power dependencies and conflicts will grow around them." The question is, How much did this ritualized meeting alter management and practice in the BPD?

The BPD had perhaps the most sophisticated data-analysis capacity present in any American police department at the time of the study. It combined the necessary databases, fiber optic cables within the department, support personnel, political resources, and leadership within and without the department. The top command were committed to crime analysis, problem solving, and sharing best practices with other police departments, according to an interview with the director of Research and Evaluation on August 13, 2002. The CAMs were the most obvious showcase within which IT could be displayed, and they were facilitated by the modern, fiber-optic-based new $70 million police headquarters building first occupied in the fall of 1997 and the winter of 1998. Nevertheless, as the case study and the following analytic chapters show, progress was not without costs, resistances, constraints, and limits.

The CAMs were perhaps a microcosm of the impact of information technology on policing. It is shaped more than shaping. The meetings were more than that, however. The full story was suggested, but only hinted at, in these public meetings. The full process of entering data, processing it, reorganizing it, and formatting it is possible because of the very well-organized and -maintained infrastructure of record-keeping storage and retrieval. The impressive, dramatic, colorful, and engaging shows that were a part of the crime-analysis meetings were a partial rendition of the information system in place, as well as a partial picture of the issues and policies that surrounded policing in the city of Boston. Most of the important ongoing decisions were not made at these meetings but in private meetings among the command staff, the superintendent-in-chief, and the commissioner, and at times between the commissioner and the mayor. Furthermore, the meeting did not reveal the work of investigators and their use of information technology. (This is an area about which little is known [see Harper 1991; Jacoby and Ratledge 1989].) Although investigators did present at the meetings, they discussed problematic clusters, described the odd arrest, or detailed a successful investigation (one that led to an arrest). What was actually done was not discussed.

On the basis of these early observations, the extent to which this information was used, as opposed to the rhetoric that surrounded its use in the meetings, was difficult to establish. The chain of evidence was weak. The process of tracking and back tracking information use was contingent on a number of factors, such as the six dimensions used to organize these case studies, the willingness of supervisors to follow up on projects and problems that were raised in the public meetings, and the ability and skills of officers to carry out intelligence-led work, in addition to the burdens of everyday police work and its uneven workload.

The structure of policing shapes the content of policing. It is clear that in the absence of standards other than the tacit ones by which "good police work" is known and said to be known and by which work is evaluated, modes of systematic evaluation on the model of crime audits, and feedback processes that are institutionalized, there can be no real assessment of the impacts of new information technologies. This is true whatever the capacity of the technology. We must return to the favored concepts of rationality and of rationality itself as situated and multifaceted and in some kind of competition within a context in the police departments studied. This is a key theme of the following chapter, which analyzes how the structure, ecology, and format shaped the very complex materials presented in the Boston CAM.

# PART III

# Appraising

# 8

# Contributions of Structure, Content, and Focus to Ordering

*Introduction*

The case studies presented in the previous chapters demonstrate the degree to which efforts to change police organizations based primarily on new IT require not only command direction (power) but also resources, skills, an infrastructure, and the willingness of a substantial number of officers and civilians to employ the technologies consistently. Technology is not a thing, solely a material matter, but is a symbolic, representing, and signifying entity. It creates modes of relating among people. As argued in the first three chapters of this book, the conditions under which various sorts of rationality obtain are not obviously powered by technologies, information, or the manifest means shown: mapping, maps, tables or figures, or crime analysis. Competing rationalities surface power and may dislodge power-based configurations.

An overt manifestation of information technology's ways is the fortnightly Friday morning CAM in the Boston Police Department. It is an exercise in which memory, facts, imagination, and social organization come together in often engaging and powerful fashion. This meeting shows the dance, with its variations, stylistics, and aesthetics. This concatenation of structure and process emerges from the ecological and structural factors, the meeting's ecology or places; the procedures that have developed, some of which are ritualized; and the content as it unfolds over the course of the meeting. These factors come together in the event, but it is not obvious how and why they do so. The question arises, How does a working consensus that allows things to be done develop over the course of a two-hour meeting? How is this consensus sustained and validated every two weeks in a differently constituted group?[1] How can such a show be mounted, staged, and then memorialized to the satisfaction of participants? These are surface features to be ordered, not the source of the order. The types of rationality identified later are not, upon close examination, consistent with one another but serve even as they are contradictory and are "good for all practical purposes" (Garfinkel and Bittner, in Garfinkel 1967). This means that the "glue" that holds together the stories, mininarratives, and explanations is not what is said or displayed directly, but knowledge *about* such matters (Wolff 1993; Mannheim 1960; Garfinkel 1967). This chapter dwells on the contributions of structure, procedure, and ecology to sense making (Weick 2000) in the CAMs. This chapter reexamines the Boston CAMs as a window into technology's ways—how the response to technology alters organizational relations and stimulates sense making. This chapter describes some of the precise ways in which the performance, sequences, and what is seen, talked about, and understood overlap but are in some loose configuration. Chapter 9 discusses how and for what purpose maps are used in the meetings.

## The Background

Because the BPD had the only CM/CA capacity realized in the three case studies, the focus here is on information processing rather than on the somewhat less visible infrastructure that is necessary to produce it. The sense making surrounding crime analysis and crime mapping is highly occasioned, stimulated by the way the problem is defined and reacted to publicly and by what follows from the definition offered. Given that the meetings were intended to address issues of a general character that bear on crime control, to what extent did the featured concept, crime, become a sponge concept, soaking up all the available meaning and meeting time? The ways in which a crime or incident was occasioned can be connected to the traditional view of police work: controlling the here and now in the event or encountered incident lest it become worse and get out of hand. The riveting anecdote—an arrest with a gun, a successful warrant serving or drug raid with results (money, drugs, or property)—always drew interest and buried any discussion of how and why this was a result of CAM or other "problem solving." This "work" and display of interest was what participants brought to the meetings, how they made sense of the particular displays, and what they took from the displays. This process of punctuating the work with crime might be called the everyday phenomenology of policing. A traditional view, based on minidramas, well shared within the police and not verbalized as such, is a mini-ideology rooted in the practices associated with the occupational culture. It is widely shared in the organization by sworn officers as well as civilians. It continues to guide what is done and what sort of rationality obtains. While facts touch off beliefs, belief guides what is taken to be factual.

The technical aspects of these meetings, the workings of computers, the software in use, the displays of photos, maps, tables, and cartoons (to amuse the audience between presentations) were never an obstacle in the performance. These things worked and worked well. The physical setting, arrangements, and sound systems were all of high quality. Amplification was excellent, no feedback occurred, and the visuals were at times riveting. The audience heard without squeaks and squawks. The technical proficiency of the crime analysts at the keyboards was remarkable; they were skillful, flawless, quietly competent, and in general masterful in orchestrating the images and maps, able to zoom in or out, move back and forth between tables and pictures, seek out previous materials shown, and so forth. Ironically, this meant that the technology was nonproblematic and the analysts quietly capable—that they faded in significance even while the visuals were the focal point of attention in the room. This suggests that a very careful prior rehearsal had been undertaken and that presenters had also been briefed and rehearsed with the CAM Booklet. It also meant that what was shown was a predetermined focus of the meeting, the undeniable and present matter that required no account or explanation. The meeting was apparently run as a result of what was seen. Of course, authority and power do not require overt and obvious displays.

In the following sections of the chapter, we will see how police placed themselves in the order of the meeting via structure, format and procedure, process, and content and how they engaged in the sense making that went on collectively. I consider only as background the excellent quality of technology used and the well-organized character of the CAM presentations.

## The Contribution of Structural Aspects to the Ordering of the CAM

"Structural" here refers to the pattern of relations or the elements working to sustain the meeting. These elements are the ecology, the rank structure of the organization as displayed, the audience and its players, the composition of the participants (gender, color, authority), and their interactions. Some of these matters were described in the previous chapter, but their significance was not highlighted as it will be here. These matters were not reflected on in the meetings directly but were constitutive of the things that made them what they were: celebrations, technical exercises, and instrumentalities.

The chairs and tables in the large departmental conference and meeting room were specially arranged for the CAM. The room was usually kept empty, and could be arranged flexibly on short notice for press conferences, meetings, or large gatherings. The meetings took place within a specific ecological arrangement that was repeated for each meeting. The top command was seated on the left at tables arranged facing the podium. Behind the podium was a very large screen. Two people were seated at laptop computers with very large memory capacity on the tables in front of the screen. The officers who would present were on the left in the audience, while the rest of the uniformed officers were spread out in the room. The ecology reflected the social organization of the police department insofar as it is based on rank. Seated at the front was the top command. They occupied about ten seats, including places for the commissioner, the deputy commissioner, called "Chief," a representative of the Detective Bureau, the head of Patrol Operations, the head of Special Operations, and the two crime analysts who operated the laptops and screens, presented overviews of crime figures, and answered "technical questions." To the far right facing the screen were three other top command figures, one a woman in civilian dress. These were among the some fifty-eight holders of offices in the department (most were above the rank of sergeant) who were required to attend the meetings.

Like the rest of the gathering, those at the top table were identified by the line drawn between civilians and sworn officers. The two top command officers, the commissioner and the superintendent-in-chief (called "Chief"), wore shirts and ties, and no coat (the Boston compromise with formality). The remainder of the sworn officers, at the top table and in the general audience, wore uniforms without hats or coats and displayed their 9 mm. weapons high in holsters on their right hips. Those in anomalous dress stood out, e.g., a sergeant who once wore a bright sport shirt hanging out over his uniform shirt and tie and took it off for his presentation on gang activity (he put the sport shirt back on after his presentation and wore it for the rest of the meeting), and officers who had been up all night on a drug raid who appeared in their flak jackets. Detectives wore coats and ties and were seated with other members of their division before presenting. Experts of various kinds, in photography, ballistics, forensics, and computer and data analysis, whose identities and ranks were not denoted by uniforms, wore a variety of outfits. Some wore the "uniform" of white-collar professionals: suits, ties, and formal clothes. They sat in the front rows, near the top table, ready to answer a technical question if called upon.

The people in the room, some one hundred, were divided into several audiences rather than one. Some of the differences marking group membership were visible; others were not. The audience for these performances included the police team and the inner circle of police-linked people: academics, well-liked reporters with a routine job to do (not reporters in a crisis mode or attending a special press conference about a recent crime), and the civilian employees of the department. No public "outside groups" made direct, personal contributions. Although they might be consulted at some point in the process of preparing a presentation, I never heard or saw anything directly reported from them or by any citizens' groups at these meetings. This of course underscores the basically tacitly defined nature of the focus and purposes of these meetings. They were about crime, not about the community, "partnerships," or realigning priorities.

The first elite audience was the top command at the front table, who were dressed as described above and quite visible to all. The second audience was the group behind the top table. This group was in turn divided into two segments: the uniformed (and plain-clothes detective) officers waiting to speak on the far left as one faced the screen, and the others. The others, in turn, included those dressed as civilians, who were academics, visitors, some of whom were officers from other departments, reporters, students, staff from the police department, and others. There were also uniformed officers sitting in the middle and right sections of the general audience.[2]

Gender and color also divided the audiences. The meetings presented an odd panorama of color (as a surrogate for ethnicity), for virtually all the audience was "white" (with a few exceptions of officers in uniform); the top table was about one-third people of color; and all the faces shown on the screen were black. (In my observations I saw only one white face on the screen.)[3] Most of the audience was male and was dressed in conventional clothes and uniforms. One woman, a bureau head, sat at the top table. I saw no women presenters except a crime analyst who was running a laptop and asked a technical question. The right-hand police audience was all men. The general (other) audience was highly male, although some crude counts yielded the information that about 10 percent of the audience was female. Depending on the district presenting, a crime analyst might be female. The crime analyst present at the front table worked with the presenting precinct. The ecology thus replicated the structural rank of people, but dress alone did not. Color and gender were strong cues to the rank held, social role in the organization, and position, as well as prestige or status.

## The Contributions of Procedure and Format to Ordering the CAM

The procedures displayed in the CAM, known, rehearsed, well understood, and laid out in a printed booklet distributed by the crime analysts are very effective in focusing attention on the topic and sustaining the order of presentations and interrogative sequences. As examples provided in the previous chapter suggest, the order of topics was set by the format, while there was variation in time given to a topic or figure. The time allocated to a district's presentation was forty-five minutes, and the meetings ended promptly after two hours. The meeting was format driven, based on the booklet created by research and evaluation people, and then rehearsed with the officers from the districts who would be called upon to present in the forthcoming meeting. The meeting, as discussed below in more detail, was also ritualized. That is, it was opened formally with a welcome, an introduction of guests, announcements of import to the general audience, and, later, the introduction of the ranking officer presenting for the district (usually the captain) and the other participants from the district who would lead parts of the discussion. At the conclusion of each district presentation, and at the end of some minipresentations, the presenters said "thank you," and the audience rendered mild applause. The meeting was closed by the highest-ranking person at the top table, and thanks were again given and applause rendered. The applause thus marked the ending and beginning of sessions, mutual appreciation of audience and speakers, and deference to the hierarchy present.

The order of discussion, as formatted, placed the top command in control of the unfolding. As in a Ph.D. oral exam, the presenter was not allowed to move on to his or her next topic until the top table was satisfied. But power was in the hands of the questioners, and this blurred the relationship among talent, knowledge, and rank. Rank's privileges were concealed in this way. As Goffman (1959: 97–105) notes, any team has a person who acts as dramatic director of a kind, guiding and directing performances to achieve an implicit purpose.

The people who made contributions to the discourse varied. Interventions at length and depth of observation were rare and uneven in their pacing. Presenters, crime analysts, and officers from the districts presenting at a giving meeting talked most and were the targets of the questions directed to them from the top table (exclusively—never from the general audience). The presenters did not ask members of the top table questions: the questions were asked from the top table, and the questioners were never questioned in return except for purposes of clarification. The only contribution of the general audience to the meeting was the occasional laugh in which they joined. The flow of interaction was thus radically asymmetrical: questions flowed from the top command to the presenters and the presenters answered. The audience behind the top table watched, listened, and some of them waited.

This pattern of sequencing and ordering, as well as of the targets or responders, was a means to make sense, to carve out an area of agreement or not, and to assert a working consensus. The verbal interactions took the form of a triad. The presenter presented, the audience, including the top table and the general audience, listened, and then, if a top table person had a question, the audience remained the same, but the presenter had to answer, ask for clarification, and/or apologize. The emotional tone of the meeting was low-key. The questions were ritualized and civil, as were the answers; typically, the commissioner was addressed as "commissioner" in response; and in general, first and last names and ranks were otherwise rarely used, except when reference was made to a person outside the room, who was usually referred to by first name and sometimes by a diminutive, e.g., "Eddie in 6." One officer called the commissioner "lieutenant" in response to a question, and the audience laughed quietly until the commissioner said, "That's okay, I was a lieutenant once." The register (degree of formality of address and honorifics [address based on respect]) was generally formal, although typical rounding of *g*'s at the end of words and the well-known "Boston accent" were heard predominantly. While there were jokes and tension relief, the banter was neither sexual nor vulgar and no "dirty jokes," racist remarks, or sexist comments were made. The jokes were male jokes by males directed to males by other males. The nature of this humor went unremarked, yet was remarkable, during the meetings.

There was a level of anxiety and tension manifested among the officers sitting stage right waiting to be called. This was indicated by their occasional soft laughter and the way they shifted in their places, made discreet faces, and looked down with embarrassment when presenting. Officers sometimes apologized for failing to see something on a table or for being unable to read their own notes. These were both literally and metaphorically scripts. The event was certainly at least partially scripted, edited, and shaped, and the presented content was well selected. Selected matters were not discussed and would not be discussed, in part because they were the responsibility not of the audience but of the top command. This gave the meetings a rather pleasant, matter-of-fact tone—the matters discussed did not touch on the broader legitimacy of the organization or its leaders. In part this was a function of the quiet style of the commissioner, who was well liked and enjoyed a ten-year tenure as commissioner after a distinguished career in the BPD.

### The Contributions of Content to Ordering the CAM

The first matter announced, if it had occurred, was the death of an officer. When an officer died of natural causes, or in an accident or shooting (as opposed to when an officer shoots a citizen or a citizen dies as a result of or in the aftermath of a chase—these were not mentioned, as noted below), the death was announced and treated with significance and seriousness. If an officer was in the hospital with a serious illness, that was also mentioned. In the case of an officer's death, the department's response was described and details of his or her funeral were announced. Thus, the death of a colleague was linked to the department and to the occupation and was placed first in the list of matters to be considered in a meeting of high-ranking officers. These announcements of a life lived are a very powerful and continuing source of comment and concern among officers and serve simultaneously to solidify the occupation, maintain the theme of danger and risk, and dramatize the heroism, altruism, and unpredictability of the work. Deaths on the job, especially as a result of confrontations with villains, are especially notable (Waddington 1999). These announcements were solemn incantations.

## Matters Omitted from the Meeting

Content refers here to what was said, what might be said, what would not be said, and what was strongly prohibited. In the meetings observed, I noted that certain events and matters of concern were omitted. These were in some ways what people on the street think of as "crime" and immorality (setting aside the media's affinity for dramatizing the rare, bizarre, and unusual). What was discussed, as in courtrooms and in family living rooms, was bounded by that which would never be discussed. Matters or topics *omitted* include the following:

- Descriptions of the most serious and heinous crimes: assault, murder, and fatal semicriminal traffic deaths. These were discussed in general, as aggregated numbers, not as cases.
- Pictures of scenes of crime, including those of the victims, the bloody circumstances and weapons, evidence gathered, and so on. These were likely to feature in murder trials and were high points in the often bloody, disturbing, and bizarre slide talks given by forensic pathologists.
- Discussions of police shootings of citizens, fatal chases, any barricade-hostage situations, and individual officers' errors, mistakes, and violations of regulations or the civil or criminal law.
- The work of teams or or news from beats or neighborhoods based on local information—in short, any of the activities related to the much-touted "community policing" with partnerships that was the central mission of the department. No mention was made of "followup" with community-policing actions. Neighborhood

groups, community associations, and others had no standing in these meetings, they did not appear, and their views were not reported or considered publicly.

- Comments from officers about their obligations and responsibilities as a result of their territorial assignments ("one-cop-one-beat"), unless featured as a special project or program in the district at the time of the CAM presentation.
- Responses of neighborhood members, community leaders, or the media to current or discussed tactics.
- Estimates of crimes prevented or disorder reduced by police efforts.
- Specific reports of assessments made of any previous tactics, "operations," or planned efforts.
- Reflections on the broad context of problem solving as a generic process. This included comments critical of suggestions made, alternatives, new data that might be considered, or flawed logic.
- Specific names of officers. Officers were mentioned in general with respect to raids and other meritorious matters in district presentations, but they were never mentioned in a negative light or context. The practice of public praise, private criticism would appear to operate as it does in the military.
- Social matters that precipitated or surrounded the incidents described were not questioned. Only in the minipresentations—for example, about gangs, traffic problems resulting from the clustering of Cape Verdeans blocking the streets, or a successful raid—did speakers go beyond summaries of figures shown on the screens.
- Announcements of a banal nature such as those associated with roll call. No roll was taken, and apologies were offered only if the commissioner could not be present.
- Negative, angry, or hostile questioning. The tone was positive, upbeat, and uncritical of what had been done in the past.

These were understandable and reasonable exclusions. Limiting discussion of serious media-attended cases and other investigations may have served best the careful working through of evidence, and not revealing the leads, directions, and frustrations of the case to the assembled audience (some of whom might be reporters or might talk to reporters after the meeting) may have assisted investigators. The circumscription of content to the format-based matters and the omission of "administrative" matters (omitted by policy in the NYPD's compstat meetings) and general announcements (other than the death of an officer) sharpened the content of the meetings. Recall that when an officer died or was shot, as opposed to an officer shooting someone or killing a citizen, the matter was announced and treated with significance and seriousness. The absence of any consistent feedback or consideration of past decisions kept the focus on the here and now. The public, ceremonial nature of the meetings was enhanced also by control of the setting and the participants involved, as well as the topics and the teamwork required to carry off the presentations.

## What Speaks through Silences

The limitations on context discussions may have been a direct result of the mission of the meeting. Its stated purpose was to make visible crime and crime patterns. Many of the other things omitted may have been under internal investigation by the department or a review board, or may have been in the courts shortly thereafter. The NYPD model was specifically designed to exclude the usual kinds of meeting content and to focus on the management of crime and on making middle management in the police department accountable publicly for official reported crime figures. Importantly from the dramaturgical perspective, the limitations may have been the result of decisions made by administrators about what would be concealed and what revealed in these very public meetings. The actual topics may have resulted from a mix of all of these (unstated) factors.

Although the content of the meeting covered many matters, they were mostly about crime, especially violent crime and variations upon the main property crimes of concern: home invasion, breaking and entering, and auto theft. Gunshots held their place, as they could indicate crime or potential crime. Crime was the focus, and questions and suggestions to presenters went directly to the presumed or supposed offenders, if any, elements of the offense (M.O., time of day, weapon used), and any pattern that might be discerned between a crime and other recent crimes. These were introduced as and when by officers who brought them to mind, not by the crime analyst or as a result of review of past problems or "solutions." These questions from the audience were complemented by "special presentations" on operations, raids, prevention, or other matters of interest. Tactics came in for some discussion, such as a raid or using ballistic data once the direction of action—what to do about the issue at hand—emerged in the discussion. Most importantly, the presentation was slightly forward looking and did not countenance backward-looking criticism or systematic evaluation.

## The Focus and the Focal Point of the CAM

The focal point of discussion in the partially darkened room was the screen and its content: an icon, a mark, a table, a set of signs, or a text projected in front of the room, to which the presenter, while holding the floor, attended (verbally and nonverbally). The effect, one of the most significant of the Power Point presentations, was an amazing concentration of attention to the surface features of a presentation, perhaps even more than to the underlying social forces that were being there displayed in some refracted manner. Always crime—its recent dynamics, especially with homicide and armed crimes, i.e., any crime involving a gun—was featured. No mention or discussion of "disorder," except as incidental to a crime, was mentioned in these meetings, nor was any explicit problem solving articulated. Implicit problem solving and imagination were features of the meetings, once a crime problem was articulated. "Crime," in the sense of a reported incident processed by the police, was the trigger for a ripple effect of considering other matters. Furthermore, if the crime cluster or problem drew a question, it was the only topic that drew more than one follow-up query. Crime spoke to the police, and the police spoke to and about crime in these meetings. The discussion was contemporaneous in focus and concern, and only partially future oriented. I did not hear "follow-up" questions generated by previous sessions, previous proposals to "do something," nor did I hear requests for evidence of what had been done previously about the problem being discussed, often without a label or sobriquet. While crime was the focus of the meeting, and indeed was part of the title of the meeting, it was spoken about in a narrow and limited fashion. That is, the discussion was focused on what had happened and how to reduce or manage it in a pragmatic and immediate way that would reduce officially known and reported problems.

## Conclusion

No single rationality, or clear exposition of ends that were to be sought as a result of the talk displayed in the CAM, was referenced verbally by participants to make sense of the flow of events. They came at sense making in a meeting not as a sociologist would, treating it as a problem. It was not. The CAM participants assumed that a working consensus would emerge, be sustained, and not break down. The order was apparent to the participants. They referred to order and ordering tangentially, working through traditional shorthand comments and using recipe knowledge (Garfinkel 1967: 262–83). They made reference to things known and taken for granted. This is the "natural attitude of everyday life" (Garfinkel 1967: 37).

These shorthand references to human motivation had very important truncating functions in the meetings. For example, it was assumed that college students "don't care about their possessions," will "drink and party late at night and not be cautious," and "leave their cell phones lying around in full view in unlocked cars." It was also assumed that gangs are composed of young black males, deal in drugs, and are violent. Such stereotypes about gangs also constituted the focus of the work of the gang unit within the BPD. It was also assumed that larger structural matters—poverty, unequal opportunities for education and jobs, disorganization of families, schools, and areas—cannot be much altered. They were seen as givens, here to stay, and beyond the reach of everyday work to change. These sociological maxims are the equivalent of the false claim that sociologists argue that crime cannot be controlled. They are based on unexamined stereotypes and reconstitutions of social life that work when applied to strangers and serve to tidy up loose ends or contradictions such as exceptions: students who are cautious and abstemious, students who are careful with their possessions, successful programs that alter areas and opportunities, and serious, scholarly minorities from disadvantaged neighborhoods who succeed.

Talk, the discourse of the meeting, was the most obvious vehicle for forming a working consensus, one that works, but it could not alone carry the day. People often use talk as a surrogate or rough index or ordering, but ordering is carried by nonverbal gestures and postures, monitoring of each other's movements, and deference and demeanor requirements. Talk is laced with modes of speaking, or tropes, in particular, metaphors, that do their work without great recognition. By a trope, I mean a way of talking about one thing in terms of another. We do this in everyday speech and writing when we note similarities either of a part to the whole (called "metonymy"), as in saying that the attack on the World Trade Center (part) was a part of a "war on terror" (whole) or the whole to the part (called "synecdoche"), as in saying that the war on terror (whole) is working when we attack and occupy Iraq (perhaps a part); when we treat something ironically or sarcastically, displaying distance from feelings; and when we use myths and allegories, such as claiming that "God is on our side."

Although irony has a major role in setting out the limits of police efforts and knowledge, pointing out incongruous or anomalous matters is only one way of punctuating what is otherwise unquestioned. While the major powerful tropes were at work in the meetings—irony, synecdoche, metaphor, and metonymy—and the narratives weaved the tropes together wondrously, it was the sequencing and the engagement of the discursive bits (the stories, the tables, the figures, the icons) that emerged as the basis for the kinds of situational rationality that powered the meetings.

The maps presented in the CAM were somewhat standardized. The colors used, the scale of the maps, the size of the tables and figures, and the displays routinely presented did not vary from week to week. It would be possible to dramatize selectively certain crimes of concern by use of color (red always cries out for attention, blue does not) or by showing selected crimes or spikes of crimes in recent weeks (no crime declines were shown). The icons used could be inflammatory in themselves (using roaches for gangs, or gorilla pictures for robberies, or bags of drugs and hypodermic needles for drug crimes); bloody crime scenes and bodies of victims could be shown; or voices or pictures of victim's families could be attached to crime reports. The aim of the Boston meeting, both verbally and in the visuals shown, seems to have been to downplay the dramatic, extraordinary, and shocking, and to focus on the routine and common and that which can be suppressed and perhaps reduced in the short term. In short, the visuals were not used as a means to create emotional swings or moods but to focus on the cognitive, the immediate, and the "doable." This meant that the emotional tone of the meeting was fairly light-hearted and that irony and humor were common.

This chapter has addressed the sociological questions of what contribution the structural aspects, procedure, format, and, to a lesser extent, content of the meeting made the order work. What was omitted by policy also made the meetings more focused and coherent: routine matters, bloody and extreme aspects of crimes, and matters that were under investigation, in the courts, or part of the high politics of the department were not on the agenda and were not discussed. The silences that were observed kept the meeting on topic. In many ways, the maps were a kind of stimulus producing conventional police talk.

# 9

## Seeing and Saying in the Boston CAM

### Introduction

These meetings were orderly and ordered, and much of what made the meetings "work" was not on the screen. There was a drama of the meeting, a result of differential presentation of materials and of the ways in which the meeting maintained front- and back-stage areas and their simulation. While the meeting was a public or semipublic affair, it also had an intimation of a back-stage event because of the unscripted remarks, informal interactions, shared topic of crime control, and presence of the highest-ranking members of the department. In some ways, the presentation was a ceremony that celebrated policing and its active, detailed, electronically sophisticated and scientific capacities. Yet it had a magical aspect because many things were concealed and kept secret from the meeting's participants, those in charge set the format and the emotional-sentimental tone of the meetings, and others were celebrants and participants without a deep understanding of events as they unfolded. Sequencing was an essential aspect of the ordering and taken-for-granted order of the meetings. The sense making that went on, the drama of the meeting, was not a function of what was seen alone. What was seen had to be grasped as relevant to action. It had to be "actionable" information to be of interest in these meetings. Police in the audience brought to the screen what they assumed about crime, its causation, its control, and its covert manifestations. Finally, the maps shown were used in a principled fashion, in line with unspoken assumptions, to make them relevant to the work. The maps stimulated repeatedly the use of standard police tools and tactics.

## The Drama of the Meetings

These meetings were dramatic, and they conveyed dramatic messages. Drama was produced by the differential elevation or suppression of symbols (arbitrary, conventionalized signs) in the course of a performance that maintained an impression for an audience (see Goffman 1959; Gusfield 1989). Not all of life is a drama, and the ways in which it is perceived as such are social; the assumptions that people are acting, that there is a front and back stage, that the action is scripted or role specific, and that the audience "suspends disbelief" make true theatrical performances quite different from everyday life performances. To study something using the dramaturgical metaphor means an emphasis on impressions made by performers, usually in team relationships (groups who share secrets), and on the symbols used to convey these impressions. While the public aspects of a performance are the visible and the verbal, which can be easily manipulated, there are always "back channel" communications, communications given off that are less easy to control (nonverbal matters such as gesture, posture, dress, and props). Now consider these CAM sessions. They were formal, public meetings governed by tacit rules about order of speaking, pauses, question-and-answer sequences, and deference and demeanor that combined the rank of participants with the general code of public discourse. There was a front and back stage, the materials were largely scripted, roles were well understood, and teamwork was well acknowledged. The meetings were theatrical.

## Front and Back Regions of the Meetings

The CAMs had a front and back stage that was well understood by the participants. Team performances were enacted in "front-stage" regions for audiences, whether they were police officers, tourists, students, or patients, while the team members could relax, be themselves, and prepare in a "back-stage region" (Goffman 1959: 144–45). The idea of a front and back stage is conceptual, from the perspective of a performance, not physical, and this division led MacCannell to argue that there are three roles: those who perform, those who are performed to, and others, outsiders who neither perform in the show nor watch it. In effect, then, performers have access to front and back regions, audiences have access only to the front, and outsiders are excluded from both

(MacCannell 1973: 590). As we shall see below, it is possible to *simulate* the front region, and create or construct a series of barriers, each of which reproduces the performer/audience/outsider triad, yet suggest a kind of binary front/back division rather than a subtle and manipulated pseudo-back region or regions. The entire effect is layered.

Because any performance is somewhat fragile, it requires cooperation between audience and performer, acceptance of the tacit rules of performance, deference (accepting others' claims to self) and demeanor that permit the often uncertain character of an unfolding scene to be realized in some fashion. Since the performance is "on stage," teams must work together in some way, and audiences must conjoin and conspire not to damage the flow or, if a disruption take place, to cooperate, produce remedies, and reshape alternative versions of the reality being presented.

Not surprisingly, dramatic discipline was maintained in the CAMs, i.e., the teams as formed maintained control over expression and joking and did not reveal "secrets." Much was not said about what was wrong, the mistakes, the errors, the egregious "cock-ups" that take place daily on the streets and in offices. Avoidance of awkward matters prevailed and was maintained—people did not question limited presentations to the point of breaking down of fronts, or loss of deference. Give public praise, give private criticism was the rule of thumb. Even the marginal players, the civilian crime analysts, were loyal to the team even when their intervention could radically change the dynamics of the public interactions in the meeting. They did not intervene to offer interpretations of the data shown. They were clerks for the machines. There was little tension between the people with discrepant roles and the teams, as the teams were limited and visible in this long-term drama. Further, the players in the CAMs were regular performers of the role and likely to have built up a selves that were invested in this role. Crime was the theme that organized the narrative structure. The sequence of topics, that is, their order and the salience of crime, made crime a topic and a resource for conversational references.

This notion of the idea of crime being a topic and a resource is important. Assumptions about "crime" as an expression (one part of a sign) link the things talked about as a cluster of relevant and unquestioned objects (content) of professional concern. This connection of an expression and a content forms a sign, making crime a closed notion in this social context. No one asked, "What do you mean by crime?" "How do you define that?" "What sort of crime are you discussing?"

The CAM was not a college seminar in criminology. These assumptions —that crime is well understood, that its types are known, that it can be talked about in general terms without reference to more detail—were "resources" to be called upon when crime was a topic (Garfinkel 2002: 112). The topic stimulated the resources and the resources made the topic meaningful. In this way, the talk was tautological and redundant. It can also be said that the appearance of crime and its vicissitudes was a subject of humor as well as serious comment.

Note also that the props were in place for a master performance. The meetings were engaging. The power of the screen, the glowing computers, the projection box, the fantastic, instantaneous graphics, the fast-moving shifts between images, and the dramatic impact of villains' faces projected at larger-than-life size above the heads of everyone cannot be denied. Upon close examination, it was clear that the actual front work that went on was facilitated by the props, the lines, and the elements of a proper performance: idealization, mystification, realism, and dramatic realization (Goffman 1959: ch. 1). There is of course naturally engaging and exciting drama around crime—the violations of norms, the often-violent contours, the losses that it signals, the fear that it engenders, in perpetrators as well as victims and onlookers, and the often narrow, good-or-bad, binary morality that is commonly a part of the police worldview and deciding. It need not be said that crime is wrong, that criminals are bad, that crime should be eradicated, and that policing is the primary way in which control should be produced. There are no real secrets in everyday policing, and the secret is just that.

## Staged Authenticity

The meetings, as the omissions and commissions reveal, were carefully staged presentations. They played on the idea that this was a back-stage meeting in which quasi secrets, well-kept plans, tactical maneuvers of an essential sort, and operations against major threats to the city were discussed, analyzed, and set in motion. The easy quality of the interaction suggested a casual yet attentive attitude of major city planners at work. Setting, structure, procedures, and format as well as the content of the meetings were conducive to ordering and rational discussion. Yet, several things reveal that the CAMs were in fact public, staged performances that sustained the idea that they were back-stage meetings, semblances, and that they actually staged authenticity (MacCannell 1973).

MacCannell, an expert on the tourist experience worldwide, has asked questions relevant to the dramatic effects of the CAMs. MacCannell asks, How is it that staged presentations, such as the tours of Williamsburg, Virginia, and Sturbridge Village in Vermont and other historical sites that simulate actual places and their imagined lifestyles for tourists are so well received? How do they produce such continued fascination and attract such large audiences? Perhaps people like being "back stage" and in on the team secrets of the past and the ways in which life is said to have been lived then. What is called "reality TV" is, of course, a fabrication of reality—staged , filmed, edited, managed, and packaged to appear to be "real." Reality TV shows, like Williamsburg tours, are immensely popular. Several sets of cues in the CAM produced the impression that a back region had been entered by all participants and that they were witnessing real big-city police work in the raw, were being made privy to the unfolding, real, and complex managerial decisions made in real time. The performance was designed to produce this belief, but it was a partial, staged, and framed dramatic performance. As Goffman writes of frame analysis (1974: 124), experience that is seen as "dramatic" is staged as such, with a script, players, well-defined and fixed back and front areas, designated roles, and figures to play them. Social life is not dramatic in this precise sense; it is so from time to time and when understood as such but is not in any essential fashion dramaturgical. What was staged in the CAMs appeared to be an opportunity to participate behind the scenes in a drama, but it was only a partial and managed view.

Dramaturgical principles govern the seen and the unseen. Consider what was not shown:

- Mundane matters essential to running the police organization were omitted from discussion by design, planning, and rehearsal. This served to give the CAM what MacCannell (1973: 595) calls an "aura of superficiality," though he adds, "albeit an aura that is not perceived as such [by the tourist]." The everyday was set aside for the focus on crime and its management.
- Most of the details of the performance were written out, scripted, and rehearsed. Content was formatted and routinized. In this precise sense, the CAM was theatrical and in the theatrical frame (Goffman 1974: 124–25). Spontaneity was limited to answers to

questions posed by the top command, and thus they remained in control of what was talked about.

- The actual back stage in respect to this performance was the "mini-CAM" rehearsal meetings held in the police districts, which were based on the work done in preparing the data and the books in the Office of Research and Evaluation, and in the meetings of the commissioner and his top command and staff.

- While some groups were banned (reporters from time to time), excluded, or simply not invited, officers from other departments were welcome and were announced at the opening of each meeting. They were one of the primary target audiences, along with the top command staff. Visitors could bring goodwill to future encounters in which cooperation between departments would be required, and they were an important audience.

- The meetings worked to convey transparency in deciding, but little was actually decided because what was discussed were suggestions, and implementation rested on later deployment by district captains. There was no feedback on the results of any suggestion, operation, policy, or tactical maneuver.[1]

It has been argued by MacCannell that there are at least five kinds of back-stage areas (or back-stage-like areas). They range from the most constructed and openly available simulations (which appear quite unreal to the observer) of a back region to those that are in fact back regions. In effect, the simulation gives a peek at the apparently open and available, and this peek conceals what is actually going on in the other backlike regions and back region. This is not a model of endless regress, because that which is necessary to put on the show at whatever level, finally, must be present if there is a front stage or performance. Each layer is known only by the presence of the other. There is no inner sanctum.

If we expand this idea one step further, it is clear that Goffman in *Presentation of Self in Everyday Life* (1959), when he employs the concepts of "front" and "back" stage, is modifying and perhaps playing on Durkheim's (1961: 52–63) fundamental distinction between the sacred and the profane. This distinction is contextual and not absolute in any sense. The two work in contrast to each other. The front is a kind of secular play area or arena in which public decorum is required, and the back regions are the sacred or more concealed and emotively loaded places. Between the two are interdictions, rules, barriers, taboos, and physical obstacles that serve to sustain the regions and make crossing or transversing them somewhat problematic. The ideas are relative and constituted situationally by actions and gestures. The sacred is that which reflects the sentiments that groups hold about their own intimate group relations. Durkheim in effect says that societies, large or small, worship themselves when the sacred is involved. The substantive and ethnographic power of this observation is precisely that the police are consummately based on secrecy and they reproduce this in their buildings, their cars, their uniforms, and their maneuvers. They are armed, uniformed, and set apart, distant, awesome, and violent. Exploring these traits in more detail, I point out that the armaments of police in the last twenty years have increased in a striking fashion—from high-powered arms to semiautomatic handguns and long guns; from soft uniforms to a variety of armored, insulated, covered (now with hazmat options, including full body coverage and oxygen) uniforms; from the occasional warrant service by a few officers to SWAT teams, dynamic-entry groups, and heavily armed tactical squads; from personal operations to the use of robots (for bomb detection and surveillance), helicopters, and surveillance cameras. Police stations themselves appear more open architecturally, but are in fact defended castles without the parapets. They are also positioned electronically to monitor with more expensive electronic equipment now than in the last twenty-five years (Ericson and Haggerty 1997: 57–58). In this connection I have reference to the barriers at doors of police buildings (even prior to 9/11); the desk sergeants seated in a high, protected perch; the central and concealed placement of the jail in the inner, innermost sanctum of the police building; the distinction drawn between visible, uniformed policing and secret or high policing; and the use of public relations, press releases, and conferences designed for the media and largely used to conceal police purposes (see also Ericson and Haggerty 1997: 57–58).[2]

### Magic at Work

Let us consider the drama of the performance further, pushing the meaning of the rite or ritual. A ritual is a means of celebrating that which is valued by means of redundant and repeated movements. The ritual here described as the CAM celebrated the sacrifices people make to deter crime.[3] The front- and the back-stage regions of the performance were well understood by some of the audience and the performers—employees of the BPD. The distinction between front and back, as MacCannell has shown, is not a single, sharply drawn line but a variable line based on perspective (the roles occupied), the setting, and the situation. The audience in the CAM could be analytically divided into those "in the know" and those who stood outside the particular, somewhat esoteric knowledge being conveyed. The distinction was not about "crime" or its vicissitudes but between those in the audience who were knowledgeable about what was going on back stage prior to or at the time of the performance and others. There were few in the audience who were fully aware of the meeting as a façade. Recall, these were not the performers, officers, and civilians, who know full well that the performance had been scripted and rehearsed. I would include as fully aware officers who had previously participated but were not performing on this occasion; academics who had prior knowledge of the process of preparation; and any top command or people from OR&E who were present.

These audience members could be called the colluding audience because they saw the CAM as a kind of performance resembling magic. By this I mean that magic is a rite that is carried out for technical reasons to achieve an end. Magic is a rational performance for a clientele, and aims to carry them along in the rite; the magician, in turn, views the role as a self-conscious one, not as a carried-away member of the congregation or audience (Durkheim 1961: 58–60). In the magical performance, a problematic situation is presented by the technician for a clientele under conditions of mystification and high dramatization and in some isolation. It may involve elaborate props and costumes, alternative shapes of appearance and forms, and representations. The magicians and the magicians' assistants do not share in the mystical, communal feelings of the audience. For the vast majority of the audience, the situation is viewed as a religious ceremony, and they are the pure audience. They believe. However, for the performers and their assistants, the few in the know in the audience, the show is a bit of magic; it is magical. This is not to say that the generalized feelings of the rest of the audience do not have communal and religious meaning. They do, and the magical and instrumental feelings are interacting.

To distinguish among the feelings of the performers in the occasion and the audience suggests that like the idea of front- and back-stage regions, they must be further differentiated in respect to the feelings generated and shared and the technical role of some of the performers. These distinctions suggest why the compstatlike meetings have taken on a religious-contagion character, widely promoted and widely emulated as a source of power and, as suggested here, of magic. Why are they magical?

The French sociologist Marcel Mauss, a colleague and student of Emile Durkheim, was the author of the classic monograph on magic. In the penultimate chapter of the book, a survey of the elements of magic worldwide, he (1972: 125–26) wrote,

> it is only those collective needs, experienced by a whole community, which can persuade all the individuals of this group to operate the same synthesis at the same time. A group's beliefs and faith are the result of everyone's needs and unanimous desires. Magical judgments are the subject of a social consensus, the translation of a social need under the pressure of which an entire series of collective psychological phenomena is let loose. This universal need suggests the objective of the whole group. Between these two terms [magic and religion], we have an infinity of possible middle terms (that is, we have found such an extreme variety of rites employed for the same purpose). Between the two terms we are allowed a degree of choice and we choose what is permitted by tradition or what a famous magician suggests, or we are swept along by the unanimous and sudden decision of the whole community. It is because the result that is desired by everyone is expressed by everyone, that the means are considered apt to produce the effect.

Mauss's summated arguments here sustain the general points of this chapter. Recall that magic can be used in a piacular rite, or rite of sacrifice to a god or gods. The magician knows that a cucumber, used by the African tribal people, the Nuer, in times of near starvation to represent an ox, is not an ox, as do the participants, but it becomes an ox through the rites (Evans-Prichard 1956). Mauss characterizes magic as shared ideas combined with voluntary rites (Mauss 1972: 127). If religion is the essence of the worship of the social, magic is a rational variation on the same. In the quotation above, Mauss argues that it works under special conditions and pressures and that by implication it does not work by tapping, mobilizing, or expressing "everyone's needs and unanimous desires." It can be further noted that there are mixed occasions—"between the two terms" of magic and religion—of religious fervor in a setting like a "church" (Durkheim 1961: 56). Mauss means by this a metaphoric congregation, not a physical one. It is a community. In a sense, the performers are effective as "famous magicians." But of course, "if magic is to exist," he writes (Mauss 1972: 127), "society has to be present."

If these arguments obtain, the consequences of the meetings were not designated effects or outcomes, the putative consequences of police actions on crime, disorder, or traffic, but but rather, they were about the sentiments that were stimulated and shared by police about policing. This was true because the community at large in the meetings, what Durkheim would consider a church of a kind, shared feelings, whether because they were under some special pressure or because they were carried away in the generalized sentiments occasioned. On the other hand, the meeting displayed a form of magic, for all the performers did not share the same definition of the situation as the rest of the audience. Like priests and preachers, those who "ran the show" were magicians of a kind.

This is not to claim that the meeting was a ceremony celebrating policing's grasp of the uncertain. It served the instrumental purposes of information sharing, of some speculation, and of a nonranked discussion, but its actual impact on crime, disorder, and community quality of life could not be determined, and no one could say what it was because no data were gathered on the consequences of the decisions made. Would one question whether a church service achieved purity of thought and deed in a congregation? Is the size of the offering collected on a given day an accurate prediction of forthcoming good deeds, grace, and altruisim?

When pictures are shown, clichés come to mind—"a picture is worth a thousand words," for example—and the notion that displays are obvious to any viewer is assumed. Yet, it does not take an art historian to know that disagreement, confusion—a range of emotions and reactions—are what makes pictures "work" or have a collective effect. The question here is, How did these displays work to produce collective deciding on matters as complex as "crime" or "disorder"? How was what was assumed, what was invisible, made visible? The maps, tables, figures, graphs, photographs, and other visuals were visible; however, the meanings and the attributions had to be revealed rather than assumed. In a public meeting, what is seen must be seen together in some fashion. It is a shared collective enterprise that resembles jazz more than the performance of a string quartet. It is this phrase, "in some fashion," that I attempt to explain here.

## Social Objects at Work

What is seen must be a *social object* that can be reproduced without question again and again. By an object I mean a socially shared something that can be called upon to refer to what is going on in the situation. Possessed of an enduring social reality, it is distant, restraining, and objective; it has an intersubjective reality to participants—others are seen as having the same view one would have if one were in the others' place. By using the word "something," I mean to indicate that it functions without a specific name, in the ways that in conversation people say "well . . . the thing is . . ." It, the something, can be a word, a picture, an icon, a shorthanded remark, or a bit of interaction. The construction of an object must take place over time in interaction and must result in the following features: it must have a morally constraining feature and must display something. It must also be intended as such in the past and must be again intended and displayed in the same fashion in the future.

The maps displayed in the CAMs were produced with an aim to convince others of something—something that was unstated and did not need to be stated. Stating or asking requires an account, and the object discussed is accountable, or could be explained well if necessary. However, an account is an indication of some failure to be engaged in recognizable practices. While the particular display varies in salience, importance, and complexity, the object should display something—show something to somebody (this is one definition of a symbol). Whether the given object is a practice or a visual object, the display of it should be intended as such in the past and should be again intended and displayed in the same fashion in the future. What is displayed is indexical—a product of language, pointing, and naming. It has social and shared features so that it is a matter that works for self and others as seen and not as a function of biographical particulars or a unique personal history. It is characterized by at least some features that are private, unstated, and unshared, so that more can always be said about it. It is variable in the sense that features attributed to it may vary among witnesses. It may have a factual base or not; it is always partially constituted by taken-for-granted facts.

On the other hand, an object in use cannot be idiosyncratic in meaning or a nonce symbol (one understood only to a person on the basis of a personal experience). While there are things that could be said, etc., etc., these variable matters are not relevant to the public constitution of the object. The object must be set in a context of interpretation such as (a) a commonly entertained scheme consisting of a standardized system of symbols and (b) "what anyone knows," i.e., a preestablished corpus of socially warranted knowledge. The more the object is repeatedly framed, the more easily it can be reproduced. While this is in part a tautology, most of social life is tautological.

These features of a social object are abstract, but such a list of features means that in operational terms, any object has meaning only if it is named, accountable, or explicable, has intersubjective reality and reproducibility, is surrounded by facts that are assumed and not spoken about, is a publicly represented idea, and is seen as part of a shared interpretive scheme that can be indicated, brought to mind, and reproduced. All of this interpretive work is a way of pinning down the drifting nature of representations, their complexity over time, their shifting and blurred boundaries, and the many ways they can be represented.

The facts relating to making something affordable or accessible is a critical aspect of the work of making objects *useful*. One must be able to imagine objects and to grasp them, to hold them and use them and thus create their ongoing meaning. They must be imagined, and the parts that are not on the surfaces (What lies behind the computer's screen, its face?) must be made visible mentally. This is in part a function of context of memory and repetition. The work of showing what it means may produce the memory and the repetition, or the imagery may make routinization possible. Both work. There may be surface reminders—icons, marks, symbols, or signals—that permit the translation of the representation into the action, but this is a complicated process.

## Maps and Mapping

Because this chapter concerns the use of mapping, and the way maps are used, it is important to define "map" and distinguish it from the territory it represents. Dictionary.com defines "map" as "a representation, usually on a plane surface, of a region of the earth or heavens." The map is an abstract version of a physical expanse or a space. It is an icon, or a miniaturized version of the space shown. It is shaped and coordinated according to assumptions about mapping and the reproduction of maps. Consider the displays on Mapquest.com (a trademark corporate website) that allow a person at a computer to vary the scale and to "zoom" in or out from an arbitrary selected spot or center. Or think about the verbal maps that are now in luxury cars—they speak from the position of the car as seen from a global positioning station, as the station sees it, not as the driver sees it. What is seen is not what the reality of the thing displayed is. A map is a miniaturized, stylized (by color, lines, divisions, notes, etc.) picture laid out and orchestrated to produce an association with something else. What you see in a map is not what you get or imagine as a result. Think of reading a map as a process intended to get you from one place to another. Each of the indicators on the map must be known (color, size, font, labels, scale); the roads, for example, in turn, must be related to speed limits (and possibilities), mobility, access, lights, stop signs, and imagined traffic on such surfaces. The map reader must imagine where he or she is on the map and recognize the things seen along the way as indicative of that position on the map. It can be said that people are not lost, that they know where they are, but that they do not know how to get to where they are going. One can know how to get to a place but not know where one is presently. A territory is that which is represented. From looking at the map, one can imagine the territory, but the two are not the same thing.

Perhaps the most important distinction is between the surface features of a map and the facts that are conveyed. The scale of the map can be varied to produce highs and lows, peaks and valleys, spikes and troughs that exaggerate the differences over time or between areas or districts. Maps covering a brief period of time such as two weeks or a month will not reflect the same trends that are captured in long-lagged maps covering months or years. Regression to the mean is a well-understood process and is rarely reflected in small samples or samples reflecting short time periods. Spikes in given areas are used to characterize those areas—i.e., areas in which homicides occur in a brief period of time are seen as areas of high violence. The particular is used to generalize metaphorically about many square miles of activity and about thousands of people. Colors communicate emotion and are seen as emotional: green and brown are calm colors; red is an exciting color; yellow is more neutral; white and black, not colors, are a baseline against which colors are judged. Bright colors, such as red, associated metaphorically with blood, when used in maps have an expressive and stimulating effect and draw attention to some crimes or disorder more than others if colors are used to designate crimes or disorder by areas. The particular sign vehicle, or that which carries the expression, be it a shape, sound, picture, icon (a miniature of something represented), or arbitrary sign such as *, #, @, or ^, conveys information that has a communicative effect. Thus, using a picture of a burglar in a mask carrying his swag in a bag over his shoulder as indicative of a burglary contrasts with using a slug crawling away; using a cockroach to indicate gangs has contrast with a name; using a splatter of blood to indicate a homicide contrasts with a picture of the victim; using a derelict car to indicate a stolen vehicle contrasts with using a picture of a BMW or an expensive SUV. The use of the zoom function can suggest closeness or distance from the event reported upon, whether it is a trivial crime or a horrendous rape. Creating imaginative maps with pictures and lines connecting gang members or co-offenders has powerful effects that reify their actual connection, guilt, or status and contrasts with a list or set of offenses. Finally, the use of Power Point is a simulation of logical connection between items. It does not produce an ongoing logical connection, or linear argument in fact; it does not sharpen an argument that has not been stated; it cannot clarify the connections between items in the list. Crime has many faces and is a tangled web of causation, consequence, and costs. Lists of crime obscure these matters and thus destroy complexity. Perhaps, on the other hand, the simplicity of the presentations in the CAM via maps made for mobilizing stimuli.

## Sequencing and Meaning

The order of the meeting set some parameters of interaction, as the above analysis demonstrates.[4] The opening and closing were ritualized, as were the transitions between districts and the breaks (whether for coffee or fire alarms), and were set by the chair of the meeting (generally, the commissioner or his appointee). Then the crime analyst spoke, updating crime figures for the preceding two weeks and comparing them with earlier trends, and then a district captain generally spoke, announcing who would be participating (they were usually sitting uneasily to his right). The representative of the detective bureau, with the assistance of the crime analysts showing the images as his instructions, would discuss crime in the district in the preceding two weeks. He would discuss the major crimes in order of importance (homicide and other violent crimes, though rape in itself was not discussed as a unique problem), focusing first on crimes with guns, then on property crimes. In each case, the trends of the year to date were mentioned, for the district or the department as a whole. Then, usually, two other officers took up a special topic—crime prevention, gangs, a successful drug raid, arrests and seizures—and then the district's presentation ended. This took around an hour and ended with "thank you" and applause from the audience. The chair of the meeting announced a break after the first set of presentations. After coffee, the second district was announced and the same format and order of topics obtained. Granted that the format and the selected role players gave an overt structure to the discourse, as did the logic of crime based on reported, police-processed crime and its disposition, there were other aspects of the ordering of the interaction that yielded cues to forms of situated rationality.

In this section, I argue that the previously articulated factors—structure, social organization, procedures, and to some degree the rank structure of the department—provided cues to order. These cues were indexical, indicating what might happen next, what had happened, and the ways in which this and that, the next thing to come along, might be shaped to carry on as usual (cf. Garfinkel 1967: 273). "Indexical" means simply that the meaning of the word is taken from the context, which can shift when the context changes. Think of the differences between saying, on the one hand, "the way he treats his car is a crime," "to lose the game that way is a crime," or "wearing a skirt that short is a crime" and, on the other, "he was charged with a crime." Crime is indexical. A focus on the indexical is a way of saying that people regard the "sense of the conversation" rather than the precise referents of the words, as a guide to its meaning. Even with a plan, a project, and a well-focused agenda, the order that emerges over the course of events has nuances and bumps and has to be carried along tacitly.

There were features of talk-as-work that constituted the sequencing and ordering that evolved in these meetings. Since it was impossible to predict the next sequence of questions and answers, or content, or the length of any intervention, much of what took place was a process of negotiated order through the cues and signals embedded in the discourse.

## Silences and Sequences

Silences, even longer-than-usual pauses in speech or in taking up a turn, are notable and noticed. They communicate powerfully in a formatted meeting. The important silences in the CAMs were those between segments of the meetings: the opening, the closing, the main break, and the period between presenters/speakers. There were also important silences between presentations and the first question, if any, and between the questions and the answers. These did not last long, as there was "pressure" to have the answers in hand, to appear decisive, and to be in command of the data. There were pauses of a second or so between sentences or at changes in topic within the minipresentations, which suggested reflection or preparation for the next comment.

Perhaps the most important effects on shaping the discussion came from the sequencing of questions and answers and the ways in which the trope, irony, came and went over the course of the meeting. Here are some examples of irony:

- Question-and-answer sequences. If the commissioner or anyone at the top table asked a question, it had to be answered, even if to say, "I don't know, Commissioner." In general, a response was made to the query. This might take the form of a joke, of buying time and pleading for some forgiveness, of admitting puzzlement, or of supplying a direct answer: "yes, we have a suspect" or "no, we have made no arrests." Another question could be asked by the first questioner or another person from the top table, and again the presenter was obliged to answer. At times, this led to a question to the crime analyst. The dialogue was hinged upon the image before everyone, even if other examples or details were being examined, elaborated, and explained verbally.
- Jokes. The tension could sometimes be punctuated by a joke, such as when a detective sergeant called the commissioner "lieutenant." In another case a sergeant apologized upon taking the podium, saying, "I am sorry, I am not really prepared, I thought I'd be off in Maine this morning," and then laughing. The commissioner then said, "You may still be sent to Maine," implying, I think,

banishment for a poor performance. On another occasion, an officer presenting said, "We are looking at the forensic evidence on this," and the commissioner asked, "Do you have any blood?" The officer replied, "He [the burglar] seems to get flustered and cut himself every time he gets into a building." His remark was greeted by low laughter from the audience, and he went on to say "yes." Finally, a detective sergeant was noting that a rash of auto thefts had been committed in one part of the district that abutted another city, Somerville (across the Charles River from Boston). The commissioner asked, "Have you made any arrests?" The answer came back, "Well, no, but the police in Somerville think that they have a guy who did them there and in Boston." The commissioner quipped, "That guy in Somerville is a busy guy," and the audience laughed. These were attempts, perhaps unconscious, to deflate the claims and give some guidance—a kind of two-sided sword—sanction, and a direction.

- Requests for facts or more facts as a means of clarification. At times, someone seated at the top table would ask for facts associated with a crime or crime patterns. For example, the director of Special Operations once asked, "Are any of these [incidents] gang related?" "No," said the head of the gang unit. At another point, as above, the commissioner asked about blood evidence. In another case, the commissioner asked if any overtime cars or shift cars were being used to pursue the problem (a series of auto thefts). The answer was, "Yes, we'll do that." These requests or questions were usually brief, but some topics could solicit questions and comments for five minutes or more.

- The interaction between presenter and top-table questioner maintained the topic and the focus (but see above about reasons for excluding some events). In addition, no one from outside the team entered into the show; only the top table, crime analysts, and the presenter introduced a new topic or variation on the question, or opened up a new line of questioning.

- Analogical moves based on the data presented on the screen surfaced other matters. For example, one could go from a crime to a crime pattern (for example, "are you seeing a pattern?" was asked about robberies on Commonwealth Avenue) or from a pattern to a particular crime if a villain was shown. A pattern could lead to discussion of another pattern, for example, Are these shootings gang related? Are these addicts dealing also? Is prostitution involved with the drug use? Sales? An incident could lead to connections being drawn by the presenter among, for example, gang members, or co-offending robbers or burglars (pictures being shown). A pattern such as "burglaries" or "auto thefts" could be broken down in comments about similarities, e.g., "These kids at BU [Boston University—a large university surrounding one of the major avenues of Boston] just leave things in their cars . . . cell phones, radios, CD players, etc., and they're taken. . . ." A part, a gun, could be linked to a series of shootings. (A picture was shown of five people shot and the ballistics showing that the bullets were from the same gun. Unfortunately, the gun had not been found and none of the shootings had been cleared at that time.)

- Irony linked one of the above crimes or patterns to the others, as in the commissioner's remark, "That's a busy guy over in Somerville" or the remark about being sent to Maine. The fact that returning arrestees from prison and younger people were now committing crimes (this was the current ideology, though no data were shown to demonstrate this point) was seen as ironic. "Now, the young guys are taking up after the others were sent to prison." When vests were found in a raid on a drug house, the drug officer smiled and said, "Fortunately these were not ours, they were from the Cambridge PD." (This was followed by low chuckles and exchanged smiles in the audience.) In general, citizens were seen as vaguely stupid or contributing to their own victimization—being out at night on the street drunk, leaving things in their cars, walking alone home late at night.

- Maps elicited comment, were dramatic and engaging. But: the maps and figures were ciphers. Some dots were just dots on the screen, for example, a series of burglaries. No comment was made after they were shown other than "you can see them." Some were seen as important if they were in a known area, e.g., a known housing project. Some were signs of other matters. That they continued to be clustered (undefined) meant that they are "resilient" crimes. Some clusters were picked out for lengthy explanation, as was the case when the gang sergeant discussed shootings and "beefs" between gangs in an area of the city, or when a lengthy discussion of drug dealing in another area took about five minutes. In both cases this involved showing pictures of people shot or shooters and discussing their gang links. But no explanation for this lengthy discussion of gangs, these young boys, or the current antagonisms was given other than the incidents of shooting. The discussion did not include further details, about the gangs, the boys, the housing projects, the links between these gangs, and churches or ministerial activities. The implication was that this situation would lead to more shootings.

- Presenting official reported crime statistics was an open-ended matter, something of an emotional trigger that could lead a discussion anywhere. The idea had tenacity and durability as a stimulus and topic. This was the other side of the expression (part of a sign that is the point seen on a map) that elicited no connection to any particular content (above, the silent observation of a map). This was the case where the crime statistics became an "open text" subject to virtually any reading or interpretation within the context of police discourse and police culture. That is, the discussion could go to guns used, to gangs, to housing projects, to overtime funds, to shift cars (cars on the 3:00–12:00 P.M. shift), or to the larger issues of immigration and multiple-family dwellings (all of these were observed in dialogues in the crime-analysis meetings).

- As noted above, the content of the meeting and its general lively and inquiring tone suppressed the work of information management, which put the best face of policing before this semipublic meeting. Crime animated the discussion, but it would be impossible to predict the sequencing and algorithms of questioning that took place. The meeting rewarded a kind of anticipated spontaneity.

### What Was Seen and Why?

In order to distinguish what was meant from that which was seen and shown, a preliminary distinction between what was seen and what it meant to the attendees must be made.

### What Was Seen?

What was seen was less important in the long run than what was understood as a result of seeing. One must keep an eye on what is out of sight. In a meeting, the maps stood for things that were in fact not there. They were elsewhere, and the icons created associations with the social world "out there." What was being talked about were events, people, processes, and places no one sees, even though the iconic signs, maps, contained or represented features of the thing they represented— streets, parks, housing estates, intersections. The natural events being referred to as one aspect of "crime" were natural events occurring in the world. They were being represented, symbolized on these screens. What could be taken from the screens, the images, and the talk? It appeared to be largely what came to hand—what one could grasp from the screen, take from it, and say about it. If one could talk, the topic might lead to another screen being shown. The material presence, a picture of someone, an intersection, or a crime scene (typically not shown), might touch off associations. The place had to be imagined somewhere in some place in some kind of action. The same was true of the angry black faces that stared out at one from the screen. Who and how could they be? We had nothing but our imagination and the descriptions provided with which to fashion a context within which the described actions were meaningful. To some degree, the ironic and playful atmosphere of the crime-analysis meeting permitted people to vary the script and its meaning without straying from the path of deciding something.

## What Was Grasped?

How does someone grasp something, make it available (Sellen and Harper 2002)? In an occupational context, a meeting of police minds, the underlying sentiment was based on the craft assumptions of policing —what it means to be a "good cop" or do "good police work" on the streets or in reference to a case, within the constraints of the task (that which everyone knows and takes for granted). What was seen in this sense was what could be brought to hand (and said) over the course of the meeting that on balance everyone assumed and understood to be pertinent. One of the most important sources of continuity was mininarratives, or stories that connected incidents.

One reading of the question of what was seen that departed from the narrow crime focus was what might be called mininarratives. These are stories that made sense of the pictures, maps, renditions of problems, and banal reports of gunshots fired, usually with no suspects, no context, and no outcome other than that a report was made by some-body in some district in Boston at some time in the previous two weeks. A mininarrative is a story that makes sense, with a beginning, middle, and end. It sums up common experiences and makes them general and memorable. It takes observations, comments, reflections, and bits of life and wraps them in a linear framework (Czarniawska 1997; Culler 1997: 78–89). In many ways, of course, by elevating some facts and bits, including others, amplifying and expanding some elements of the stories, and reducing or suppressing others, stories dramatize life. In the sessions I attended several mininarratives unfolded:

- A detective reported that a Boston newspaper had claimed that a "prostitution ring" was working in an area around a methadone clinic. Investigation ensued, and it was discovered that it was not a prostitution ring but people from the methadone clinic selling their methadone to others just outside the clinic or on the buses passing by. Pictures were shown of the clinics, a white prostitute (the only white face shown that day), and the gathering of addicts/methadone users outside a clinic.

- A gang squad member from a district presented the tale of three gangs and a history of their animosities (girls, guns, and compe-tition for territories). A few members' pictures were shown, su-perimposed on the areas in which their gangs were dominant. They were linked additionally to public housing projects, said to be the source of much gang recruitment. They were described as an emerging problem, by implication for their violence toward each other. No mention was made of drugs, guns, specific crimes, or past records—merely their gang-member status (based on his story).

- Five shootings of young black teenagers were linked by the crime analyst for a district in his general overview of crime in the previ-ous two weeks. Pictures of each of the people shot were superim-posed on a map and under the picture was a text: the address at which the shooting occurred. Lines drawn on the visual connect-ing the pictures of the men were based on the finding (established by a ballistics report) that the same gun had been used in each shooting. Approximately six weeks later, it was revealed (accord-ing to my interview with the crime analyst on August 13, 2002) that a police response to a "home invasion" call to 911 had netted the gun and other guns. It was still not clear who did the shootings, but the gun was seized.

• In the series of crimes reported below about the possible car thief working in Boston and in an adjoining area (about which the commissioner made a joke), a tale was told that linked unexplained crimes and pinned them down to a suspect, thus tidying up an otherwise worrying set of crimes.

• This narrative mode was used also in the example of the burglar who cut himself and left blood at the scene.

Of less interest perhaps was the thin line of continuity provided by the statistics that were shown at each meeting; they suggested a mininarrative of continuity and stability in banal and ever-present evil, punctuated by little ups and downs, largely unexplained, stabilizing the need for policing and the vagaries of the public and of criminals. This (people being caught, justice being done on the street, good work being recognized) was in a sense the vulgar and droning background, like the hum of bagpipes that makes the little harmonies and melodies more pleasing. The more obvious cliché was captured in the police officers' most stable refrain: if crime is up, more police are needed to bring it under control, take back the streets, and make neighborhoods safe, and if it is down, as it had been in the preceding ten years in most large cities, police must be rewarded for keeping cities safe, officers must be hired and trained, and numbers must be kept up because the threat of rising crime lies always just out of sight. This was the ready-to-hand explanation for sustaining and/or expanding police power and numbers.

Conversely, the little epiphanies, good stories, successes, a successful arrest (a drug raid was reported a few hours after it had taken place, the officers having been up all night executing the raid, booking the suspects, cataloguing evidence, and taking statements) were greeted with smiles. No one asked if the arrest altered the drug markets, drug costs, the quality or types of drugs being sold, the users, or the dealing structure.

In these ways, the story of crime control as a drama was punctuated and sustained by mininarratives that validated its existence, memorialized its vicissitudes, and made plain the costs of crime and the ever-watchful vigilance of the police. This formulation, in its turn, permitted the irony of failed arrests, botched surveillance, errors, and mistakes to be amusing and sustaining as well. Failures were embedded in successes.

### What Was Brought to the "Seeing"?

The presenters from the districts carried with them to the meetings a thick book. It was the basis for the rehearsal and for the performance at the meeting itself. The support of the crime analysts was appreciated, and they stood ready to assist in the presentations. The format was well known, as I noted above, and was replicated in each meeting. The question is, Given the book, crime analysts' help, and rehearsal, how did the content make sense from the perspective of the participants? To some degree, answering this question requires returning to the themes resident in the police organizational-occupational culture. .

The world of an occupation is something like a set of lenses through which the world is viewed. The closer one comes to matters of interest to the work, the more likely it is that the perspective of the occupation will come into play. A craft requires tools, and the tools of police are those at hand: good judgment—the ability to make good assessments of the here and now and of the trustworthiness of people, as indicated by their voice and body—as well as the material tools of the craft. These are practices, and the practices and the perspective are brought inside, to the meetings, and there applied.

Police work, as is often noted, is craft work—it takes the matters at hand and shapes them to a reasonable outcome. This is not often the best, or even the sought-after outcome, but rather that which is possible given all that could go wrong. Police work is concrete in the sense that it makes do with what is possible, and adjusts, shapes, cuts, and shims things until they cohere, or at least (a) do not fall apart, (b) come back "banana shaped," as what happens when "the shit hits the fan," (c) allow one to cover one's ass in the event that something goes wrong, and (d) work in the here and now. Police work is an intentionally conscious, present-oriented doing (or not) something such that things will not get worse. If one can, one avoids paperwork and further complications, violence and the related complaints, investigations, and the rest (if anticipated)—the work should be untraceable when in low-visibility circumstances. That for which a record exists should be flattering and compelling to those who read about it. There are no absolute standards. What is acceptable to one group will not work with another. For example, threats and exhortations may work on the street but do not suffice for middle-class people; good manners and etiquette work in the suburbs but may be dynamite and lead to ridicule and violence in disadvantaged areas. Violence, for example, is highly contextual in its appearance, targets, and consequences, and police are well aware of this. While policing is governed by standards, it is not a science, there are no written general rules, and local traditions and history shape the practices. These may appear to be basic observations, but the point is that there are no transcendental theories, systematic propositions, laws, or tenets that hold across all situations and against which an officer can be held accountable (Klockars 1996). The extension of this general rule (the one general rule is that no general rules hold) is that legal standards are highly contextual. In general, these rules provide protection to the police so that they can carry out work that is capricious, vexing, and confusing—a game that one cannot not fully understand, that in general is something to be avoided, and that must be accepted as a tool in the craftsperson's box. If one thinks of practice as a kind of habit, a habit that blinds us to its contradictions and self-serving features, then it is not surprising that habit obscures and makes misrecognition readily at work (Bourdieu 1977).

There is no unified or even coherent police culture in the sense that is often referred to in textbooks. Even this reified picture is drawn from limited research, focused on the white, male, urban patrol officer and his work-based oral culture, and in that sense is a misleading gloss on complexity. What is usually called "police culture" is talk full of hyperbole and exceptions, a kind of tool kit, on the one hand, used to resolve the fundamentally incongruous aspects of the work, and, on the other, a configuration of warning signs about how to keep out of trouble. This means further that much of what is talked about is exceptions, stories that are meant to express cautionary tales (Hughes 1958), ways around trouble and all those things to be thought of as a deep pit. Doing good police work, ironically, is dragging something out of chaos and making the best of it. This might be called applying flair. "Flair" is a matter of managing and anticipating all those things that any reasonable person would manage and anticipate in such a situation as the person doing it saw it (not as you, the outsider, after the fact, might see it).

It is very important to underscore that this meaning-making mechanism is not "the police occupational culture" that is trotted out as a caricature that appears in virtually every criminology, criminal-justice, and police textbook (sometimes citing incorrectly my own 1977 [reprint 1997] work). Waddington (1999) points out that "police culture" is a label based on talk, stories, and derived from the "canteen culture" ("canteen" referring to the cafeterias in police stations where uniformed officers eat and take tea and coffee breaks). It has been used incorrectly by researchers as a description of police behavior. Waddington argues, with very close reading of the research evidence as well as his own experience as an officer in the London Metropolitan, that when police behavior is examined, it shows great subtlety in action choices, and that behavior is a compromise formation based on the structural position of the police in democracies, not on their "attitudes," "culture," "stories," "figurative culture," or the mythical caricature that is the "policeman's personality." Agency, he argues, in effect is action "on the streets" and in behavior. However, Waddington acknowledges that, as is shown in these descriptions of crime-analysis meetings, the drama of policing does unfold in such public meetings in part because the work on the streets is so dreary.

Finally, the presentation of aggregated data, the overviews of trends and patterns on which the CAMs are based, is in conflict with another sort of rationality of the officer and is consistent with the rule of thumb that "you had to be there." This brief and elliptical phrase means that the decisions made were based on readings of the people, the place, the time of day, and other matters at hand such as workload and stress that the observer, a neutral and distant person, might not fully appreciate. Abstractions are in conflict with this incident-based rationality. It is easier to tell stories about an incident than about a pattern, a trend, or an algorithm. Stories, in short, are rooted in the concrete and call out for generalization, resonance with experience, and the next story. Memorable aspects of life are often captured in the second story.

This rather long listing is a coherent rendering of what can be seen and done when an image appears. What can be seen there is rooted deeply in the assumptions of the craft as practiced in public before a large audience. It is not police work; it is the dramatized, public versions of the craft as seen in words and abstractions—a certain kind of compromise formation based on the limits of what can be done and said to be done in this job. Thus, the images must be translated into the question, What can I do about this now? This formulation in turn leads to what is the nature of the job: controlling the work and keeping things moving. How do I resolve a problem—do something? What do I do and when—now, or as soon as possible? What means do I use? My fists, my feet, my body, my head, my weapons, my car, and the rest of the world as it comes to hand. What is the cause of crime? Who knows?

It might be bad families, racial inequality, the economy, bad moral values, etc., but all this matters not. I am faced with something about which I must (I feel I must) act or be seen to act. Crime and evil are easily reified and seen as these shown people doing the named things. Motive and cause have no place in such discussions. Arrests, prior convictions, field stops, and other past records merely substantiate what is known. Gangs, and pictures of gang members, mean potential crime about to happen. The person on the screen, the named person, the listed person I see is the next villain. When a crime of this kind is reported, this person is on the horizon now and will be sought and questioned. There is little reason not to pursue this "hypothesis."[5] Thus, the alliance between the probation officers and police becomes a powerful means to screen, monitor, and control probationers, especially since one random drug test that shows positive results sends them back to prison. Once an arrest is made, of course, a crime is managed (Both may lead to jail time if a conviction results, but an arrest will suffice.). This in turn validates the ideology of crime control and the binary world of crime/criminal/evil and absence of crime/noncriminal/good.

## How to Use Mapping in an Occasioned Fashion

We can see from these examples taken from the CAM that in order for a map to be used it must be understood—grasped as useful and ready to hand (Heidegger 1977). It must be seen as part of the dance and consistent with the usual steps. This, in turn, means that, like any displayed analytic tool, it will be shaped by the current practices and routines that are thought of as the taken-for-granted essence of the work. To say that a map is "occasioned" is to say that it is part of an occasion in which it "works" and that the occasion is characterized by containing a map. Several rules of thumb or principles order the meaningfulness of maps in the CAM.

### Principled Use of Maps

It may be useful to see the use of maps not as a series of scenes shown but as something governed by unseen social "principles." These are not "rules" but rough, unspoken guidelines for application. They are used without reflection (Heidegger 1977a: 182).

The first principle is that the map must incorporate and represent familiar, named, and retrievable *objects* that are themselves "seeable." I do not mean that they are available visibly (Sellen and Harper 2002). The objects immediately relevant to the meetings—places; persons (usually past offenders with records) as suspects; crime as reported to the police or seen by them; named acts encoded within the vocabulary of the police-UCR (Uniform Crime Report) categories; and victims or assumed victims—were all familiar objects. Using these terms was accomplished without concern for or speculations upon motivations, causes, etiology, prognosis, or cure.

The second principle is that these matters, these analytic tools, must be available, affordable, ready-to-hand, and visible. Tools and a tool box require objects on which to work. These tools and their objects are symbolic in the case of the police.

The third principle is that the matters represented in speech and on the screens must be linked by known trajectories (Halsey 2001: 414) that connect familiar objects (or objects constituted in a familiar fashion). That is, several things are assumed to be required to talk about the matter: events that are labeled as "crimes" are seen as connected to one or more offenders and a victim. Crimes are not committed by witches, aliens, or other nonpersons, and unless revealed by a vice investigation, must have a known victim (even if known as John Doe) and be actionable. They are not cyber crimes, or crimes of a terrorist sort (from whatever source). There is considerable pressure on police, in their view, to act on information received that points to a possible crime that they can imagine, that they have encountered and investigated before, and that they believe they can encounter and investigate again in the present case.

One can argue conversely that if these principles were not observed and seen to be observed, the meetings would produce nonsense for the participants.

## Maps Stimulate Tools-in-Use

The tools at issue, when seen in the context of the crime-analysis meeting, must be connected to the dominant current practices and be seen to expand and clarify them as well as to simplify them. This requires working through the tasks and charting out the natural history of their issues and the expected outcomes. As Halsey (2001: 414) writes rather poetically, "For to trace the world is never to leave the security of the known." He means that representations of an iconic variety are particularly powerful in eliciting responses and memories and reestablishing the prior constraints they had exercised on thought. But they also permit reconfiguration of the multiple signs (expressions and contents) into simple versions, stories and tales, or more complex narratives with dead ends, algorithms, and expressive structure.

While tools have a conservative function, and those used must be seen as relevant to the core values of the occupation, they can be transformative because the particular context or situation always presents new surface features and new aspects of the ensembles that are displayed and talked about. Thus, on the one hand, maps and charts make visible a unity that was not visible before: robberies using a gun, or daytime robberies as opposed to nighttime robberies, now group into emergent or resilient clusters or areas in need of service, but these clusters are part of yet other configurations and unities suppressed by the maps' color, their animation, or the speed of the operator in pointing and clicking.

The resistance to use must be seen as the other side of the acceptance. What features of the tool are not seen, not imagined, not graspable among those made marginal or among those who decided to be marginal? Once a connection is made, it can be remade, erased, displayed with new, vivid colors, set in another map, moved to one side or the other of a screen projection, or reconnected to other matters, e.g., burglaries can be collapsed with other property crimes. The lines between the objects can vary in strength, color, or content. The outcomes of the uses of tools must be made visible and rewarded in some fashion.

## Operative Rationalities

What sort of rationalizing was going forward in these three police departments? Clearly, the infrastructure was being built: the experts, the software, the databanks, and the linkages were leading to the creation of more links across large data banks and making more federally based data available to local police departments (e.g., FEMA, INS, and Homeland Security shared data with the BPD after July 2002). Support staffs were becoming more skilled at manipulating and presenting data, some of which was context based and local. Top command and the experts within police departments were more likely to know the recent research, at least in general terms, as well as the success and claimed success of compstat in reducing crime (Kelling and Coles 1996). The extent to which these processes produced change on the ground, such as changes in disorganization, the distribution of crime, repeat victims and offenders, and the quality of life in cities, is as yet unknown. The changes in regard to management, according to the work of Weisburd and associates (see, for a summary, Weisburd and Braga 2006), appeared to be minor. The kind of rationalizing that was in place was that which flows from the viewing of and commenting upon crime figures in ecological or geographical-territorial areas for which responsibility is nominally assigned.

Discourse, using maps presented at meetings and featuring the term "crime" as a multifaceted shifter, varying in meaning by unstated context, organized and made sense of the very complex matter of social control via crime suppression. The unstated, unremarked-upon, and taken-for-granted assumption was that these figures represented what should and could be controlled, whether or not they bore on underlying social causes and consequences.

In this process, the figures and maps were both topics and resources for the discussions and the data that was presented. In other words, people assumed that others knew what they were talking about when they asked about crime (a topic), and these assumptions were resources that could be drawn upon to sustain conversation, sequencing, and ritualized control over the topics. The fact that in Boston the discussion moved away from and around the presentations opened up avenues for exploration and action that were far superior to the other arenas in the trade, such as the shift-based roll call, video screening, general orders, or meetings of squads.

The idea that many rationalities obtain in organizations means that given an end, one can approach it in several acceptable ways, all of which are understood by others as "something we could and should do." Organizations feature rationalities, not rationality. This array, in turn, makes them accountable—things one can explain if need be (or not). The working rationalities that appeared in these cases were context bound and temporal. Nevertheless, even at its most visionary, any mode of rationality will be short term because policing as an occupation values immediate action taken in case something might get worse (paraphrase of Bittner 1990).

## Rationalities Revisited

If change is to take place in police organization, a timely rationality based on set objectives, goals, evaluation, feedback, and correction based on the success or failure of the plan has been assumed by most writers to be necessary. Thus the popularity of management talk (seen in Bratton's planning in the NYPD; Bratton 1998). In fact, there are several rationalities at work. Consider these shown in the case studies.

One way to get things done is to follow the rules, go through channels, defer to the office (not the person holding it), and do what is implied. As in the military, orders are rarely given, and most of what happens is based on an unstated implicature. What might be called order-based rationality is not about orders denotatively. It does derive from rank and associated "bureaucratic power." Ranking officers use formal, down-the-line orders and rules and regulations to sanction (positively or negatively) officers' actions. This was found in and dominated deciding in all three organizations. This source of rationality was in fact based on compliance with rank and seniority, not on the value of the ideas in achieving an end. Rules were understood and orders followed because of the context of the order, the suggestions or directions read into it. This rationality was situationally justified (Manning 1997: ch. 6) and seen as a matter of duty, obedience, keeping a low profile, or even, cynically, "covering your ass" (CYA). In many respects it did not refer to or value content but rather valued the source of the command or order. Conversely, officers at sergeant rank and above felt they had to "chase the troops," "keep after the slackers," and force the troops to "keep the numbers up." In many ways, the use of such rules and order created a "mock bureaucracy": one that only appears to function according to rules and orders but in fact works through other means: personal loyalty, grudging acceptance, indifference to the command and/or the commander, or a wait-and-see attitude toward the order given.

A form of emergent rationality that is based on using data, maps, and statistics in a short-term, action-based fashion was present. It was found at times, and on occasion, in Washington and Boston. One memo with data was used in Western to guide the actions of vice officers and encourage them to be more productive of arrests. In the studied sites, resources enabled some shifting around of priorities, using overtime and "details" or curtailing them, to present the appearance of energetic order maintenance and crime control.

An occasioned rationality in which talk and problem solving was focused by the maps and information was present in Boston. Some new avenues were opened for imagining the opportunities presented, and innovation popped in and out of the Boston meetings. This rationality was situated, local, transitory (not transcendental), and loosely connected to the next problem-solving exercise, and it drew on the invisible power of the new forms of information technology. The value of such discussions and uses of maps was predicated upon the assumption that the usual traditional tactics would be employed and that the target was offenders and their crimes.

A kind of pragmatic rationality was the most dominant rationality and was found in all three organizations. In philosophy, this meant a constant refinement of the known and accepted means to achieve unstated, and in that sense traditional crime-control, ends. Police pragmatism hinged on the unstated notion that one must "reduce" crime through direct action of a visible, obvious, and conventional sort. If a "rash" of auto thefts broke out, then the solutions imagined were more overtime for police presence, more undercover officers and surveillance in the area, and increased pressure to clear the crime reported. This was the rationality of policing as usual, elaborated and dramatized by meetings, maps, pictures, icons, photos, and Power Point presentations. Pragmatism was sometimes combined with the rhetoric of community policing in public and with the media, although it was not manifested in the meetings.

Partnership rationality sometimes played a public role in dramatizing crime control.[6]

A prevalent and short-term rationality used in all police departments but not observed in this study is "damage control." The BPD specifically avoided discussion of such tactics in its CAMs, and the other two departments had no meetings. Nevertheless, damage control is frequently used to reduce loss of prestige and to increase legitimacy. This is done by mounting a campaign to actively manipulate the media (Chan 1996: 167–89). It includes expedient actions to quell media meretriciousness and dampen public curiosity. The tactics may include misinformation (lies and facts that are wrong), disinformation (intentionally directing attention to other facts that do not bear on this case or incident), closing off of information by using "no comment" after media raise questions, and hinting at alternative story lines or causes that deflect attention from the police. When damage control is required, concealing and distorting information, lying and avoiding direct answers, and hidden agendas are the order of the day. The surface announcements often have little to do with the facts or problems at hand and more to do with police "face saving."[7] That is, how does one deal with mistakes and failure?

These rationalities, derived from the interviews and meetings in the departments, were an odd mix. The rationalities emerged and were used as and when they were needed. In general, order-based rationalities replicated the structure of police command and control, in which the right or the truth was equivalent to the rank of the source of the message. Partnership rationality and damage control as general rationalities also draw on institutional beliefs. These were "institutional rationales," explanations for why policing itself is done—to maintain control of the organization by the top command, insure citizen trust, and reduce damage from the media. They tapped or displayed beliefs that were part of the canopy that enveloped legitimate policing. Another set of rationalities consisted of more "practice-based rationales" in that they referred to the things that should be done or were being done about the matter discussed. These were the practice-based rationales and included emergent, occasioned, and pragmatic rationality. Here the shifter, crime, and the context-based meanings of crime animated the discussions. The power of CM/CA was that it tapped both kinds of rationalities and permitted the merging of what could be done with what should be done, or what had been done.

### Grounding the Rationalities

The several rationalities were acceptable because they were all grounded in the natural attitude of policing. The form of rationalizing associated with Weberian transition is based on comparing and contrasting evidence, looking for a theoretical and coherent ordering to the elements, correction and feedback on the comparison of outcomes, and so on (Garfinkel 1967: 272 ff.; see below). What is done then is considered good for all practical purposes. The public accept the value of police organizations holding compstat-type meetings and assume that scientific rationality drives them and that this scientific rationality is based on management theory, social science data, and careful analysis (Kelling 1995; Kelling and Coles 1996; Henry 2001). It is more likely that it is a particular kind of short-term management tool that coerces more attention to crime and disorder among precinct/district captains than that it alters the fundaments of policing (Moore 2003). There is no evidence that it assists detective work, proactive crime preventions or vice policing, antiterrorist–homeland-security work, or any intelligence-led policing with an anticipatory or planning function. This is no accident.

## Summary

This chapter is an attempt to capture the flow of events in the meetings as instances of the natural attitude of the police while performing this task. The rationalities displayed were those consistent with the unfolding craft of policing and the constraints necessary to sustain the working notion of reciprocity of perspectives. The problem with this concept, which assumes that I assume that the other person would see things as I do if the other person were in my place, is that evidence of this "seeing" is still needed. The structure, procedures, ritual, and expected content all contributed to order and the ordering of the CAM, but order was sustained by the natural attitude and displays that were brought to the events as they unfolded. Watching CAMs unfold required an analysis of how making sense was done and of the subtle ways the process reproduced the ideology and crime concerns of the occupation. Technology was a necessary aspect of producing the very dramatic and engaging CAM gatherings. Nevertheless, the work of making sense of the maps and figures had to be undertaken and be seen to be undertaken.

To what degree does the introduction of information technologies alter the practice of policing? It appears that a number of small changes are taking place. The first is that the visible display of figures and cases and examples of problem solving brought by representatives of the police districts provided a shared body of knowledge that could be applied, or a crude ensemble of best practices. Granted that this was based solely on "what works" rather than on a contrast of failed practices with good ones, it nonetheless made visible the craft. It may be that this also brought low performers at the higher levels up to standards or made them more aware of their failures. The infrastructure of data was known to be there, and the familiarity of officers with laptops, MDTs (mobile data terminals), and electronic file preparations rapidly accelerated the potential for queries that were broader than a quick check of outstanding warrants, traffic citations, motor vehicle information, and drivers' licenses. The speed and efficiency of the retrieval made magical the processing of such information, but it made it visible in ways that searching for paper documents could not replace. One of the most powerful effects that data may sustain is that the same faces appeared in the meetings, black men rearrested on probation violations, burglaries, and armed street robberies. These were the people committing twentieth-century street crimes and being rearrested; they often had long "RAP" sheets and were the "usual suspects" in any series of burglaries, robberies, or auto thefts in an area. The likelihood of being rearrested would appear to be increasing as sex-offender lists are being developed and posted on websites; ex-offenders, returning probationers, are monitored by police–probation-officer teams; and shared databases are beginning to be found in regions, rather than within a city department. Conversely, no discussions of computer crime, white-collar crime, embezzlement, or the like reached the CAMs. The facility shown with the IT equipment suggested that the inverse relationship between skill and knowledge of IT, on the one hand, and street skills, on the other, remained and was dramatized by the trained skills of the crime analysts and personnel in the Office of Research and Evaluation. They could produce the show but had no ability to sense what should be done with displayed information.

# 10

## Generalization

### Overview of the Argument

Consider again the police and their long-standing functional role, the music. The police react to something that might get worse, the emergent, the unanticipated, the potentially damaging to the social fabric. They do so as things happen and when they happen and rarely before. As Bittner (1990) has so eloquently put it, they respond when someone "calls the cops." People call the cops because they perceive, intuit, feel, know, or wish that something should be done by someone willing to control a situation, perhaps with violence. This means that it is not possible to fully imagine what might be next. Imagination arises as needed. Police value and admire good work done in the episode, in the here and now, and work that is done with some aspect of parsimony. Immutable facts result from this music and the dance that results: they shape any attempt, no matter how well conceived and implemented, to alter policing. In policing as practiced, there is no need for a theory of crime or its causation—that is for others to cogitate; it is sufficient to be there soon after being called. There is no urgent need for "crime prevention," whatever that means in practice, because the need to respond, to act, is encompassing, engaging, and all that is needed day after day. There is no evidence that the public is concerned about crime prevention. It would appear that formal control using the criminal sanction driven by "fear of crime" rules the day. This means that spikes and peaks in recorded serious crime and exceptions in the short run govern the concerns of the police command. Whatever passes for policy is labeled an "operation," usually with martial connotations—a short-term, focused, labor-intensive, visible sequence of police work for a few days or weeks. These operations and tactical maneuvers are telling because they are in effect long-term planning. They are repeated as a vision of the future. Whatever technology increases the officer's sense of efficacy will be used and modified, and what is not useful will be destroyed, sabotaged, avoided, or used poorly. The penetration of technology into the contours of the job is almost entirely dependent on its perceived utility on the ground. The only exposure of officers to these data, as we have seen, was in the meetings, now abandoned (see the epilogue), in the Boston department. The meetings in large part were ritualistic reaffirmations of policing tactics, with some attempt to make managers accountable for brief changes in officially reported data. This is what the quotation from Lichtenberg at the beginning of the book refers to: mistaking the sign or merely the expression (officially recorded crime) for the referent (the content) or what it points to: social order, quality of life, security, and feelings of trust. Variations in these matters have crudely and variously patterned the relationship of public trust in police, public fear or lack of fear of crime, or disorder (Weitzer and Tuch 2006). Beliefs override facts in a world dominated by trust. The information and information processing seen in this book were adapted to the police organization and its characteristic practices: IT and its supporting features did not change any significant practice in the three organizations studied.

What is called the reactivity theme of policing (see chapter 2) confers sanctity upon traditional strategies and tactics, the music of policing. By "sanctity," I mean the patina of the sacred, the unquestionable, the taken for granted that is beyond words. Imagine the police organization. The modern police are a conservative, reactive organization resistant to innovation and invested with trust from the public. In spite of using inexpensive, readily available information technologies, the police remain a fairly traditional organization with respect to their fundamental perspectives, a theme of responsiveness to public demand, their structure, strategy, and tactics. What of new technology? Police claim scientific sophistication in such matters as laboratory science, ballistics, and crime analysis. However, the primary technology is verbal—the words used to persuade and control others in interaction. The budget reflects investment in technology as third or fourth in priority behind personnel, transportation (fuel, repairs, replacement of vehicles), and weaponry. There is no comprehensive platform from which the various data sets and databases can be drawn. IT remains scattered, a midden heap of electronic files, data retained on daily calls for service, management information, budgets, case files, and physical evidence in vaults, labs, safes, and bank accounts. Thus information is shaped to suit its host.

This ethnographic study of organizational change focused on an information technology called crime mapping, often joined with crime analysis. Six features of a CA/CM capacity and the process of sense making in the meetings were primary foci in the fieldwork. Certain features had to be present for the CM/CA capacity to be realized. The central question was, What impact did information technology, crime mapping, and crime analysis have on three police organizations: those in Washington, D.C., Boston, Massachusetts, and a midwestern city I call Western. IT is one aspect of the rationalizing of policing. Were the police being swept along into newer and smarter modes of management and data analysis? Did these new modes guide deployment, evaluation, and readjustment? How does this new technology fit into current police everyday work? Is CM/CA merely a trendy fashion? Are police organizations changing as a result of the introduction of information processing? How? To what degree and how do crime analysis and crime mapping as implemented create a conflict in rationalities and power relations within police organizations?

The degree of external political influence, the field and the surround, have not been studied in previous work on technological change in policing. Previous studies by Weisburd and colleagues, and the study done primarily by Willis in Lowell, Massachusetts (Willis, Mastrofski, and Weisburd 2004), do not describe the content or interactions in the meetings. Rather, these researchers are interested in the putative allocation of personnel resources and, having not deeply probed into the matter, assume that the meaning of the maps and the problems discussed emerge in the course of the meetings, that the infrastructure of traditional policing suffices to produce consensus, and that organizational or command intention is solely to alter the environment and hold managers accountable. Outcomes remain a quagmire, or bureaucratic mystery, as the processes by which the deciding is done are not explicated. Instead, an instrumental view obscures the diversity of social interactions taking place (and those not taking place) and the interplay among structural features of the meetings, the process, and content. As this research has shown in respect to the way crime mapping is used, the meaning of the problem of which the surface features are shown, that which might be solved or managed, was not discussed; the tactical results were conventional in every respect; the maps simply reified or objectified what was assumed to work and be "good police work" (Willis, Mastrofski, and

Weisburd 2004, 2007). Organizations do what they have done well in the past. Political support and the necessary resources were only in place and the meetings were only realized in Boston. Maps and tables were presented to assembled officers of various ranks and duties twice a month. These fact-based, abstract, reproducible sources of data as presented and diffused widely can capture trends and identify anomalies across time and space, in theory challenging the traditional logic and practices of policing, which are based on the overvaluation of control of an incident and the reactive pose. The juxtaposition of "police logic," or the way things should be done, and abstract rationalities can create incongruities and reflection within the police organization.

In Boston, the CAMs were orderly and reproduced the rank, gender, and color ratios in the organization. The ecology reflected the actual authority and power of those seated in the room. The format constrained random, imaginative, or innovative responses or questions. Top command remained in control via deference to their rank, personal charisma, and control of the timing and the format. Meaning was sustained in the process. Variations in speech, such as the use of irony and jokes, were well understood and the tactics suggested were viewed as obviously the correct option. There was no "problem solving" in the exchanges. The officers and all seated at the meetings viewed the meaning of the maps and data as clear and unproblematic. What was taken to be a problem—that is, anything underlying the data as presented—was not discussed; actions were suggested almost immediately after a rise in a kind of crime or disorder. Reducing the rise was the problem to be attended to, not the causes of gangs, the availability of guns, the ecology of areas, the current state of the economy, or the like. The ways in which the actual maps were understood and used by officers was not talked about. The ways in which "problems" were defined and identified were not included or discussed by participants in the meetings. Short-term crime suppression was not discussed, but merely assumed to be valid and necessary. No negative consequences of a crime-attack mode were discussed.

Since there were no rewards for changing behavior and no feedback about what had been done or what its effects were, there was little or no reason to believe that any change in the basically undirected and entrepreneurial work of patrol officers changed in Boston. Standard tactics—reallocation of officers by shift, saturation patrol, authorizing additional ad hoc allocation of overtime pay, and other exercises in traditional police tactics—predate World War II and cannot account for trends in reported crime. Since the CM/CA process remains in place in 2007 in many departments, and crime continues to rise, claims by the police that they are masters of the streets, have taken them back and are now in control, and other rhetorical flourishes of the late 1990s are no longer heard. The null hypothesis, nothing proven, must be accepted.

## What Change?

While being shaped and constrained by the music or structure of the organization and its historic commitments, a modified dance based on IT could possibly emerge. The case studies suggest that the process is time bound, and that the steps of development do not fall in a linear fashion. Rather, some parts were present, such as the software and computer capacity, while others, the problem-solving approach, the skills in use and interpretation, and the availability of the information (the ecology of distribution) were most often absent. Except in the BPD, some but not all of the necessary elements were present. The labels applied to programs based on CM/CA are misleading, as most of them did not contain the elements that are essential to producing an evidence-based kind of policing based on visuals and group presentations. While the claims for the program have been exaggerated and the evidence of success is thin, the Boston meetings provide evidence that internal coherence around crime concerns can be made public and shared.

A theme of continuing interest is the study of organizational change based on a phenomenological view of organizational work (D. Silverman 1971). This view assumes conflict, contradictions, divisions in meaning and rewards within the organization, and negotiation of the place of IT within an organizational and political environment. The place of a municipal police force cannot be understood outside the part it plays in the political economy and ecology of a city. The police are a political force, shaped by and shaping political action. This is also an ethnographic study of the introduction of a technology into an organization. I have used the metaphor of music to capture the background against which any innovation is a foreground. The music, I have argued, is constituted by the traditional police mandate, organizational structure, strategy, and tactics. While the mandate, seen as the way policing is viewed in a surround of politics and particular field of agencies, is discussed, the primary interest in this book is discovering the choreography or logic that makes the dance, what is done, appear to work. The question is, Does the introduction of information technology, in this case, crime mapping and crime analysis, change the dance steps and the style with which they are executed? Given this question, I have focused on the situated or occasioned relevance of this technology, rather than its global impact on policing. In the situation of use, in which the IT is a part of the occasion or situation in which it is displayed, CM/CA becomes a stimulus for the police to talk about doing policing. On balance, the music and the steps remain the same, but some aesthetics and poetics have emerged about how to display talk about policing in a semipublic setting. I have suggested that actions are often confused with accounts or justifications for what is done, and that these accounts themselves are indicative.

## Implications

The three case studies outlined above have sociological implications beyond the particular cases. They raise basic questions about the links between theory and practice in policing; about how such technology and information can be interpreted and used given the present ossified social organization of the police; and about changes in the direction of prevention and problem solving. The case studies suggest that map reading can be better understood as a methodical semiotic process than as a matter of merely looking attentively. Much was brought to the presentations that was drawn from the occupational perspective of policing the streets. The studies also suggest the utility of seeing rationalizing as a process with several faces, each of which is situated or occasioned, rather than as a single mode of connecting known and stated ends using understood means to achieve a relatively clear objective.

In Western, CM/CA had top-command support and political support, but the department had neither resources nor demand conditions (sufficient crime) to make the innovation of crime analysis and mapping a high priority during organizational change driven by the community policing ideology. While the reforms in Western had political support, some funding, leadership, and interest, there was no urgent and apparent need for officers to use it, nor any broad-based way to disseminate the information. This may in part have been due to the scale and size of the organization: a large formal meeting was not necessary for the police to debate problems and approaches and to draw a colluding audience into the process. There was strong resistance to the practice of mapping and crime prevention among the patrol segment. The series of changes in the leadership and the external events, in part related to leadership in the city and in the police department, drained energy and time from the officers and slowed organizational transformation. While a minimalist software-server combination and two operatives were in place, the absence of ecology of distribution, meetings, training, and civilian staff meant that the crime mapping was a very early prototype. Clearly, the rationality of working the street and of dong it here and now, the pragmatic "crime control" approach, ruled the organization.

In many respects, the MPDC is the most fascinating case because some of the necessary elements were present while others never materialized (literally). Leadership was present, but strong internal political resistance remained, and a system of crime analysis and crime mapping was not realized during the time of the study. In Washington, there was a plan and support, but supportive, consistent internal politics and a supportive technical infrastructure were lacking. The field and surround were in constant and almost chaotic change. Meetings around the problem of information infrastructure were planning meetings, and the project as imagined was never implemented. The innovation was connected to the legitimacy of the current chief and his supporters, and resistance to a planned, integrated approach to crime analysis and mapping was only one part of a departmental power struggle.

In Boston, the necessary elements had been forged some six years before the CAMs were introduced. They were in place when the innovations associated with producing shared statistical information, compstatlike meetings and processes, came together. Sense making rarely was pushed beyond the use of conventional tactics and strategies. The lack of theorizing, the lack of awareness of the interpretive work necessary to link the signs on the maps to broader social processes or intervention strategies, meant that the range of problems identified was narrow. Most of the actions taken were performed to demonstrate graphically and dramatically evidence that sustained much more of the same type of policing. While the Boston meetings and process illustrate an advanced form of rationality-dialogue, the tactical focus remained. In the crime-analysis meetings, when broader aspects of problems were raised and discussed, they did lead to some information sharing and did make visible some "practical" solutions. Nevertheless, since there were no standards against which the results were measured, or the matters at hand were contradictory—e.g., crime was up (bad) but trust in police was also up (good); a few visible crimes raised public concern and anxiety, but the overall rate dropped—and because there was no feedback on the results of the solutions or programs presented, every spike or drop in crime was viewed as an anomaly.[1] The problem solving done in Boston was largely carried out in the here and now with present resources, and focused on "crime" in its various facets. The police arrested the same people repeatedly because they believed those people were committing the crimes, since they were being tracked by probation officers and sex offender registries, as well as detectives and uniformed officers (see *Boston Globe*, Aug. 22, 2002; and the review of Boston's programs in the 1990s in chapter 7). Where problem solving is public or at least semipublic, as in the case of Boston, it is highly edited by topic and data presented to demonstrate a clear, organized, and controlled effort. The edited, rehearsed, and selectively presented data sustain the impression that the police are fully in charge, holding back the tide of crime and preserving property and lives. As was shown in the analysis of the Boston meetings, the uses of maps were occasioned, their meaning was situational, and those attributed meanings were rooted in traditional ways of viewing the problems of order and social control. The meeting was disconnected from any formalized feedback processes and standards that might establish best practices, benchmarks, or any of the buzz words used to characterize crime mapping and compstat processes.

## Return to the Dance

The dance of the police has little changed if these studies are representative of large, urban, North American forces, in spite of the new wave of IT-based innovations and managerial strategies, including crime mapping and crime analysis. It would appear on the basis of the evidence presented here that in order for change to occur that reflects managerial and pragmatic rationalizing, several elements, named in the case studies—infrastructure, skilled personnel, administrative power, distribution, and access to data and relevant soft- and hardware—are necessary conditions. One factor, neither obvious nor in the control of the police, is political support. Rationalizing based on information technology requires external support from politicians, city councils, and, indeed, citizens in the form of information and taxation for budgets and overtime costs. Of the most obvious recent innovations, CM/CA, problem-solving policing, community policing, and crime-attack approaches, CM/CA and community policing were most favored, although the configuration called "community policing" varied in the three sites. Problem solving was evident and public in Boston. CM/CA was used exclusively tactically in Boston.

The combination of promotion of the ideas of CM/CA in the media and the appeal of apparent success in reducing crime made the ideas popular with police chiefs and their staffs. The previously mentioned survey and fieldwork carried out by Weisburd and colleagues in 2000–2001, and published subsequently (Weisburd, et al. 2003; Willis, Mastrofski, and Weisburd 2004), found that the dominant and preferred use of crime mapping in most departments surveyed, and the three in which their observations were made, was tactical, short term, and conventional: the departments reported deploying officers to an area-employing saturation patrol and/or undercover work. It had little effect on management, promotion, careful problem solving, or use of crime data except as indicators of unwanted spikes in known crimes. Crime analysis was seen as displays of simple clusters of crimes by area in a given time period. No problem solving was observed or reported. A careful and extensive analysis of compstatlike meetings in Lowell, Massachusetts, by Willis, Mastrofski, and Weisburd (2004) showed that even with consistent efforts and most of the elements in place, resource deployment was rarely accomplished and resistance remained among the patrol officers. The effects on management, crime, and organizational change were nugatory. Willis's study, published after this book was drafted, found similar patterns. In none of the organizations was information from citizens directly or indirectly introduced into the dialogue of "problem solving." There was no "coproduction of order." "Accountability" seemed to refer to the obligations of middle managers and precinct-level captains or lieutenants to the top command, not to the citizens or their elected representatives, politicians, in individual or collective fashion. Crime attack, as a systematic planned program, was not featured, nor was any experiment of this kind ongoing.

There are many rationalities, or ways to approach achieving an end, in policing, but they are always partially affected and shaped by nonrational, belief-based ideas. Means are discussed, but ends are not. The ends move around silently. The ends or purposes of policing vacillate in salience, making it impossible to establish rational deployment based on resources, evaluated and reassessed as to consequences. In addition, whatever means are used are seen as being connected to the tacit and unspoken ends. The contesting rationalities identified are not in explicit conflict because they are all clustered as means to the unspoken, tacit end—crime control. Crime control is never defined or explicitly outlined as to its character—its priorities, salience, durability, or time dimensions. Even simple matters that focus on displaced concern for means rather than ends, matters such as reducing response time, increasing queries to databases, or counting numbers of field stops or clearances among detectives are not discussed. Beliefs are transcendent ideas about what is best and are often counterfactual. Ends may be in conflict as well as means to agreed upon or tacit ends, such as crime reduction. The process of silencing one or the other is a question of power as well as dramaturgical expertise. The dialogue of rationalities moves slowly. The networks, cliques and cabals as nodes, within the organization must coalesce, and there must exist less resistance from the cabals (the conservative forces within the department) and more power for the cliques supporting change. CM/CA produces an aura. It radiates a kind of contagious or sympathetic magic. It pleases, and emulation results, but it is not clearly the cause of a reorganization or transformation of large-city policing. If the police intend to move beyond reactive calls for service-based policing, the same misleading standards—crime figures based on reported crime, vetted and processed by the police, unaudited by outside sources, and slavishly and misleadingly reported by the media—will not suffice. These figures, commented upon by experts, are granted prima facie legitimacy and serve as redundant measures of police claims that they control crime and disorder. The meetings were important as a performance, a bit of staged authenticity, a well-rehearsed play with some extemporaneous dialogues.

## "Refrigerators on the Desk"

Policing is not entirely information driven, but patrol, the activity that is the core of the organization and absorbs most of the time, energy, and wages, is powerfully incident and demand driven. Information is a bit that makes a difference, but this must be understood in the context of matters in policing that shape or pattern information. Primary data are gathered by officers. The data are shaped by the readings of the interactional context in which they are gathered. This includes tacit understanding of what is relevant; the formatting effect of the forms used, or the online menus supplied; and a variety of social and spatial facts that could be relevant when viewed as an analytic problem-solving exercise. The channel by which the messages are sent is an important shaping matter; face-to-face communication is most trusted in police work. Once these primary data become processed as information, their use is mediated. In policing, a job of assessing trustworthiness, any mediated communication is suspect, and as a general rule of thumb, the more abstract and distant from the officers' experience, the less it is trusted. The database to which the message is sent and from which it comes is also a matter shaping the nature, amount, and kind of information that will be sought and used. Software contains the categories and classificatory system into which the information will be placed. The linking of this software and database to others is problematic as well. To restate the point made earlier, the entire organization is shadowed by the incident focus of the patrol division and the salience of the here and now. This makes gathering systematic needed information that reflects past decisions, aggregated materials, or future planning something of a crisis, or a refrigerator on the desk.

Maps become another visible visual that can stretch back and forth in time, but they are not used that way. In policing, maps are only relevant when they are seen as valuable in use, needed for something. Metaphorically, databases and their links, the terminals, even computers, are really only "dumb pipes" through which data flow. They represent capacity, future utility, but they must be implicated in some process to become useful. Lists of strategic uses of crime mapping are academic exercises. Capacity is not the critical matter, but actualization through imagination—the problem to which the data are to be attached must be imagined.

Maps are occasioned in the sense that they only make sense when one has a use in mind. The need for them makes their relevance come clear, or emerge. They come into being when an explanation based on the conception of the future that one wants realized is required. Demand can arise from many sources but is typically handled as an incident, an encounter, or a case. A map requires that one imagine and make an imaginative adjustment forward and backward in time. Maps can also be created as a result of having done something that one now sees as having resulted from the map. An account can be based on already-known outcomes. If we bear in mind that maps can be drawn from any number of databases that are integrated invisibly, data source shapes the meaning of the maps. Use is thus situated as well. Turning this around, we can imagine that reading a map means making it *transparent*, reading back through how it came to pass and forward to how it might be and has been used. Thus, the practical and the abstract find a common ground.

Now, let us return to the big white box, the refrigerator on the desk. Sam McQuaid was working in the Metropolitan Washington Police Department when I undertook the study. He facilitated the work in every respect. When I asked about the progress of his planned crime-analysis unit within the department, he smiled and said, "We are always dealing with the refrigerator on the desk. . . ." I did not get it. He explained that police departments operate in a crisis mode and that the crises reverberate up and down the organization. If the chief is concerned about the city council's questions about how the service areas were defined and delineated in the city (the smallest units within the districts and within the beat or patrol areas), he sends down a lieutenant to explain to the Research and Development officer that the chief wants this information.[2] He appears in uniform from the chief's office. This personally delivered message is a refrigerator—it covers everything else on the desk once it is placed there; it cannot be easily moved and may stay for a while before anyone can move it; it obscures other work under it (and that work cannot be pulled out to be looked at); it is not wanted or asked for; and it may in the end be impossible to shift. Nevertheless, the Research and Development office is expected to produce an immediate response. The staff is shifted from other problems—budgets, grant writing, map making, meetings to plan future activities, and crime-analysis meetings—to attend to this. These short-term demands ramify within the top command and administration, while minipeaks in serious crime or disorder—or a series of crimes of the same kind in a local area—roil the uniform division and may lead to changes in patrol or personnel. But they are not of the same order, since they are more of the same; refrigerators are not more of the same, as they are qualitatively and quantitatively different. They cannot be easily moved.

## *A Future*

One could begin with the cognitive, operative, natural attitude of policing and work "up" to organizational change as a result of CM/CA. One might come to the same conclusion by beginning with the technology and seeing what changes take place. Police organizations are sensemaking clusters of authority and deciding that occupy space and have a material reality. They are stabilized in part by routines and assumptions about the nature of the work and its cause and consequences. These are largely unexamined. When change is introduced, reflection ensues, and situations in which uncertainties are manifested become focal. In organizations, one finds rationalities, not rationality. However, seen in the context of the Weberian idea of rationality in organizational context, the three case studies showed that organizations are complex, dynamic collections of power networks partially connected to city politics, field and surround (see above overview of case studies). These networks ascribe to different rationalities but are bound by a public ideology that ascribes to pragmatic crime control as central to the mission, whatever else is undertaken. These ethnographic case studies, the first two perhaps more dramatically for their protean form, suggest at least that the ways of technology and their role in organizational innovation are many. The argument claiming that the police are now an information-based organization, focusing on managing risk and enhancing security, is both premature and flawed (Ericson and Haggerty 1997). There is considerable general resistance to crime prevention in policing and among the citizenry. In part the lack of sympathy for change among police has to do with the changing conception of "prevention" in policing. Historically, the police have engaged in primary prevention: altering the opportunities for offenses or offenders, using many sanctioning strategies, highlighting or dramatizing the penal sanction of arrest. Secondary prevention, or changing people, has never had any purchase on the police mind or practice, while tertiary prevention, which is based on the application of sanctions, is the domain of prisons, probation, and parole. Crime prevention is almost impossible to assess: it deals with something absent.

The studies also highlighted the diffusion of a very popular idea and suggested the basis for its popularity. The potential of crime analysis and crime mapping as means, combining a technology and a technique, is greater than any other innovation in policing in recent times. In spite of the very limited applications seen here, it has explosive potential. This may be the case because it raises questions about the basic contradictions in the mandate: that policing can control crime and reduce the fear of crime and yet be an almost entirely responsive, demand-driven, situational force dispensing, just in time and just enough, order maintenance.

As an examination of kinds of rationalities, the three case studies have a troubling theme. Emphasis on scientific rationalizing means that the sacred canopy that has obscured policing and granted it legitimacy except in rare crisis periods is being eroded. Some speculation may be valuable at this point. In broad brush strokes, here are some changes that may occur in the future:

- The myth of superordinate "command and control" leadership will be reduced in salience as abstract knowledge rather than charisma and power is required to lead.
- Police organizations and their leadership will accept their own limits, constraints, and reliance on the public, other agencies, and the goodwill of the executive and elected governmental figures, local and federal.
- Crime as a key and continuing focus will be moderated by demand for the management of lifestyle issues such as the environment, noise, and civility.
- The essential components of policing, the trust of the public and reassurance rather than fear generation, will be made more matters of public debate.
- The public will continue to equate crime control with sheer numbers of officers "on the street." There is no evidence that more officers reduce crime. Any large organization requires a stable core of administrative and supervisory staff to function.
- The obligation of public organizations to account to the public will increase. Police in this country are not accountable to people or politicians. This is a historic choice for localism and tacit guidance and provides an umbrella of common law that protects police against their mistakes. Vague mission statements, lists of values that have no operational meaning, and public statements with no enforcement aspects or referential properties do not constitute rational management. Nor can they be the bases for accountability.

If these predictions are true, police will be forced to reexamine, if not relinquish, the public relations ploys that have permitted them to accept responsibility when crime drops; to blame other factors when it rises; to blame the victim for being vulnerable to crime; and to call on "forces beyond their control" whenever criticized.

If we look at the social organization of the police, we see their reactive nature, their concern with demand management, and their "bracketing" or setting aside of the question of the causes of crime or, indeed, what might prevent or reduce it. The causes of crime have never been a concern of modern policing. This concern is unnecessary as they define the job, and is not required if a reactive stance toward crime is taken. Crime causation is seen as a matter for criminologists, while crime control is neatly assigned to violent, random-patrolling functionaries. What are now called "incidents," even if defined as "calls for service," cluster in time and space and by type of crime and disorder and can be dramatically displayed via figures, maps, or texts. These representational documents display the obvious and rather trite idea that clusters arise and can be attended to, but more importantly, they are signs pointing to something else that is more abiding.

These factors, taken together, point to several general organizational changes, some of which might be considered in due course in any organization. Some are relevant to the personnel and skills needed. These include several matters. Some sensible training would have to be undertaken in both crime analysis and mapping by relevant personnel, and perhaps even among patrol officers and detectives who might use the system. Some skills in the interpretation and use of maps to deploy officers either strategically or tactically, or even to advise individuals, would have to be developed via training. The external aspects, community liaison, neighborhood associations, feedback and priorities and the lines through which such information flows, largely patrol officers in districts or beats, would have to be developed as sources of valuable informatioin. The major databases would have to be identified, cleaned, and formatted consistently. This one might call the trimming and curtailing as well as the integration of the various databases in the department. Databases would have to be planned in some way, mirrored in each other and interconnected so that tables, graphs, and narratives could be constructed with the relevant data. This may be technically possible using Oracle and developed software (some of which is commercially available). In addition, the ecology of the operations (where databases are kept, where servers are located, who has access to them, and the specific rooms allocated to these functions), would have to be considered so that the various databases, servers, groups, and users would be configured in such as way that information could flow in, be transformed, and flow out efficiently. Clearly, an infrastructure of support would have to be fashioned, including the plumbers, the data managers, the technical people, and the primary data analysts (crime or otherwise). The level of these persons could vary from computer repair people to high-level programmers.

# Epilogue

Events since the end of fieldwork in December 2003 throw some light on what was occurring during my time in the field. While the fieldwork revealed that little in the BPD had changed, soon after the study period, the power balance in the organization shifted in the direction of more traditional modes of "doing business." One acting commissioner was forced to resign and the first female commissioner was appointed in early 2004. In the absence of a commissioner, the CAMs were abandoned. A consultant was set to be hired early in the term of office of newly named Commissioner Kathleen O'Toole to reshape and reorganize the crime-analysis meetings. The consultant had worked with Bratton and others in planning and organizing crime-analysis meetings. The *Boston Globe* discovered his tentative contract and publicized it along with the contracts given to another consultant at a nearby university. While he was paid and worked in the department for almost a year, the contract for fully reorganizing the meetings was never executed. After O'Toole's resignation, a more crime-in-the-street focus emerged.

A new role-call approach—a daily meeting featuring brief, cryptic, and non-map-based reports—was institutionalized under the rubric of homeland security. The meetings were held in a room with computers called the Boston Regional Intelligence Center. A similar repository called the state's Fusion Center was also established in a nearby city. Two sergeants were given an adjoining office and were nominally in charge of organizing these new meetings. Daily briefings were combined with a new, relatively loosely organized and formatted meeting focused on "homeland security." This brought together the gang and school squads, one reporting crime analyst, rotating representatives from nearby police departments, the state police, the U.S. Attorney's Office, ATF, DEA, occasional visitors from the State Executive Office of Homeland Security, federal officials, and others given current local problems and concerns. This roll-call daily-report format has also been institutionalized in the Washington, D.C., department. Western remains a well-organized, medium-sized police department.

The allocation of resources has shifted in the BPD to more street-based crackdowns. While the former CAMs required no realignment of resources, skills, or tasks for the lower-ranking participants, this direct, unmediated approach is more in line with the conventional wisdom about how to police a racially divided and segregated city. From late 2005 through late 2006, the media no longer focused on reported crime in the city. The new media focus for amplification and constant stories was a rising number of homicides (still under five per one hundred thousand, or about ninety per average for the last forty years, making Boston one of the safest cities in America), gangs, and "shootings." The years 2005 and 2006 saw seventy-five and seventy-six homicides, respectively. Media interest was no longer on the rather modest increases in crime in general and the overall decline in the key crimes, but rather on youth homicides in selected areas of the city, now highlighted by maps, names, and pictures of victims. Two areas densely populated by first-generation immigrants and largely African American, as well as an area in which over 50 percent of the returning offenders resided in 2006, were targeted for attention with additional patrols by bicycle and car. Meanwhile the clearance rate for homicides in the city hovered around 35 percent, and witnesses were hard to locate.

The key themes in the media were "hot spots" or clusters of homicides (hot spots were not defined, but in every case shown they were located in the poorest areas of the city). These clusters were the result of mapping one, two, or at most three homicides or shootings in an area of a square mile or so within a given week or two. After each cluster police offered brief comments on the dynamics and promised more police presence. No reference has been made in the last two-plus years to "crime analysis," "crime mapping," or any other preventive measures based on analysis or data.

Causes of the shootings have been mentioned, such as rumors, violations of respect, revenge, conflicts over girlfriends, and loose associations of young men. Unlike in many cities, few mentions are made in the newspapers of "gangs," "drug dealing," or other general explanations for youth violence and homicide.

Each time a series of violent incidents such as a high-speed chase, a homicide cluster, or a drive-by shooting exceeds two, for example, the media in Boston declare a crisis. In July and August 2004, for example, a series of youth murders, culminating in three homicides in one weekend and a nonfatal shooting, led the *Boston Globe* to quote a local celebrity saying that the previous spike in early winter should not lead to panic. However, they quote him later in the editorial (August 5, 2004) as saying that gangs are "ready to live for today and kill for today." No evidence was adduced to support this idea, and the celebrity had no qualifications as a gang expert or data to support his clever answer to the question of why boys kill each other. As is typical, the commissioner called a press conference, assembled the troops (a group of state police on motorcycles was lined up behind her), called for federal agencies' aid, and mobilized an area-specific crackdown. The *Globe* headline (August 7, 2004) trumpeted, "Law Enforcement Agencies vow, 'We've had enough,'" and the story declaimed that law enforcement agencies would put on "a massive show of force." The issues of what exactly state police officers on motorcycles could do to reduce youth homicide, or how a "massive show of force" improves the quality of neighborhood life, enhances partnerships with neighborhoods, or improves the security of Boston neighborhoods (this is a paraphrase of two of the values of the BPD and its mission statement) were not discussed at the press conference. It was, as the British say, an opportunity to "show the flag" and rally public support for the police. In the winter of 2005–2006, attention was paid to guns, and claims were made that guns had been brought into the city from other New England states. No evidence was adduced to show this, and attention shifted to a gun-buy-back program funded by gift cards exchanged for guns turned in.

Other less dramatic changes were also institutionalized:

- The Research and Development team, which staffed the crime-analysis meetings and employed all the crime analysts in the department, was cut radically to about one-third its previous level.
- The previous head of R&D, who had moved in the fall of 2003 to become chief of staff for Commissioner Evans's office, left the department with the appointment of Ms. O'Toole.
- The former large auditorium location on the first floor of the headquarters was abandoned, and with it the visual aids, projected maps, laptops and technologies, rotating division representatives and detectives, bimonthly meetings, preparation and rehearsals using the CAM books, and media interest.

These oscillations in focus show several important points that substantiate my argument concerning the reification of traditional practices in the CAMs, their ritual aspects, and their absence of impact on what is done and how it is accounted for or explained. If they had been effective in changing the thinking of police and their actions, if they had been the cause of reduced crime, why would they be abandoned and the entire program gutted? Why would "smart management" be abandoned if it works? What new tactics resulted from the data and its application? How were these matters known? In part this change in program was due to the appointment of the new commissioner, dissatisfaction with the results of the meetings as crime continued to rise, and a new focus on homicide. The politics of the city and of big-city departments and their chiefs, who are minicelebrities, people with imagined lives, shape police organizations' public rhetorics and known strategies. As I edited this book for final submission to the publisher, a new commissioner, Ed Davis, formerly chief in Lowell, Massachusetts, and host to a Police Foundation field study of crime mapping (Willis, Mastrofski, and Weisburd 2004) was named by Mayor Menino.

# Appendix A
## Data and Methods

### Case Studies

This book is a comparative case study of three police organizations that were introducing information technology–based innovations. This appendix outlines the case method in some detail, my previous research, the case selection process, and details of the fieldwork done in the three sites.

The case study method adopted here connects the individual instance or study with processes and patterns that are general, thus providing a basis for developing cumulative knowledge and honing generalizations (Becker 1970). This requires consideration of the matter of definition of case and even "caseness," the unit of analysis employed, dimensions of comparison, and the data gathered in the three sites studied. The basic question, the focus of the study, was how to identify the conditions under which certain types of rationality shape deciding with reference to the use of information.

The term "case study" (Becker 1970: 76) comes from medicine and psychology, where it refers to the use of detailed facts about an individual incident, person, patient, or experiment to illuminate the etiology, pathology, diagnosis, and prognosis of a specific disease. It is assumed that close examination of a single case will permit understanding of a phenomenon more generally. This investigative strategy and the mode of presentation of such materials, when rooted in the determinism of medicine and psychology, and indeed by extension such sciences as linguistics and forensics, are valid in part because the aim is to establish the outliers or exceptions that prove the rule. Nevertheless, clinical case studies, especially those of individuals studied in the context of a larger research project, have long been rich sources of sociological insights. As Becker (1970) also notes, studies using the case method or presentation of materials usually rest upon participant observation in one of its forms, along with other methods (such as documents, interviews, and newspaper clippings). The aim of the case study traditionally has been to penetrate into the everyday worlds of the groups or organization studied—by observing their round of life, their key routines and emergencies, and the resultant "culture" or adaptive modes. It may include attention to material culture. The descriptions are social forms that should in time be part of a larger puzzle that when configured produces a whole. In this sense, too, the case study is an inductive approach that seeks to build up a coherent and plausible picture from bits and pieces of observation, interviews, talk, records, pictures and texts. This must compel the observer-writer to use metaphors, or analogies—ways of seeing and expressing visions that communicate aesthetically the parameters of experience that guide and constrain others.

The dance is the dominant metaphor of this text. The pattern that persists and communicates is the link between experience or the fragments of life one culls and gathers, and collective, joint, shared life. To speak of epistemological breaks, crises and turning points, dilemmas and contradictions that arise in the course of a life of work life is to explicate modes of doing and being that persist, perhaps because they are seen to operate collectively. The foundation of the work is in the "common sense" observed, rather than the statistical regularity, frequency, or absence of a pattern. My aim in this appendix is not to assess the merits of or generalizability of case studies, but to use an analytic scheme to compare case studies of empirical units (see Ragin and Becker 1992: 9).

In this book, I have argued that the way into understanding the work is not via normative caricatures, snippets of talk, or official discourse of the institution or organization but via the situated deciding that takes place. As Goffman wrote (1964), the situation is a fundamental social form of constraint that may be characterized by talk, but what takes place is not solely a function of talk.

The fitting together of the evidence of cases in a comparative design requires a theoretical question or problem, in this case how various forms of rationalizing exist and are sustained in police organizations adapting new information-drive technologies. This task is always subject to refinement over time as new aspects are revealed, unanticipated results emerge, and the underside of the metaphors used are disclosed. In addition, the theoretical enterprise as it unfolds requires that comparisons within and among the cases be used to further refine the questions. This refinement aims to further make the results general and re-producible in other places, times, and settings. Implicit in this is the fact that levels of social organization and change are ongoing and should be explicated during the course of the study. The claims to generality and representativeness of the case study do not lie in the distribution of a phenomenon discovered or described, but in the pattern of integration within and across the cases that holds and in a sense provides multiple versions of the same processes. The task is translating the symbolic manifolds of the actors into some conceptual framework that captures the varieties of the pattern one sets out to explain. In this way, theory emerges through the work, rather than being "tested" or "validated" by the research.

The consequence of this approach is that one must find a way to sort out and distinguish the everyday clichés, comments, and rationales of people from the practices they manifest and display. I am committed to a phenomenological analysis that seeks the forms of perception and imagery that give meaning to social action (Becker 1992: 210–12). In some respects, one is always observing what people do, not imputing imagery, and this tension remains in all observational studies. In the crime-mapping meetings in Boston, the perception became the reality. I believe that the strength of the Chicago school case studies arose from the broader *object of study* they sought to understand: the processes by which cities grow, differentiate, die, and are renewed. The object of this study was the patterns of rationalizing that are found in three police organizations, and the target of the research was the work of these organizations. The link was provided by seeing the meetings as arenas for the display of what every police officer takes for granted.

## Case Selection

All case studies are assembled as a result of many factors, not least of which is time, cost, and convenience for the researchers. In every case I have read about in the anthropological and sociological literature, the choice of a site or sites is made for reasons that may be unclear to the researcher at the time, one or two being known and salient, and always involve a serendipitous event, sponsorship, meeting, or decision. The reasons why one is given or not given access are rarely fully known, and most published studies are based upon "successful" access. Because sociology has been deeply and profoundly shaped by the influences of positivism and statistical techniques, issues of sampling and of whether the cases represent the variables one is studying are always in the background of the methods section of a fieldwork-based study, even when they are not discussed directly. Anthropology, on the other hand, has been focused on the detailed understanding of cases per se, with only a few fundamental matters governing all such studies: knowledge of the language, the kinship system, the basic institutions, and the ecological features of the setting. Its comparative dimensions have emerged slowly and painfully. Usually a given problematic, e.g., cannibalism, magical practices, a brutal ecological niche, or a coping system, is dramatically exemplified in the chosen case and taken to be the rationale for gathering the necessary institutional detail.

In first articulating my focus I drew on several important ethnographic studies of the introduction of new information-based technologies in policing (Meehan 1998; Ackroyd, et al. 1992; Newburn and Hayman 2001) and in other organizations (Zuboff 1986; Thomas 1994; Latour 1996). I did a basic review of the literature on technology and change in policing (Manning 1992). I gathered systematic data on police uses of technology in a large American police force in 1979–80 (See Manning 1988: ch. 2); in London in 1973, 1979, and 1984 (Manning 1977) and in a large constabulary in the English midlands, the BPD, in 1979, 1981, and 1984 (Manning 1988: ch.2). Some materials were gathered at the Texas Law Enforcement Management Institutes in 1991 (Lubbock) and 1992 (San Antonio). My fieldwork in 1999, in Manchester and Cheshire, England, and Toronto, Canada, focused on the rationalization of policing via information technologies such as crime analysis, geo-coding of crime, management by objectives, and performance indicators. With Albert "Jay" Meehan, I studied the natural history of the adaptation of IT in two police departments in middle-sized Michigan cities. Both departments had advanced IT and used cellular phones widely. Two focus groups on community policing were done in the summer of 1998 by Albert Jay Meehan and me for a COPS-funded study of community policing in a midwestern city I called elsewhere (Manning 2003) Tanqueray. These studies are a backdrop for the cases presented here.

In the three studies I developed, I intended to explore again the impact of new technologies on policing practices. My primary aim in this research was to describe and analyze the "fit" between police practices and the CM/CA technologies, and to develop means to assess the resultant changes. Information technologies, in the form of criminal intelligence and crime analysis, crime mapping and victimization analyses, are means to convert "facts" into useful and actionable information. While these innovations were widely touted as a revolution in policing, especially since the introduction of CAD (computer-assisted dispatch) in the early seventies, little evaluation research had been done (as of 1996). It was not clear how much crime-mapping and problem-solving approaches had altered police practice (see Weisburd, et al. 2003).

I imagined a two-part study of which this book would constitute the first. I imagined doing a comparative case study in which I would work through the organizational requirements, infrastructure, and politics, and see what the core of a crime-analysis/crime-mapping center might look like. I imagined a companion book that would focus on the extent to which the innovations at the center of the organization had impact, if any, and what that impact was on the work on the ground of the uniformed officer and perhaps of investigators. In part this research strategy was based on a considerable doubt that the claimed changes to policing, those rendered by community policing and other innovations discussed in the introduction and chapter 1 of this book, were in fact altering basic tasks and routines. My sense at that point, not having yet undertaken the second research, was that some change in skills, perspectives, and routines, was going on but that this change was occurring more in the top- and middle-management segments than at the "sharp end," the work of patrol officers.

The book contains case studies of three cities: Western, which has a police department of about 263 officers and about 100 civilians, in a medium-sized midwestern city of about 127,000 people; the Metropolitan Police Department of the District of Columbia, an organization of 3,600 officers and 600 civilians, in Washington, D.C., a city of about 572,000 people; and the Boston Police Department, an organization of 2,044 officers and about 600 civilian employees in a city of some 590,000 people, according to the 2000 census. Although it would have been possible to create a logical scheme that would have orderd these cases, and they did in fact have a cumulative or almost "evolutionary" aspect to them, I assembled them over time as a result of acquaintances, opportunities, expediency, and good fortune. This is not a study of the evolution of these units. My aim was to make a comparative study to increase the chance of seeing what features of the process of rationalizing were organization specific and which were more general features. I hoped that this would be a cross-national comparison, but a proposal to do a study in the Staffordshire Constabulary was turned down in 1996. After I made a formal application, and wrote a letter requesting permission from the chief constable to carry out a study of the crime analysis unit, it was turned down summarily. This was a surprise, as several very warm preliminary talks had been held.

Some general points guided my final choices. Although the process, the dance of change, has general features, it also takes place in a specific surround or set of national political issues, as well as in the field in the city. Each police organization had its high and low politics—on the one hand, matters connecting them to the city, its politicians, elites, and minority communities, and, on the other hand, the internal politics of advancement, careers, rewards, and job control. While the technical features of the IT and the infrastructure varied in the three organizations, in each case I found it was "retro-fitted" to the organizations' practices, structures, and routines. The three organizations did range in size, in scale, and in the state of development of the IT systems. I began with the most primitive and nascent changes and moved to the Washington efforts. I then took up the Boston innovations in rationalizing and their sharp differences from others that emulated the NYPD process.

My focus from the beginning was how and to what degree the IT surrounding and enabling CM/CA was changing police practice, but in the end it became a study of how, once in place, CM/CA activities were seen and used. I did not see the study of Western as a "crime mapping study," but came back to the setting after I had done work in Washington, D.C. Thus, I formulated the bases of my study when I wrote a small, informal proposal to the MPDC:

> New forms of policing, based on community-oriented work, problem-solving and prevention, anticipation and intervention as well as patrol, are now facilitated by combining crime mapping, crime intelligence and linked data bases. 30 years of development of complex, linked data bases, management systems for storing, retrieving and aggregating data, geocoding (TIGER files), GPS, MDTs, laptops and other software, reduce pass-through time, and may enhance problem-solving. If policing is to shape effective community problem-solving it will require integrating information technology such as crime intelligence and crime mapping with investigation and problem solving in a focused fashion.

In effect, the fieldwork looked back to the Western data and analysis and forward to the Boston data and analysis. I did not write up a proposal for the Boston study as I was sponsored and much of the data were gathered in public, open meetings. In each case, I wanted to see how the dance of change was a reflection of both the internal politics of the organization and the external politics of the city. I managed to gain access and sustain it over a long period of time in part because I had internal normative sponsorship for the project. In Western and in Washington, D.C., I had worked in the department in previous fieldwork projects and knew the people who sponsored me. Once I was inside, ethnographic research on police organization and cultures requires working close up, observing and describing activities in detail, and asking those observed to reflect on their experiences and practices. I wanted to use this approach to address these questions in the context of the practices and routines of police, and show how their beliefs and values shape their everyday decisions. I assumed that successful problem solving requires information, analysis, feedback, and evaluation, and I hoped to chart these. Introducing an information technology puts a new symbolic entity in the game—both a means to process and acquire information and a means to conceal it. The meanings of the technology are built up over time through use, through collective definitions, and through its role in the work. These meanings can be gathered through observations and interview data and displayed in tables to map changes in attitude, use, and understandings of the functions of the technology.

There were some unique and personal features of the case selections. I was asked by colleagues to participate in a COPS-sponsored study in Western that included interviews with key command staff, down to the rank of sergeant, and two long focus groups as well as some observation by me and other members of the project. We did focus groups in the Detroit PD. I was involved in a second COPS grant concerned with training for community policing involving some seven departments as partners in 1997–1998. I followed up later with a series of interviews with the key players in the crime analysis unit in the Western PD, and the then deputy chief (who later became chief). I published a paper on the subject of crime mapping in Western (Manning, 2001b). When in England to present a talk on the application of zero tolerance and "broken windows" policing in the U.K. in 1999, I appeared with a deputy chief constable who had worked in the COPS office in Washington and studied the crime drop and compstat process in the NYPD. Later, I discovered she had moved to Washington, D.C., and was working as a civilian in the Metro Department. I called her and arranged to meet with her while visiting Washington. She in turn put me in touch with the director of a new project just beginning in the department. After several telephone conversations, it was arranged for me to do a small study of the emerging COPSAC project. This I did. The opportunity to do the third case study emerged when I was asked to be a visiting senior scholar at Northeastern University in the winter of 2001. I had been to the university twice in 2000 and on a visit in the spring of 2000 was a guest at the Boston CAMs. Upon taking the Brooks Chair in the late summer of 2001, I began to make plans to carry out further fieldwork in Boston. This I did in the summer of 2002.

## Aspects of Access, Methods, and Fieldwork in the Three Sites

The following section is divided into a series of topics, and under each topic I discuss the sites and settings. This facilitates comparison across the sites. Although I tracked changes in the organization after the formal study ended, I had specific beginning and end points for each study. Although I have been in contact with people in the departments studied since the 9/11 terrorist attacks on the World Trade Center buildings in New York City, NY, this is essentially a study of CM/CA in local policing prior to those horrendous, axial events.

There are some general points that hold for all three sites. I made at least three clustered visits in each site to try to track developments and changes in practices and rhetoric. Boston, until the resignation of Paul Evans in December 2003, remained relatively stable in the form and context of the CAMs and the role crime mapping, crime analysts, and crime analysis played. In Western, the primary changes were in the installations of servers, faster and better links between data sets, and the actual capacity to produce maps and reports. In D.C., the COPSAC (Community-Oriented Problem Solving Analysis Center) scheme was a failure during the time I studied it. This was due to the internal politics and conflict between the chief's cabal and others, the power of consultants, the inability to afford the total replacement of the computer/information system within the department, the resistance of the crime analysts' coterie and their sergeants, lack of training and skills, and the data czar who was working to convert the Chicago mapping system to the MPDC's present needs. A minimal infrastructure was beginning to emerge at the completion of my study, but the key player in the grant and in the crime-analysis movement, Mr. Smith, completed his Ph.D. and took a university position in the fall of 2001.

In a sense, I have used several kinds of fieldwork and data in this book. These include interviews, observations, newspaper and magazine clippings, the observations and interviews of colleagues, and television viewing. I kept a clippings file from the local newspaper for almost three years, from fall 1995 to summer 1998. I drew on my own undisciplined television viewing. I coded and filed newspaper articles using such topics as "cybernetics," "social control and the visual," "the modern [computer-assisted] house," "computing and the self," and "policing" (with subheads on the media, on selves, and on technology). Some of the analysis of "high politics in Western" is based on my clippings file (for 1996–98) from the local Western papers and television newscasts. I have a file of clippings from Boston, primarily from the *Boston Globe,* from 2000 to 2004. I inquired at the websites of each of the departments studied and downloaded maps, boundaries of police districts, precinct and service-area locations, mission statements, and crime data. I observed in the three departments for various times and in strategic places in which deciding takes place. I used the six dimensions for comparing organizations that emerged in the D.C. study to organize my presentations in chapters 5–7. The interview schedule was designed to inquire about the background to the innovation, the key players in this process, the setbacks and little wins, the current state of play, and the present strengths or weakness of the system. I took notes by hand and did not use a tape recorder. I did not type my field notes but kept them in handwritten form as I did not intend to quote any one source in detail and at length. I kept separate my interviews, field notes and observations, analytic memos (to myself), and documents. As my primary data were interviews and observations, I will discuss them in connection with each site.

The questions of writing ethnography and of writing it up have been broached in recent publications (Van Maanen 1988). This is an artificial dichotomy because on the one hand one is always condensing, organizing, and drawing inferences in the field, and in many respects the analysis does not emerge until it is written. The project unfolds partially and in segments, and ideas, inferences, and even conclusions are changed as one writes. For example, I began the study thinking there was one sort of rationalizing, and I was influenced by Weber's framework (Sica 1998) After observing the CAMs, reading Wendy Espeland's remarkable and insightful book, *The Struggle for Water* (1998; see also Carruthers and Espeland 1991), and revising my own book, *The Narcs' Game* (1979, 2003), I saw that several rationalities were intertwined in the meetings and in policing, and that these were all understood through practices and displayed collectively. The links between these rationalities and modern politics are important but little explored (see Edelman 1967, 1988; Merelman 1969, 1991, 1998). I also saw that logic in use changed easily and expediently. Organizations are domains in which rationalities and power are contested. The situated and occasioned nature of sense making is layered and circuitous, and the accounts for why something should or must be done are flexible. The dance is a dance, and one cannot anticipate much in detail before the dancing begins, nor even after it has finished. As I wrote, I also began to expand the case studies with concerns for the political field and the surround in which the urban police organization operates. In each organization, I interviewed people at various levels and ranks, both civilians and sworn personnel. With a few exceptions, the interviews were fairly formal, done in the office of the informant, and lasted about two hours. When sources were reinterviewed, I checked on unclear points, asked them to clarify what they had said, and tried to understand better the subtleties of the conversation.

The writing was done sporadically and, unfortunately, unevenly. I first wrote a little draft of portions of the book in the summer of 2001. I revised in the summer of 2001 and was again able to work on it in concentrated fashion in July, August, and September 2004. In the course of that writing, I came to see that the impediments to innovation were more tacit than acknowledged, and the change was perhaps due more to changes in skill level than to organizational change. It was finished in "final" draft in Boston in late September and early October 2005.

## Washington

I wrote to the Research and Development office in the MPDC as follows:

> A grant received recently by the Metropolitan Police of the District of Columbia from COPS to establish a Community-Oriented Problem

Solving Analysis Center (COPSAC) using link analysis and crime-mapping presents a unique opportunity for evaluation research. The aim of the Center is to enhance problem solving capacity in the Department, as well as increase interagency cooperation. This project is an effort by the MPDC to strengthen its community policing program by integrating an infrastructure of crime analysts, with access to relational data bases and crime-mapping, with analytically-based problem solving.

At this time, I proposed a two-stage (before and after), approximately fifteen-month, ethnographic-observational case study of the functioning and impact of the COPSAC project on police practice.

I intended to observe COPSAC personnel as they use crime mapping and analysis and note the functions of associated software and databases, and resultant patterns of information flow. Fieldwork (interviews, observations, and records) would identify what types of information were in use, the information used in decision making and problem solving, where information goes, and how it is stored and retrieved.

I intended to chart the flow and use of information produced by the center.

I proposed a pre-post design based on ethnographic fieldwork, interviews, and archival searches of records. This design would allow comparisons of patterns of use, analysis of problematics in these patterns, and description of the range of accommodations made at two points during the first fifteen months of the study's operation.

I intended to carry out a baseline or "pre" study, working for one to three months, in late spring 2000, to create a natural history of the acquisition of the necessary infrastructure, personnel, training, and other resources. I intended to follow with a post-ethnography some twelve months later. This second or "post" period would last from one to three months. At that time I intended to interview crime analysts in the districts and a sample of patrol officers. This was not feasible, given my limited time and a nonfunded project. Further, as the center was never in operation, there was no point is tracking information that was not produced and distributed.

In effect, I was reshaping the study in order to gain access to the MPD. This work reflected forward on the way I developed the Boston study (it was unfunded and did not require a written proposal to the BPD). When I returned to Western, I used my rationale and focus to guide my interviews and observations there.

A turning point in sharpening up the research questions was setting out the orienting questions I was hoping to answer in the MPDC study. These questions concerned how technology was defined and used and with what aim and impact on skills and values. I wanted to chart the physical location of technology and the spatial/ecological distribution and storage of information, as well as skills, authority, practices, and tacit knowledge emerging. My questions were, How does this technology shape police work? Does the technology create new social divisions, unification, and/or conflict? What are the key points of interaction and exchange among groups and the sources of conflict, accommodation, and cooperation? I was interested in the routines of those who work with the relevant technology: What routines, access, and working rules arise around processing and using CM/CA? What values, beliefs, and working rules of the various groups using the information shape the information "outputs"? Are any new routines being learned, innovated, and created? What, if any, key interfaces (turning points, contingencies, blockages or cul de sacs) exist between policing craftwork and IT-based channels?

This natural history approach would allow inference of the unanticipated results of introducing IT—the "ripple effects" and their extent and emotional charge. What resistance strategies, sabotages, misuses, and possible abuses of authority were facilitated or reduced by IT? I intended to gather information on the attitudes of a sample of officers and investigators toward the present and proposed crime-mapping innovations. I did not do this. My study would also include drawing on the present data showing the crime-mapping facilities in the department, beginning with observations in the Communications Center and in COPSAC.

*First phase.* I first worked in the MPDC from June 26 to 28, 2000, spending a total of eighteen hours on site. I interviewed and observed and set up subsequent interviews for another visit in late July. I returned on July 25 and spent until July 28 interviewing and observing. I spent some forty-five hours on site. Upon return, I spent some forty hours in reviewing notes, writing analytic memos, producing preliminary outlines, and writing a first-phase preliminary report. During this period, I interviewed fifteen people, some a second and third time (N = 17 interviews). These interviews ranged in length from one to three hours. I observed meetings, informal conversations, and phone conversations during my time on the site. The duties of those interviewed were as follows: consultants (two), officers in the Communications Center (four), members, both sworn and civilian, in the central crime analysis unit (two), members of the COPSAC staff (two), other members of the RRDU (four), and the head of the Office of Professional Integrity (one). I collected several documents: annual reports of major crimes for the preceding ten years; crime analysis sheets for one day; an organizational table of the MPDC and a revised organizational chart being considered at that time. This chart is discussed below; it included a central location for data analysis, including the COPSAC project and its relationships to other units in the MPDC. Observations were carried out in the Communications Center and office, the COPSAC office, the Crime Analysis Unit, and the consultants' office. Each night on site I went over my interviews and field notes, adding and elaborating points (I did not use a tape recorder), wrote brief summary comments, and noted matters that required further interviewing, observation, or documentary support. My focus was on trying to connect the project with the broader reform and politics of the department.

*Second phase.* I returned on April 5 and 6, 2001, to assess progress in the preceding nine months. I spent some 13.5 hours on site and an additional six hours on my notes. I spent an additional three days on writing the report itself. I interviewed the head of the COPSAC project via phone. I carried out interviews (N = 8). These included lengthy interviews with the key people in the project, including the head of the research division (twice) and the supervisor of the central crime analysis unit (twice). I observed in the crime analysis unit for several hours and talked with two support people, Mr. Smooth, who was in charge of preparing the UCR (Uniform Crime Report) data for the Bureau of Justice Statistics (BJS), and the administrative assistant who was funded by the grant. I spoke briefly with two consultants who were involved in designing the IT changes in the MPDC, and asked their views on the changes in place. I read and took notes on several documents, memos, and general orders bearing on the progress of the grant. I returned for two days in August of 2001 and reinterviewed key people in the Research and Development area. In all, I carried out thirty-three interviews; observed in meetings, at the Communications Center, at the crime analysis center, at the office of Research and Development, and in several lunches with members of staff in the Research and Development office; gathered documents from the websit;, and had six lengthy phone interviews, including a "debriefing" call with Mr. Smith in August of 2001. I spent the equivalent of about twelve days on site during the four separate visits.

Following this research, I wrote a number of analytic memos and drafted a paper concerning the attempt in Western to develop crime-mapping capacities. That summer and fall (2001), I began pulling together work I had done for *Policing Contingencies* (2003) and *The Privatization of Policing* (with Brian Forst) (1999) as basic background on policing, technologies, and change for the book I was planning.

## Western

In the fall of 1995, I held lengthy, unstructured interviews with a sample (six) of command and supervisory officers in Western, including three captains, the chief, two sergeants, and a lieutenant. I also interviewed a retired captain in that department. My interest there was on command conceptions of community policing and related problems of evaluation and supervision. These interviews ranged from one hour to two. I took notes. I interviewed a set of officers about the crime-mapping capacity of the department in the fall of 1999. My focus was upon patrol officers in Western PD who underwent a command-led reform labeled "community policing" or "team policing." In many respects the case study revealed some of the institutional contradictions in organizational reform and the vulnerability of the chief during such a transition. In the period 1996–98, Joe Schafer undertook fieldwork relevant to organizational transformation, and some data were gathered by Tracy O'Connell Varano. This research was funded by two grants from the Community-Oriented Policing Services Agency to Michigan State University School of Criminal Justice and to the Western Police Department. Four focus groups (two with sergeants, two with officers) were conducted by Tim Bynum, Joe Schafer, Steve Mastrofski, and me in Western City in December 1995. We discussed community policing, its strengths and weaknesses, problems of training, evaluation, and supervision, and the role of technology in community policing.

There were two other phases in this research. I returned to Western in 1999, 2001, and 2002. I made a final visit in August 2004. In the 1999 visit, I interviewed Chief B, the acting deputy chief, the computer person in the research and planning office, and the lieutenant in charge of the nascent crime-mapping operation. I spent a day on site. In August 2003, I spent the day with Chief C and his primary advisor in the informational technology area. On August 19, 2004, I spent the middle part of the day with Lt. Babbage. In all, I spent the equivalent of seventeen days on site; did thirty-nine individual interviews with civilians and officers; attended four group interviews (focus groups); gathered documents and clippings; and participated in meetings with academics and officers in the course of the COPS partnership grant.

## Boston

The CAMs were the central drama I observed, and I followed up with interviews with a crime analyst, civilian staff in the CA office, and two colleagues at Northeastern who have been closely involved with research in the BPD for over twenty years. I spent the equivalent of five-six days on the site doing systematic observation or interviewing. I collected relevant clippings from the *Boston Globe* from 2000–2004. I had intended to follow up on the problem solving and deciding in CAMs to see to what extent it was passed on to patrol officers and investigators, and what, if any, differences it made in police practices in Boston. However, I was unable to do so by the time the study ended with the resignation of Paul Evans on Dec. 1, 2003.

# Appendix B

## Professional "Faery Tales" and Serious Organizational Ethnography Compared

### Overview

The aim of this appendix is to specify some key differences between various writings that are seen as professional or policy making. I include works that are (1) written for organizational promotional purposes, e.g., reports from organizations, annual reports, and explicit policy-driven statements aimed to persuade via rhetoric alone, (2) hortatory and proscriptive—those that claim to show what one must to do to achieve a goal or objective, (3) programmatic—a description of how I did it, claiming this works and will work for you, and (4) descriptive (and often laudatory) or polemic-critical and one-sided, such as autobiographies and op-ed pieces in newspapers or magazines. All four are "professional" faery tales—they serve to reinforce dogma and ritual and are not based on scientific evidence. They are professional only insofar as the writers are paid directly to make such statements. The writers personally benefit from the publication of these works. They are "fairy," "faerie," or "faery" tales because they rest on ritual assumptions about the way the world ought to work, are cautionary tales (do not do this!), and are subject to modest review in advance of publication. They are based not on science but on a predetermined policy end that is supported by selected materials gathered and published, sometimes in scientific journals.

These works should be distinguished from ethnographic and other sociological work that intends to create critical knowledge, is subject to professional peer review, and meets standards of competence and procedural strictures.

I want to emphasize that my point here is not to assert that these writings are useless, wrong, inappropriate as bases for public dialogue, or stifling intellectually. I wish to emphasize that when such works are taken to be based on empirical research that can be acted upon, disconfirmed, and seen as scientific, the documents are being "misread." This kind of misreading can lead to spirals of contagious imitation such as that behind the spread of the rhetoric of community policing, the broken-windows essay-cum-perspective, and the fantasy of building a deeply experimental criminology.

## *(Professional) Faery Tales and Ethnographies Compared*

### Faery Tales

Let us first consider these writings. The aims of these exercises are often not stated, but they imply evidence and analysis and are written by those with academic degrees. They have important political and persuasive functions, and are often associated with institutes, centers, and "think tanks." They are functional insofar as they

- serve to gloss facts and stereotype complex, contradictory, and recurrent problematics of organizational actions, decisions, and policies;
- use hyperbole to elevate and dramatize certain aspects of the working and to suppress or avoid others, and make no effort to point this out;
- provide guidance in a complex world (Like fairy tales generally, they serve as way stations of the lost, assurances that fundamental human error and malice are unlikely and that sin, death, veniality, birth, and death, can be managed.);
- imply that these emblematic stories are durable, resilient, and resistant to change, that they are transcendental truths;
- play on redundancies and the repetition of themes and responses, each of which reinforces the inevitability of the final and well-expected outcomes.

### Ethnographies

There is nothing innocent or pure about ethnographies, and they are often misleading. They emerge from a different sociopolitical tradition insofar as they

- reveal contradictions between policies and plans and outcomes, rhetoric and actions, the ideal and the "real";
- identify the various modes of coping with identified underlying problematics and their range of effectiveness;
- show that these coping and management skills, abilities, and outcomes vary and perhaps suggest why;
- suggest some of the variables associated with the problematics and the coping and the outcomes;
- display in the writing variation in complexity in spite of surface similarities or differences;
- note that while problematics remain, and are situated, they may produce or be associated with quite different responses and outcomes;
- shift perspective within a social organization from seeing as it is done from the top, or from the bottom, from the center or the margins, from the elite and their burdens to those affected by organizational decisions;
- elevate the ambiguous, the mystified and mystical, the unanticipated, and the negative consequences of well-intended works and decisions;
- embed findings and analysis in theoretically valid perspectives that are themselves subject to scrutiny, analysis, and ratiocination;
- can fail, be judged inadequate, poorly written, or unpalatable, rejected for publication, disconfirmed, or subjected to further careful study as a result of peer review.

## An Example of a Hypothetical Professional Faery Tale

A number of books written on the NYPD's compstat program have elements of professional faery tales.[1] In these books, although not in real life, one finds harmony of purpose, execution, and outcome:

- All promises were kept in the course of developing the program.
- All duties were performed, or if not, the offenders were caught out and disciplined.
- All requests for joint action, sharing of operations, and actions by specialized units were filled unequivocally.
- All warrants, plans, documents, data, and other information re-

quested from internal or external sources was available, valid, and reliable.

- Cooperation was always and reliably forthcoming from all city agencies, other police departments, and federal agencies, e.g., the FBI, DEA, U.S. Attorney's Office, Customs, state police, and elected officials.
- No clear, stated resistance to programs and policies existed. There was no public or private resistance to the ideas, management approaches, or styles that were features of the process and/or the meetings within the top command or among the other segments of the organization. Everyone was "on board" and "on the same page" all the time.
- No active resistance or sabotage arose against any plan, approach, or operation except by the unions with respect to merit pay and assignment.
- There were no incomplete databases, no problems in gathering or presenting data, no failed repairs of a problem once identified (crime was controlled), no computer crashes, loss of data, incomplete information, outages of power, or other unpredictable obstacles in the way of the never-ending war against crime.
- There existed completely integrated databases in the city and shared information within the police and its various databases, the city fire departments, the emergency rescue teams, and other city agencies. Henry (2001) reports that data were gathered from the precincts after being hand tabulated and screened, put on disks, and delivered to One Police Plaza for the meetings. They were later shaped for UCR, checked by detectives for "unfounding," and so on. They were "raw data."
- There existed no systematic and continuing power struggles among top command, between top command and precinct commanders, between the commissioner, Mr. Bratton, and others or other key groups within the organization.
- All the key players were in tacit working consensus on every issue or at least were not in opposition consistently.
- Rage, envy, jealousy, ambition, revenge, and other emotions had no role except as a basis for an implied consensus to eradicate crime.
- The detective division was in agreement at all times and fully on board with the compstat program.

- There were no increased costs, resources required, efforts expended, or other kinds of costs to the NYPD of developing this program. It cost nothing and was nothing but a total and complete success.
- The statistics and crime figures were not massaged, altered, shaped, or reduced in any way, e.g., by refusing calls, failing to send a unit, units not responding to requests, failing to take reports, reclassifying calls (downgrading) after the initial classification, reclassification by sergeants (shifting felony arrests to misdemeanors rather than felonies), and so on.
- There were no complaints, public or private, from judges, jails, prisons, city council members, probation officers, or officers and clerks of the courts about the increase in arrests, affidavits, warrants served, prisoners resulting, and so on.
- Previous red tape, bureaucratic fumbling, and bureaucratic resistance to booking and arrest vanished, and resistance of "bureaucrats" and courts suddenly melted.
- There were no known negative consequences for the public as a result of this "crackdown" except the unfortunate incidents, complaints, and suits.
- No data on arrests, patterns of stops, misdemeanors, clearances, or other official records were relevant to the "crime drop" except the reduced official figures of crime during the brief period when Mr. Bratton was commissioner, followed by a few years when other commissioners held office (they were, it is to be assumed, the beneficiaries of his leadership and the transformation of the NYPD).
- No additional data from other sources was relevant, e.g., other measures of quality of arrests, stops, and so on, such as rejected arrests, quality of evidence, failure to indict, arraign, or prosecute, clearance rates for the reported crimes, percent unfounded (was it rising, falling, or stable?).
- The judges and courts were compliant with the new massive wave of misdemeanor arrests.
- No proof of the flow of evidence from report to compstat decision to outcome was needed; the "black box" notion sufficed. How, logically, empirically, did reporting crime and processing it in these meetings reduce reported crime? There was little evidence of what the processes might be for the most notorious "nonsuppressible" crimes that are private; semi-consensual, such as drug use; typi-

cally unreported, e.g., rape, assault, and homicide; and "domestic abuse crimes" that have received attention in the media and require mandatory arrests.

## Some Functions of Professional Faery Tales

There is little doubt that faery tales have long-lasting, euphonic functions for both the writers and the audiences of these exercises. Some of them are as follows.

- They resound positively into the short term, usually echoing already agreed upon premises about what works in the organization.
- They make consultants "look good" and police "experiments" are shown to have produced unequivocally positive results.
- They provide feedback into the risk-adverse ambiance of police organizations—the wish to keep a low profile with respect to crises and manage damage control—and give comfort.
- They maintain an atheoretical approach to change and to evaluating its purposes, impacts, and consequences. There is no need for a theory; just do it.
- They sustain the organizations' natural wish to appear successful, and the sponsoring agencies' (e.g., the National Institute of Justice) wish to diffuse successful innovations.
- They promote as truth myths within the department among the lower participants who must act on the changes in their everyday work. These are such views as that top command is always doing the next popular thing, the "flavor of the month," with no regard for what works or how it affects workload and job control, and not attending to what the public and the patrol segment think about the problem or the innovation.
- They advocate change based on science and on consultants (some of whom are academics and scholars), which gives top command prestige by association.
- They produce useful additional stories. It is easy to "sell" something to the media, the city council, and/or the mayor, absent data, theory, and concepts, and consistent with the current version of the police occupational ideology.
- They reinforce in written form the primary conceit of the police:

that they can and do control crime. They show that criminologists, whom the police claim wrote that crime cannot be controlled, were wrong.

- They reinforce the myth of command and control. In the case of compstat, they show that even change comes through the initiatives taken by the chief or the "CEO."

The difficulty in a field that is partially a moral enterprise, partially a policy-making and -shaping enterprise, and partially a science (criminology in particular) and that is composed of bits and pieces of many disciplines—law, sociology, political science, economics, history—is that the forces and pressures to do some or all is great, and the driving force is not always scientific. While criminologists doubtless hope to reduce crime, and have read their Durkheim, they do not claim that they have the tools, will, or knowledge to do so, nor do they claim the police can't. In fact, no criminologist ever stated in print that the police cannot control crime. What is often written is that the causes of crime are economic, social, and psychological and that these deeper forces produce variations in crime that are not modified by police actions. There are three other points glossed by such a false claim.

1. The police rely on their data, which capture at best less than half the known crime reported in victim surveys. Any change is insignificant statistically, but important when writing faerie tales.
2. The police are uninterested in causes, and perhaps need not be. Their job is to sustain a trustworthy position and function in the society.
3. The vast majority of crime is minor, unsolved, and of little concern to middle-class people in an affluent society. The most serious crimes, or incidents reported or unreported, such as rape, homicide, and drug crimes, are few in number and are resistant to direct reduction by police action. The claims for reduction of crime are typically for short-term interventions or cross-sectional reductions.

Several powerful critiques of the crime-control efforts of the NYPD and the flawed broken-windows thesis have been written (Harcourt 2001; Sampson and Raudenbush 1999), but they have not been featured with the awe, shock, and welcome surprise that greeted the NYPD's initial claims of smashing crime in the 1990s.

# Notes

1. I include here the works of Wilson 1942; Leonard 1980; Larson 1972; Colton 1979; Abt Associates 2000; and Dunworth 2000. These studies demonstrate little structural change resulting from alterations in systems of information processing.

2. Weber in this argument is isolating the ends-means continuum while holding out a value-free view of rationality. Values are always a part of the choice of ends, and value-oriented actions can alter formal schemes. But rationality absent a logical scheme cannot determine the relative value of ends. Ironically, rationality and associated techniques cannot easily defend a choice of ends because they are values. Weber uses the distinction between a "fact," defined as something assessed with reference to a means used to accomplish an end, and a "value," defined as something that is intrinsically desirable (Gerth and Mills 1958: 129–86). See also the magnificent critical analysis of Alan Sica (1998).

3. The arguments for a situational view of deciding can be found in the works of Karl Mannheim, Egon Bittner, Harold Garfinkel, Martha Feldman (1996), and Hawkins (2004).

NOTES TO CHAPTER 2

1. Here I draw on the work of Burns (1953, 1955, 1958), Goffman (1959), Crozier (1972), Van Maanen (1974), and Manning (1997, 2003).

2. P. A. J. Waddington (1999) has best captured the way in which the rhetoric of the uniformed patrol officer has been taken as *the* occupational culture.

3. A recent example of conflicting interests that became public in Boston (July 2004) was the threatened strike of the patrolmen at the time of the Democratic National Convention. The high politics of the nation, the state, and the city, the power of the mayor and city council, were involved. The interests of the segments of the organization were visible because the commissioner (head of the Boston police) was newly appointed by the mayor; the unions had been without a contract for several years; and supervisors might have been called upon to act

again as patrol officers without overtime pay. The strike was resolved at the last minute by the intervention of the mayor and the governor.

4. I use the term "surface features" because in most respects policing was not changed in form, i.e., structurally. The processes of deployment and mobilization, procedural refinement and discipline, have become more refined and focused. To some degree its knowledge base and appreciation of legal niceties has also expanded.

5. August Vollmer crystallized this model at the University of California (Carte and Carte 1975) and had a hand, through his protégés and his own work as chief in Berkeley, Los Angeles, and Wichita, in spreading his doctrine.

6. The apparent successes of private security (and their claimed lower costs) became more salient as attention turned to crime prevention in addition to claims that police were capable of lean, confident, focused crime control and "crime fighting." Historically, private security, including corporate security, guarding, and watchman functions, had emphasized loss prevention since their origins were in transporting money and gold, and later in strike breaking and industrial-asset protection. There remain moves to "privatize" some aspects of policing (Forst and Manning 1999; Johnston 1993).

7. This means surveillance without the permission or knowledge of the persons or groups watched; increasing use of simulations as a basis for social control; abstract models or profiles that reify the complexity of human choice, such as expert systems; "smart profiles" and "smart personnel systems" for early warning of incompetence; and profiling of all types.

8. Policing aims to protect lives and property, yet loss of these, as well as complex disorders of urban freedom, are inevitable consequences of the division of labor. These broad aims have been operationalized as providing random patrol for the untoward event and responses to calls for service. Proactive crime control, in the form of investigation, intelligence gathering, and application—and to a lesser extent vice-control policing—have been poorly funded relative to the other functions and are poorly developed and resourced. "Responsiveness" now incorporates the idea that citizens have a direct obligation, like the police, to react to and perhaps even anticipate the dynamics of crime and disorder in their neighborhoods. But the fondest hope has been placed in technology, especially information technology, to solve this paradox.

9. Here, I include the work of reinventing government (Osborne and Gaebler 1992) and serious scholars like Mark Moore (1997), who argued early for the introduction of new modes of management in the public sector. This is the second generation of scholars who build on the earlier work in management by objective (MBO), zero-based budgeting, and other modes of tracking decisions. Their addition was the theme of decentralization and innovation and responsiveness to short-term trends on markets and a serious addiction to the buzz words of business and high-tech gurus.

10. Community policing is a peculiar rendition of policing growing from Anglo-American conventions, culture, and law, and in no sense captures universal or even fundamental principles of ordering cross-culturally or historically.

11. This is contentious in any case as there was no agreement at that time on how many officers were currently employed in public policing. This is still debated; see chapter 2.

12. Some of these are mandated by the Home Office in the U.K, and others are indigenous developments in England and in the United States.

13. I have not attended these meetings. My description comes from interviews with two people who have attended and the published materials.

14. Karmen (2000), Harcourt (2001), Taylor (2000), and Sampson and Raudenbush (1999) have explored the virtues of the broken-windows thesis, the impact of police actions on crime and disorder, and their relationship empirically. The debate continues in scholarly circles.

NOTES TO CHAPTER 3

1. This definition of democratic policing raises several significant issues, which can only be indicated here. Many agencies at federal, state, and local levels act as police, but few are authoritatively coordinated—that is, bureaucratically structured to insure compliance with command. "Standing ready" to use violence echoes sociologist Max Weber's terms; when used, violence creates negative spirals that damage legitimacy. The specification of political territory is itself a problematic issue in practice. In theory, it is used to define the domain of police forces. The trends to transnational policing, in the form of agreements, task forces, and ad hoc "policing actions," as seen in Kosovo, Bolivia, Columbia, and Haiti, are ever present (Sheptycki 2000).

2. The vicissitudes of demand management vary. Some departments are highly and visibly committed to rapid response and service, while others, such as large rural counties, state police, and some cities, due to ecology, tradition, and the land mass they serve, cannot deliver such service. Moreover, some large urban departments screen and reduce demand internally by policy more than others, e.g., by use of firm priorities or by introducing 311 and seven-digit service numbers in addition to the 911 number, and others reduce it through powerful tacit rules on the ground about what is answered and how calls are up- or downgraded (changed in importance by association or distance from crimes).

3. Some of these ideas originally appeared in Manning 2003 and have been modified and edited for this book.

4. The Anglo-American model is found in the United States, Australia, Canada, New Zealand, and the United Kingdom. Each country varies from the ideal in important ways (Brewer 1996; Bayley 1975, 1985, 1992).

## NOTES TO CHAPTER 4

1. Some of the material in this chapter appeared in Manning 2005.

2. While many articles and professional journals yearn for dramatic and directly visible change as a felicitous result of introducing new information technologies, little research evidence supports this claim (Weick 2000; Thomas 1992; Orlikowski 1992, 1996, 2000; Orlikowski and Tyre 1994). Information technologies do not inevitably produce the positive, expected organizational change in the direction of efficiency (Thomas 1994; Roberts and Grabowski 1996).

3. Janet Chan's (2001) work on the Australian (New South Wales) police is suggestive. She finds that use is patterned by age and rank such that younger officers are predisposed to using technologies well and in that the primary valued uses are the already trusted ones concerning seeking past criminal records, licenses, number plates, and outstanding warrants. The perceived virtues of the IT in her study were not that it expanded vision or imagination but that it was faster. Senior officers used it for administrative tasks, were self-taught, and had a positive attitude toward its future uses and effects. In effect, the technology worked in two quite different contexts and created different modes of relating to the work.

4. Capturing change in organizational processes is difficult at several levels. Change echoes in social, political, and cultural dimensions. Studies that narrowly view change—evaluating a new program, a short-term effort, or a task force—miss the contours of change over time. Organizations are echo chambers in which goals are proximal, tacit, and unrecognized (Mackenzie 1993: 162; Weick 2000: 148–75); goals are unclear or in conflict (Mackenzie 1993: 237); goals are made visible by routines rather than clear statements of purpose and accomplishment (Feldman and Pentland 2003); and organizations, whatever their goals, are characterized by competing rationalities or sanctioned ways of getting things done (Espeland 1998). Directives coming from the top are subverted, sabotaged, redefined, and redirected by those implementing them (Roy 1952, 1954).

## NOTES TO CHAPTER 5

1. Some of the material rewritten and summarized here appeared on Manning 2003, chapter 8.

2. The events were quite dramatic, consequential, and public. They included a series of dramatic murders; killing of unarmed citizens by the police; violent deaths in custody (mentioned above); a series of dramatic protests of the deaths in custody; and gassing of strikers (and residents of nearby neighborhoods) at a large factory in the city.

3. As of the present writing (August 2006), the "Plea for Justice" group no longer exists, a former city council member who is Hispanic is mayor, and the largest auto factory in the city, employing more than six thousand workers, is now closed.

4. Evidence from San Diego, a department known for its advocacy of problem solving and community policing, suggests that even when such problem solving is done and viewed as valuable, it is superficial, limited, evaluated by word of mouth or gossip, and seen as marginal to the "real work" of answering calls for service (Cordner and Biebel 2004).

5. Since 9/11/01, the federal government has made efforts to provide computer-based software that permits local police departments to communicate via radio.

6. Some of these points were made in Manning 2001b, "Technology's Ways."

7. The reward system of a police department is not a one-dimensional matter. It includes rank and related salary rewards, informal rewards such as time off and overtime, ecological niches (photography, evidence handling, research and planning), and prestige derived from community respect (more likely to flow to chiefs and deputy chiefs, who are in the public eye, attending public functions, visiting groups such as the Rotary Club, the Lions Club, and churches, and having external political-media obligations).

## NOTES TO CHAPTER 6

This chapter is based in part on my analysis of a funded project in the Metropolitan Washington Police Department in 1999–2001. Previously, I did fieldwork on drug law enforcement in the District and a nearby county (see Manning [1979] 2003).

1. All the names used except those of elected officials and the chief are pseudonyms.

2. This unfortunately includes shooting citizens at one of the highest rates per capita in this country *Washington Post* series, Nov. 1998).

3. For a brief summary of the politics, racism, and policing in the District, see Kappeler, Sluder, and Alpert (1998). In particular, chapter 8, pp. 188–213 of this book provides a useful overview of scandals and corruption in the District police through the mid-1990s.

4. I was told in interviews that the number and perhaps influence of these people would doubtless increase after the letting of the new series of contracts in the fall of 2000.

5. When I went to interview the director of personnel/human resources in her office, I noticed a copy of my book, *Police Work,* resting askew on a bookshelf in her office.

6. I am indebted to Sam McQuaid, who discovered these databases and their location by careful interviewing.

7. See Mazerolle, et al. 2002. They found little change other than increased calls for service and a distribution of problems that did not conform to the 311/911 priorities scheme. Absent organizational change, adding an additional number, redirecting patrol activities, establishing new and firm priorities in operator and dispatcher behavior, and focusing analytic capacities within the department have no chance of altering the distribution of resources to increase efficiencies (whatever that might mean).

NOTES TO CHAPTER 7

1. These meetings were loosely modeled after the NYPD compstat, but differed in a number of important ways. The differences are implicit in the narrative in this chapter. They are discussed in this and the next two chapters.

2. Figures regarding the current strength of a police organization are always estimates, as a known number of officers are on temporary disability, maternity, or sick leave, or have announced they intend to retire, while still others can retire, return from leave or disability, or are being processed or trained.

3. The Quinn Bill (a Massachusetts law passed in 1970) is arguably the biggest welfare gift to policing since the LEAA agreed to pay college educational costs in the late seventies for police officers. In 2003, it cost Massachusetts taxpayers $100 million. The law requires local governments who choose to pay up to 50 percent of the costs to augment police salaries in accord with officers' educational attainments—signified exclusively by a criminal justice degree. This means an increase in base pay of 10 percent for officers with associate's degrees, 20 percent for a bachelor's, and 25 percent for a graduate degree. The cities and state split the costs equally. As of 2007, efforts to amend this law always failed. A second law, called the "Heart Bill," provides 75 percent pay and retirement for any officer who suffers a heart attack on the job.

4. The Boston Police Department (and all the departments in the metropolitan region, including the various university and college police departments, the transport police, and the state police) has a tradition of rewarding officers by assigning them to "details." An entire unit of the BPD is devoted to assigning details, monitoring their management, and processing pay from the companies that employ the officers (Annual Report 2003). Officers on details are paid by industry, and the checks are issued by the city on a union-based contractual basis ($42-plus an hour). They are paid in four-hour units, regardless of their duration, up to eight hours. They stand in uniform at construction sites and related activities that might endanger citizens. They direct traffic, and sometimes smile and wave.

5. All such statements are rhetorical, meant to be persuasive, and political rather than factual. Notice the several semantic-rhetorical points here: there is one "community," and it is able, willing, and actively seeking "partnerships" (and the police are also able, willing, and actively seeking the same sort of partnerships); fear, crime, and the quality of life cohere and can be easily shaped together, in the same direction, and in concert with the extant local definitions; and while there may be many neighborhoods, they are in agreement about all the necessary matters that lead to a happy ending. While this is clearly a political statement in the best sense, it raises fundamental questions about the mandate, contingency, focus, and theme that statements like "we protect property and persons" or "we engage in crime control" do not.

6. Two of my colleagues, Jack McDevitt and Glen Pierce, served on the commission and carried out interviews, data gathering, and analysis and wrote the final report.

7. When Commissioner Evans resigned in Dec. 2003, the superintendent-in-chief, Hussey, was named acting commissioner. He was viewed by the media as the favorite to be appointed by the mayor to the permanent post. In February 2004, after the New England Patriots, a professional football team with a stadium and headquarters near Boston, won the Super Bowl football game (the national professional championship), people took to the streets around Northeastern University and elsewhere to celebrate. The police had mounted elaborate plans for this event, including closing access to several key squares where people might congregate, diverted traffic, and began sweeps to move people out of the area in which they were concentrating. After about two hours, the crowds were beginning to disperse and began crowding in Symphony St. (a one-way street heading south from Hemenway St. to St. Stephen St.). They were burning trash, rocking and tipping over cars, and damaging cars parked on the street. Because Gainsborough St. (where I lived) was blocked by police cars at both ends, a driver turned up (north—the wrong way) Symphony, saw the crowd coming toward him, and threw his car in reverse and at high speed hit and killed two students. The media (*Boston Globe*, Feb. 2004) immediately blamed the police for lack of preparation, failing to saturate the area sufficiently, and targeted the commissioner for failure to arrive on the scene, prepare an adequate plan, and deploy enough officers that night. A media celebrity based at a local university claimed in an op-ed piece that the police failed because they should have saturated the area (*Boston Globe*, Feb. 2004), while a more reasoned commentary by an expert in collective behavior pointed out the common factors, seen on that night, lying behind such rioting: white, middle-class youth who have been drinking, looking for a public place to celebrate, take to the streets, and, as excitement escalates, so does violence (Lewis, *Globe*, Feb. 2004). Acting Commissioner Hussey suffered damage to his prestige and failed to be appointed the

permanent commissioner by the mayor a month later. He later became the chief in a small Massachusetts town. Ms. Kathleen O'Toole was appointed commissioner until she resigned, leaving the position at the end of June 2006. The position of commissioner was filled in late 2006 by the appointment of Edward Davis, formerly the chief of police in Lowell, Massachusetts.

8. In effect, the police coopted the ministers to their organizational network and added credible informal social control to the threat of formal social control. The sacred canopy of religion was pulled over the secular work of control of the marginal, violent, and powerless.

9. Key people in the TPC project were later appointed to positions in President G. W. Bush's faith-based initiatives office in 2001. This office was originally headed by John Delilio, a former student of James Q. Wilson's at Harvard. Rev. Eugene Rivers III consulted in 2003 to William Bratton, now the chief of the LAPD, on gang violence in Los Angeles. See also Omar McRoberts's (2003) analysis of the role of religion in Boston's black communities.

10. Attorney General Janet Reno publicized it as a success story in a DOJ publication; President Clinton praised it publicly in Boston; a national conference on the matter was held; and Boston was elevated for its tactics and approaches in contrast to the harsher zero tolerance approach of the NYPD.

11. An earlier media shot by former celebrity David Kennedy (2002), in an op-ed piece in the *Boston Globe* entitled "We Can Make Boston Safe Again," argued that Ceasefire was simple and direct. He claimed that it confronted targeted offenders and informed them of the risks they faced. He argued that since 2000, the key players became tired and drained by their own fame and were retired, transferred , or promoted, and that envy and resentment plagued the successful implementers. By implication, he argued that Boston was not safe in 2002 and that the police lacked intensity and the will to continue to suppress youth violence. He argued that by 2000, the effects of Ceasefire no longer existed. See also Kennedy 1998.

12. The Braga, et al. report (2001) uses the language of policy evaluation and sees the intervention(s) as a quasi experiment (an intervention line suggesting a precise, implemented point of a known and measured set of interventions was drawn in May 1996). Designating May 1996 as the beginning of this program is misleading. It was not a single intervention but a number of ongoing programs, some of which had been in place for years, some just beginning, each with different interventions, time lines for implementation, funding levels, and tactics. It was an analysis of beforeand-after measures using several surrogate indicators of violence based on police data and definitions (assaults with weapons, youth homicides, calls for gunshots). Although the data presented on homicides end at 1999, it is unclear when the various programs in the ensemble ended. This variable ending of support is probably due to the projects being funded from several sources, including the DOJ. The effort glossed by the term

"Operation Ceasefire" was entirely focused on the overt, immediate symptoms of one type of youth violence, not causes or underlying processes that produce and sustain its viability. It was aimed at suppression, arrests, incarceration (with options), and, if possible, eradication of the "gang problem." This of course is more than shootings. It is suggested in the McDevitt, et al. (2004) chapter (with Braga as a coauthor) that the effort respected civil liberties and was carefully targeted at known offenders. How it is possible to respect liberties and also track and monitor persons before they have committed crimes is not discussed.

13. This same dramaturgical thrust was shown before the DNC in July 2004, when visored, riot-equipped officers were shown on television and in the print media, and again when the threat level was raised in August 2004 and automatic-weapon-equipped, riot-uniformed officers were stationed in front of financial buildings in New York City and Newark, New Jersey. Since "terrorists" work covertly and strike vulnerable targets to demoralize citizens, they are obviously not deterred by well-armed, uniformed officers standing in the open with automatic weapons. This a form of dramaturgical realism and realization.

14. The figures on calls given on p. 1 and those on p. 19 are inconsistent. The total of 625,102 on p. 1, when broken down into the categories listed, does not compute. The total listed on p. 19 is 481,356 but no subcategories are included and no explanation for the differences in totals on the two pages is offered.

15. The following description is drawn from slightly edited field notes resulting from my first visit to a CAM.

16. This is a common term used to refer to a meeting that is a ritualistic show lacking substance and having no future implications for performance. It is also defined as an "elaborate presentation" (Dictionary.com). I think it refers to past entertainments such as the opening parade of a circus in which poodle dogs in tutus rode atop ponies who circled the ring of the big top to amuse spectators, and to the traveling road shows featuring performing dogs and ponies. It seems to connote a rather mindless, trained performance without much reflection or context.

NOTES TO CHAPTER 8

1. The term "working consensus" (Goffman 1959: 10) does not mean a close agreement based on values, personal preferences, or even normative constraints. It means that the interaction order is based on rough ideas like "to get along, go along," "get the work of the meeting done," and "avoid undue reflection."

2. Below, I point out that some of the watchers were a "pure audience" and others, those not taken in by the magic, cross-cut the division I am noting here.

3. I have no idea how this display affects long-term stereotyping of "criminals" or "villains," but it is a striking example of how "crime" and "color" or "race" are linked in America. I am mindful also of the wide range of "color"

and its meanings within the world of colored people and perhaps those seen as "white,": "high yellow," creamy, the ebony associated with West Africa, the brown of Somalia, the bright and blue-black sheen of some African-origin people, and so on. The nature of racial prejudice is such that it blinds whites to such variations in color and makes "black" or "African American" very ambiguous terms.

NOTES TO CHAPTER 9

The title of the chapter plays on Wittgenstein's distinction.

1. Cooperation, formal and informal, is critical in Massachusetts because officers have no police/arrest powers outside their own jurisdictions. There are approximately 351 local villages and towns with police forces.

2. The finest examples of the inner/outer nature of policing are found in Holdaway (1983) and Young (1991) (England) and Glaeser (2004) (Berlin, Germany). Glaeser's discussion of the differences between entrances and the ecology of the East Berlin and West Berlin police prior to amalgamation is striking. Entrances for the public to make inquiries in the buildings of the former East German Berlin police were sequestered, protected, almost buried and concealed. They were off-putting and designed to intimidate rather than to invite questions. In the former West Berlin Police Department, the stations featured relatively open reception areas. As a visit to any police station will reveal, the spartan furniture, colorless props, dark uniforms, visible weapons, ecology, and resultant atmosphere all communicate a semipenetrable secrecy.

3. Evans-Pritchard (1956: 220 ff.), in the most brilliant evocation of such matters, calls these piacular ceremonies. They are designed to offer up a sacrifice to propitiate forces of evil that threaten the group structure.

4. I employ examples from field notes, but they are not taken from a given day. Each example was used in the context in which it is presented, i.e., as part of the argument that the meaning and importance of the remark is based on the context.

5. This kind of reasoning led my colleague Glen Pierce to argue that "the police go after the low-hanging fruit." These are people who are visible and often known by members of both specialized units and uniformed patrol. I think the Boston materials show that what is seen is seen as a moral geography into which known criminals and crimes are placed to be seen as where to go to get them, not signs of an underlying cause, condition, problem, or cluster of problem families. This illustrates the tendency for the criminal justice system to reproduce itself and to provide endlessly redundant versions of social life. How could it be otherwise?

6. In Boston in July and August 2004, a series of shootings, mostly of youths by youths, brought forth a series of interventions and partnerships from the

mayor's office (extending summer programs), actions by the religious groups, such as the Ten Point Coalition noted in chapter 7, and a show of force by the police that included a press conference (August 2004) with pictures of the commissioner standing in front of a phalanx of mounted motorcycle officers with an announcement of joint partnerships with federal agencies and parole officers. That night and the following day a series of raids and arrests were made. Although this did not occur during the study period, it was a continuous theme in the community-policing rhetoric of the commissioner and the department and the media.

7. This pattern is most associated with high-profile, media-driven and -shaped cases that focus attention on police and their failures, and usually seems to involve a configuration of the following kind: the age of the victims (very young and very old are of more concern); status or class (high-status victims merit more concern); gender (women are more worrying than men as victims); and ethnicity/color (whites are valued more than Latinos, Latinos more than blacks). The most elevated combination in the eyes of the media, given this formula, is a (murdered, abducted, raped, etc.) high-status white female child. If this involves the lowest-status suspected offender, an unemployed white or black man, the stakes for the police become very high. The least important victim is a black, low-status, uneducated man. This last "profiled victim," a black man of marginal status, describes the social category most shot at in this society by police and others.

## NOTES TO CHAPTER 10

1. There are always inconsistencies among perceptions, media amplification of given shocking crimes, and the reported crime figures (whether they are going up or down in the short term—the media concern).

2. This did in fact occur while I was doing the fieldwork, and it was a refrigerator of some size.

## NOTES TO APPENDIX B

1. There are several equally useful examples of this genre. Salient examples are several other books on compstat, e.g., Bratton and Knobler (1998), Kelling and Coles (1996), Silverman (1999), Maple and Mitchell (1998), and Henry (2001).

# References

Abt Associates. 2000. *Police Department Information Systems Technology Enhancement Project (ISTEP), COPS Agency.* Washington, D.C.: Department of Justice.

Ackroyd, Stephen, R. Harper, John Hughes, Dan Shapiro, and Keith Soothill. 1992. *New Technology and Practical Police Work.* Buckingham, England: Open University Press.

Banfield, Edward. 1965. *Big City Politics.* New York: Random House.

Banfield, Edward, and James Q. Wilson. 1963. *City Politics.* Cambridge, Mass.: Harvard University Press.

Banton, M. 1964. *The Policeman in the Community.* New York: Basic Books.

Barley, Stephen. 1986. "Technology as an Occasion for Structuring." *Administrative Science Quarterly* 31: 78–108.

———. 1988. "Technology, Power and the Social Organization of Work." In *Research in the Sociology of Organization,* ed. by S. Bardach. Greenwich, Conn.: JAI Press.

Barley, Stephen, and Julian Orr, eds. 1997. *Technical Work.* Ithaca, N.Y.: LIR Press.

Bayley, David. 1975. *Police in the Political Development of Europe.* In *The Formation of National States in Europe,* ed. by Charles Tilly. Princeton, N.J.: Princeton University Press.

———. 1985. *Patterns of Policing.* New Brunswick, N.J.: Rutgers University Press.

———. 1992. "Comparative Organization of the Police in English-Speaking Countries." In *Modern Policing,* ed. by M. Tonry and Norvel Morris. Chicago: University of Chicago Press.

———. 1994. *Police for the Future.* New York: Oxford University Press.

Bayley, David, and Egon Bittner. 1986. "The Tactical Choices of Police Patrol Officers." *Journal of Criminal Justice* 14: 329–48.

Bayley, David, and James Garofalo. 1989. "The Management of Violence by Police Officers." *Criminology* 27: 1–25.

Bayley, David, and C. Shearing. 1996. "The Future of Policing." *Law and Society Review* 30: 585–606.

Becker, H. S. 1970. "Case Studies." In *Sociological Work.* Chicago: Aldine.

Becker, H. S. 1992. "Cases, Cause Conjectures and Imageries." In *What Is a Case?* ed. by C. Ragin and H. S. Becker. New York: Cambridge University Press.

Becker, H., and Donna Lee Becker, eds. 1986. *Handbook of the World's Police Systems*. Methuen, N.J.: Scarecrow Press.

Berrien, J., and C. Winship. 1999. "Lessons Learned from Boston's Police Community Collaboration." *Federal Probation* (December): 25–32.

———. 2001. "Should We Have Faith in Churches?" In *Guns, Crime and Punishment in America*, ed. by B. Harcourt. Pp. 222–48. New York: NYU Press.

Berrien, J., O. McRoberts, and C. Winship. 2000. "Religion and the Boston Miracle." In *Who Will Provide? The Changing Role of Religion in American Social Welfare*, ed. by Mary Jo Bane, Brent Coffin, and Ronald Thiemann. Pp. 266–85. Boulder, Colo.: Westview.

Bittner, Egon. 1970. *The Function of Police in Modern Society*. Washington, D.C.: NIMH.

———. 1974. "Florence Nightingale in Pursuit of Willie Sutton." In *Reform of the Criminal Justice System*, ed. by H. Jacob. Beverly Hills, Calif.: Sage.

———. 1990. *Aspects of Police Work*. Boston: Northeastern University Press.

Black, Donald. 1976. *The Behavior of Law*. New York: Academic Press.

———. 1983. "Crime as Social Control." *American Sociological Review* 48: 34–45.

Bloch, M. 1961. *Feudalism*, 2 vols. Chicago: University of Chicago Press.

Blumstein, A., and J. Wallman, eds. 2000. *The Crime Drop in America*. Cambridge, England: Cambridge University Press.

Bogard, W. 1996. *Simulation and Surveillance*. New York: Cambridge University Press.

Bordua, David. 1967. "Law Enforcement." In *The Uses of Sociology*, ed. by P. Lazarsfeld, W. Sewell, and H. Wilensky. New York: Basic Books.

———. 1968. "The Police." In *The International Encyclopedia of Social Science*. New York: Free Press.

Bordua, David, and Albert J. Reiss, Jr. 1966. "Command, Control and Charisma." *American Journal of Sociology* 72: 68–76.

Bott, Elizabeth. 1971. *Family and Social Network*, 2d ed. New York: Free Press.

Bottoms, A., and P. Wiles. 1997. "Ecological Criminology." In *Oxford Handbook of Criminology*, ed. by R. Reiner, R. Morgan, and M. Maguire. Oxford: Oxford University Press.

Bourdieu, Pierre. 1977. *Outline of a Theory of Practice*. Cambridge, England: Cambridge University Press.

———. 1993. *The Field of Cultural Production*. New York: Columbia University Press.

Bowling, B. 2006. "Transnational Policing." Delivered at American Society of Criminology, Toronto, November.

Braga, A., D. Kennedy, A. Priehl, and E. Waring. 2001. *Reducing Gun Violence Final Report.* Washington, D.C.: NIJ.

Braga, A., D. Weisburd, E. Waring, L. Mazerolle, W. Spelman, and F. Gajewski. 1999. "Problem-Oriented Policing in Violent Crime Places." *Criminology* 37: 541–80.

Brantlingham, P., and P. Brantlingham. 1981. *Environmental Criminology.* Thousand Oaks, Calif.: Sage.

Bratton, William, with Peter Knobler. 1998. *Turnaround.* New York: Random House.

Brewer, John, ed. 1996. *The Police, Public Order, and the State,* 2d ed. Oxford: Clarendon Press.

Brodeur, Jean Paul. 1983. "High Policing and Low Policing." *Social Problems* 30: 507–20.

————. 2004. *Visages de la Police.* Montreal: University of Montreal Press.

————. Forthcoming 2008. "An Interview with Egon Bittner." Introduction by Peter K. Manning. *Crime, Law, and Social Change.*

Brogden, M., and P. Nijhar. 2005. *Community Policing: National and International Models and Approaches.* Devon, England: Willan.

Burke, K. 1960. *A Grammar of Motives and a Rhetoric of Motives.* Cleveland, Ohio: Meridian Publishers.

Burns, Tom. 1953. "Friends, Enemies and the Polite Fiction." *American Sociological Review* 18: 654–62.

————. 1955. "The Reference of Conduct in Small Groups." *Human Relations* 8 (November): 467–86.

————. 1958. "Forms of Conduct." *American Journal of Sociology* 64: 137–51.

Bursik, R., and H. Grasmick. 1993. *Neighborhoods and Crime.* Lexington, Mass.: Lexington Books.

Button, Mark. 2002. *Private Policing.* Devon, England: Willan.

Cain, Maureen. 1979. "Trends in the Sociology of Police Work." *International Journal of the Sociology of Law* 7: 143–67.

Cannon, Lou. 1997. *Official Negligence.* New York: New York Times Books.

Carradine, David. 2001. *Ornamentalism.* New York: Oxford University Press.

Carruthers, B., and W. Espeland. 1991. "Accounting for Rationality: Double-Entry Bookkeeping and the Rhetoric of Economic Rationality." *American Journal of Sociology* 97: 31–69.

Carte, Gene, and Elaine H. Carte. 1975. *Police Reform in the United States: The Era of August Vollmer.* Berkeley: University of California Press.

Castells, Manuel. 1996. *The Rise of the Network Society.* Oxford: Blackwell.

————. 1997. *The Power of Identity.* Oxford: Blackwell.

————. 1998. *End of Millennium.* Oxford: Blackwell.

Chambliss, W. 1994. "Policing the Ghetto Underclass: The Politics of Law Enforcement." *Social Problems* 41: 177–94.

Chan, Janet. 1996. *Changing Police Culture*. Melbourne: Cambridge University Press.

———. 2001. "The Technology Game." *Criminal Justice* 1(2): 139–59.

Chatterton, Michael. 1989. "Managing Paperwork." In *Police Research*, ed. by Molly Wetheritt. Aldershot, England: Avebury.

———. 1993. "Targeting Community Beat Officers: Organizational Constraints and Resistance." *Policing and Society* 3: 189–203.

———. 1995. "The Cultural Craft of Policing." *Policing and Society* 5: 97–107.

Clark, John, and R. Sykes. 1974. "Some Determinants of Police Organization and Practice in a Modern Industrial Democracy." In *Handbook of Criminology*, ed. by D. Glaser. Chicago: Rand McNally.

Colton, Kenneth W. 1979. *Police Computer Technology*. Lexington, Mass.: D.C. Heath.

Cordner, G. 1995. "Community Policing: Elements and Effects." *Police Forum* 3: 1–8.

Cordner, G., and E. P. Biebel. 2004. "Problem-Oriented Policing in Practice." *Criminology and Public Policy* 2: 155–80.

Crank, John. 1997. *Understanding Police Culture*. Cincinnati, Ohio: Anderson.

Crawford, A. 1998. *Crime Prevention and Community Safety: Politics, Policies, and Practices*. London: Longman.

Crozier, M. 1964. *The Bureaucratic Phenomenon*. Chicago: University of Chicago Press.

———. 1972. "The Relationship between Micro and Macro Sociology." *Human Relations* 25(3): 239–51.

Crozier, M., and E. Friedenberg. 1980. *Actors and Systems*. Chicago: University of Chicago Press.

Culler, Jonathan. 1966. *Structuralist Poetics*. Ithaca, N.Y.: Cornell University Press.

———. 1997. *Literary Theory*. Oxford: Oxford University Press.

Czarniawska, B. 1997. *The Narrative Approach to Organizations*. Chicago: University of Chicago Press.

Damner, H., and E. Fairchild. 2006. *Comparative Criminal Justice Systems*. Belmont, Calif.: Wadsworth.

Deflem, M. 2002. *Policing World Society*. New York: Oxford University Press.

Dunworth, T. 2000. "Criminal Justice and the Information Technology Revolution." In *Criminal Justice*, vol. 3, ed. by Julie Horney. Pp. 371–426. Washington, D.C.: NIJ/Office of Justice Programs.

Durkheim, Emile. [1915] 1961. *The Elementary Forms of the Religious Life*. New York: Collier Books.

Eck, John, and E. Maguire. 2000. "Have Changes in Policing Reduced Violent Crime?" *The Crime Drop in America*, ed. by A. Blumstein and J. Wallman. Cambridge, England: Cambridge University Press.

Eco, Umberto. 1979. *The Theory of Semiotics*. Bloomington: University of Indiana Press.

Edelman, Murray. 1967. *The Symbolic Meanings of Politics*. Urbana: University of Illinois Press.

———. 1988. *Constructing the Political Spectacle*. Chicago: University of Chicago Press.

Enloe, Cynthia. 1973. *Ethnic Conflict and Political Development*. Boston: Little, Brown.

———. 1980a. *Ethnic Soldiers*. New Brunswick, N.J.: Rutgers University Press.

———. 1980b. *Police, Military and Ethnicity*. New Brunswick, N.J.: Rutgers University Press.

Erickson, K., J. Carr, and S. Herbert. 2006. "The Scales of Justice: Federal-Local Tensions in the War on Terror." *Uniform Behavior: Police Localism and National Politics*, ed. by S. McGoldrick and A. McArdle. New York: Palgrave.

Ericson, Richard, and Kevin Haggerty. 1997. *Policing the Risk Society*. Toronto: University of Toronto Press.

Espeland, W. 1998. *The Struggle for Water*. Chicago: University of Chicago Press.

Evans-Pritchard, E. E. 1956. *Nuer Religion*. Oxford: Oxford University Press.

Feldman, Martha. 1986. *Order without Design*. Palo Alto, Calif.: Stanford University Press.

Feldman, M., and B. Pentland. 2003. "Reconceptualizing Organizational Routines." *Administrative Science Quarterly* 48: 94–118.

Flyvbjerg, B. 1998. *Rationality and Power*. Chicago: University of Chicago Press.

———. 2001. *Making Social Science Matter*. Cambridge, England: Cambridge University Press.

Forst, Brian, and Peter K. Manning. 1999. *Privatization of Policing: Two Views*. Washington, D.C.: Georgetown University Press.

Garfinkel, Harold. 1963. "Conceptions of and Experiments with 'Trust' as a Condition of Stable Concerted Action." In *Motivation and Social Interaction*, ed. by O. J. Harvey. New York: Ronald Press.

———. 1967. *Studies in Ethnomethodology*. Englewood Cliffs, N.J.: Prentice Hall.

———. 2002. Ethnomethodology's Program: Working out Durkheim's Aphorism. Edited and introduced by Anne Warfield Rawls. Lanham, Md.: Rowan and Littlefield.

Garland, D. 2000. *The Culture of Control*. Chicago: University of Chicago Press.

Geller, William, and N. Morris. 1992. "Relations between Federal and Local Police." In *Modern Policing*, ed. by M. Tonry and N. Morris. Chicago: University of Chicago Press.

Gerth, H. H., and C. W. Mills. 1958. *From Max Weber*. New York: Oxford.

Glaeser, A. 2004. *Divided in Unity*. Chicago: University of Chicago Press.

Goffman, Erving. 1957. "The Nature of Deference and Demeanor." *American Anthropologist* 58: 473–502.

———. 1959. *The Presentation of Self in Everyday Life*. Garden City, N.Y.: Doubleday Anchor Books.

———. 1964. "The Neglected Situation." *American Anthropologist* 66: 133–36.

———. 1967. *Interaction Ritual*. Chicago: Aldine.

———. 1969. *Strategic Interaction*. Philadelphia: University of Pennsylvania Press.

———. 1974. *Frame Analysis*. Cambridge, Mass.: Harvard University Press.

Goldstein, Herman. 1990. *Problem-Oriented Policing*. New York: McGraw-Hill.

Gouldner, Alvin W. 1955. *Patterns of Industrial Bureaucracy*. Glencoe, Ill.: Free Press.

———. 1965. *Wildcat Strike*. Yellow Springs, Ohio: Antioch Press.

Greene, J. 2000. "Community Policing in America." In *Criminal Justice*, vol. 3, ed. by Julie Horney. Washington, D.C.: NIJ/Office of Criminal Justice Programs.

Greene, J., ed. 2007. *International Encyclopedia of Police Science*. New York: Routledge.

Gusfield, Joseph, ed. 1989. *On Symbols and Society*, by Kenneth Burke. Chicago: University of Chicago Press.

Guyot, D. 1991. *Policing as If People Matter*. Philadelphia: Temple University Press.

Halsey, M. J. 2001. "An Aesthetic of Prevention." *Criminal Justice* 1: 385–420.

Harcourt, Bernard. 2001. *The Illusion of Order*. Cambridge: Harvard University Press.

Harper, R. R. 1991. "The Computer Game." *British Journal of Criminology* 31: 292–307.

Harper, R. R., and D. Rod Watson. 1988. "Computerizing Police Work." *Journal of Comparative Sociology and Religion* 15(1).

Harring, Sidney. 1983. *Policing a Class Society*. New Brunswick, N.J.: Rutgers University Press.

Hawkes, Terence. 1977. *Structuralism and Semiotics*. Berkeley: University of California Press.

Hawkins, Keith. 2004. *Law as Last Resort*. Oxford: Oxford University Press.

Heidegger, Martin. [1953] 1977a. *Being and Time*. Albany: State University of New York Press.

———. 1977b. *The Question concerning Technology and Other Essays*. Translated with an introduction by W. Lovitt. New York: Harper Torchbooks.

Henry, V. 2001. *The COMPSTAT Paradigm*. New York: Loose Leaf Press.

Herzfeld, M. 1992. *The Social Production of Indifference*. Cambridge, Mass.: Harvard University Press.

Holdaway, Simon. 1983. *Inside the British Police*. Oxford: Blackwell.

Hough, Mike. 1980. "Managing with Less Technology." *British Journal of Criminology* 20: 344–57.

Hughes, E. C. 1958. *Men and Their Work*. Glencoe, Ill.: Free Press.

Hunt, Raymond G., and John M. Magenau. 1993. *Power and the Police Chief*. Newbury Park, Calif.: Sage.

Innes, M. 2003. *Investigating Homicide*. Oxford: Clarendon Press.

Jacoby, Jane, and E. Ratledge. 1989. *Handbook on Artificial Intelligence and Expert Systems in Law Enforcement*. Westport, Conn.: Greenwood Press.

Janis, Irving. 1972. *Victims of Groupthink*. Boston: Houghton Mifflin.

Janis, Irving, and Leon Mann. 1977. *Decision Making*. New York: Free Press.

Jermeir, John, and Leonard Berkes. 1979. "Leader Behaviour in a Police Command Bureaucracy: A Closer Look at the Quasi-Military Model." *Administrative Science Quarterly* 24: 1–24.

Johnston, Les. 1993. *The Rebirth of Private Policing*. London: Routledge.

Johnston, Les, and C. Shearing. 2003. *Governing Security*. London: Routledge.

Jones, Trevor, and T. Newburn. 1998. *Private Security and Public Police*. Oxford: Clarendon.

Jones, T., D. Smith, and T. Newburn. 1996. "Policing and the Idea of Democracy." *British Journal of Criminology* 36: 182–96.

Kappeler, Victor, Richard Sluder, and Geoffery Alpert. 1998. *Forces of Deviance*. Long Grove, Ill.: Waveland.

Karmen, A. 2000. *New York Murder Mystery*. New York: NYU Press.

Kelling, George. 1995. "How to Run a Police Department." *City Journal* 5.

Kelling, George, and Catherine Coles. 1996. *Fixing Broken Windows*. New York: Free Press.

Kennedy, D. 1998. "Pulling Levers." *NIJ Journal* 238 (July): 2–8.

Klockars, C. 1996. "Police Violence." *Police Violence: Understanding and Controlling Police Use of Force,* ed. by W. Geller and H. Toch. New Haven, Conn.: Yale University Press.

Kraska, Peter, and Victor Kappeler. 1998. "Militarizing American Police." *Social Problems* 44: 1–18.

Lane, Roger. 1967. *Policing the City: Boston, 1822–1905*. Cambridge, Mass.: Harvard University Press.

Larson, Richard. 1972. *Urban Police Patrol Analysis*. Cambridge: MIT Press.

Latour, Bruno. 1996. *Aramis, or the Love of Technology*. Cambridge, Mass.: Harvard University Press.

LaVigne, N., and J. Wartell. 2000. *Crime Mapping: Cases Studies,* 2 vols. Washington, D.C.: PERF.

———. 2001. *Mapping across Boundaries*. Washington, D.C.: PERF.

Leonard, V. A. 1980. *The New Police Technology: The Impact of the Computer and Automation on Police Staff and Line Performance.* Springfield, Ill.: Charles C. Thomas.

Liang, Hsi-Huey. 1992. *The Rise of the European State System from Metternich to the Second World War.* New York: Cambridge University Press.

Lichtenberg, G. 1961. *Aphorisms.* Harmondsworth, England: Penguin UK.

Lipsky, M. 1986. *Street Corner Bureaucracies.* New York: Russell Sage Foundation.

Loader, Ian, and A. Mulcahy. 2003. *Policing and the Condition of England.* Oxford: Oxford University Press.

Lyons, William. 1999. *The Politics of Community Policing.* Ann Arbor: University of Michigan Press.

MacCannell, D. 1973. "Staged Authenticity." *American Journal of Sociology* 79 (November): 589–603.

Macdonald Michael. 1999. *All Souls: A Family Story from Southie.* Boston: Beacon Press.

Mackenzie D. 1993. *Inventing Accuracy.* Cambridge, Mass.: MIT Press.

Magenau, John, and Raymond G. Hunt. 1989. "Socio-Political Networks for Police Role-Making." *Human Relations* 42: 547–60.

Maguire, Edward. 1997. "Structural Change in Large Municipal Organizations during the Community Policing Era." *Justice Quarterly* 14: 547–76.

Maguire, E., et al. 1998. "Counting Cops . . ." *Policing* 21: 97–120.

Maguire, M., R. Morgan, and R. Reiner, eds. 2002. *Oxford Handbook of Criminology,* 3d ed. Oxford: Oxford University Press.

Maltz, Michael, et al. 1991. *Mapping Crime in Its Community Setting.* New York: Springer-Verlag.

Mannheim, Karl. 1960. *Essays in the Sociology of Knowledge.* London: Routledge.

Manning, Peter K. [1977] 1997. *Police Work.* Long Grove, Ill.: Waveland.

———. [1979] 2003. *The Narcs' Game: Organizational and Informational Limits on Drug Law Enforcement.* Long Grove, Ill.: Waveland.

———. 1979. "The Reflexivity and Facticity of Knowledge." *American Behavioral Scientist* 22(6): 697–732.

———. 1987. *Semiotics and Fieldwork.* Thousand Oaks, Calif.: Sage.

———. 1988. *Symbolic Communication.* Cambridge, Mass.: MIT Press.

———. 1990. *Organizational Communication.* Hawthorne, N.Y.: Aldine de Gruyter.

———. 1992. "Information Technology and the Police." In *Modern Policing,* ed. by Michael Tonry and Norval Morris. Pp. 349–98. Chicago: University of Chicago Press.

———. 2001a. "Theorizing Policing: The Myth of Command and Control." *Theoretical Criminology* 5: 315–44.

———. 2001b. "Technology's Ways." *Criminal Justice* 1: 83–103.

———. 2003. *Policing Contingencies*. Chicago: University of Chicago Press.

———. 2005. "Environment, Technology, and Organizational Change." In *Information in the Criminal Justice System,* ed. by A. Pattavina. Thousand Oaks, Calif.: Sage.

———. Forthcoming 2008. "Occupation and Organization in Dialectic." In *Police Occupational Culture,* ed. by M. O'Neil and M. Marks. Amsterdam: Elsevier.

Maple, Jack, with Chris Mitchell. 1998. *Crime Fighter.* New York: Doubleday.

March, J., and H. Simon. 1993. *Organizations,* 2d ed. Malden, Mass.: Blackwell.

Massey, D., and N. Denton. 1983. *American Apartheid.* Cambridge, Mass.: Harvard University Press.

Mastrofski, S. 1998. "Community Policing and Police Organization Structure." In *How to Recognize Good Policing,* ed. by Jean Paul Brodeur. Thousand Oaks, Calif.: Sage.

Mastrofski, S., M. Reisig, and J. McCluskey. 2002. "Police Disrespect toward the Public: An Encounter-Based Analysis." *Criminology* 40: 519–51.

Mauss, M. 1972. *Magic.* Trans. by Robert Brain. London: Routledge.

Mawby, R. I. 1999. *Policing across the World.* London: Routledge.

———. 2004. "International Policing." In *Handbook of Policing,* ed. by T. Newburn. Devon, England: Willan.

Mawby, Rob C. 2002. *Policing Images.* Devon, England: Willan.

Mazerolle, L., D. Rogan, J. Frank, C. Famega, J. Eck, et al. 2002. "Managing Citizen Calls to the Police: The Impact of Baltimore's 3-1-1 Call System." *Criminology and Public Policy* 2: 97–124.

McDevitt, J., A. Braga, D. Nurge, and M. Buerger. 2004. "Boston's Youth Violence Prevention Program." In *Policing Gangs and Youth Violence,* ed. by S. Decker. Belmont, Calif.: Wadsworth.

McDonald P. 2001. *Managing Police Operations.* Belmont, Calif.: Wadsworth.

McRoberts, O. 2003. *Streets of Glory.* Chicago: University of Chicago Press.

Meehan, Albert J. 1994. "Information Technology, Patrol Work and Recordkeeping Practices." Presented to the Midwest Sociological Society, March.

———. 1998. "The Impact of Mobile Data Terminal (MDT) Information Technology on Communication and Recordkeeping in Police Work." *Qualitative Sociology* 221: 225–54.

Merelman, Richard. 1969. "The Dramaturgy of Politics." *Sociological Quarterly* 10: 216–41.

———. 1991. *Partial Visions: Culture and Politics in Britain, Canada and the United States.* Madison: University of Wisconsin Press.

———. 1998. "On Legitimalaise in the United States." *Sociological Quarterly* 39: 351–68.

Mills, C. Wright. 1940. "Situated Actions and Vocabularies of Motive." *American Sociological Review* 5 (December): 904–13.

Monkonnen, Eric. 1981. *The Police in Urban America, 1830–1920.* Cambridge, England: Cambridge University Press.

———. 1992. "History of Urban Police." In *Modern Policing,* ed. by Michael Tonry and Norval Morris. Chicago: University of Chicago Press.

Moore, Mark H. 1997. *Creating Public Value.* Cambridge, Mass.: Harvard University Press.

———. 2003. "Compstat: Sizing Up an Administrative Innovation in Policing." *Criminology and Public Policy* 2(3): 469–94.

Moore, M., et al. 1984. *Dangerous Offenders: The Elusive Target.* Cambridge, Mass.: Harvard University Press.

Nesbary, Dale. 1994. "Politics and Discretion: The Acquisition of Technology in Municipal Police Agencies." Paper presented to the Michigan Sociological Society, November.

Newburn, T., and S. Hayman. 2001. *Surveillance.* Devon, England: Willan.

Newburn, T., ed. 2004. *Handbook of Policing.* Devon, England: Willan.

Orlikowski, W. 1992. "The Duality of Technology: Rethinking the Concept of Technology in Organizations." *Organization Science* 3(3): 398–427.

———. 1996. "Improvising Organizational Transformation over Time: A Situated Change Perspective." *Information Systems Research* 7(1): 63–92.

———. 2000. "Using Technology and Constituting Structures: A Practice Lens for Studying Technology in Organizations." *Organization Science* 11(4): 404–28.

Orlikowski, W., and M. Tyre. 1994. "Windows of Opportunity: Temporal Patterns of Technological Adaptation in Organizations." *Organization Science* 5(1): 98–118.

Osborne, D., and T. Gaebler. 1992. *Reinventing Government.* Reading, Mass.: Addison-Wesley.

Park, Robert, and E. Burgess. 1926. *Introduction to the Science of Sociology.* Chicago: University of Chicago Press.

Pease, K. 1997. "Crime Prevention." In *Oxford Handbook of Criminology,* ed. by R. Morgan, R. Reiner, and M. Maguire. Oxford: Oxford University Press.

Poster, M. 1990. *The Mode of Information.* Chicago: University of Chicago Press.

Ragin, C., and H. S. Becker, eds. 1992. *What Is a Case?* Cambridge, England: Cambridge University Press.

Rawls, Anne. 1983. "The Interaction Order Sui Generis: Goffman's Contribution to Social Theory." *Sociological Theory* 5: 136–49.

Rawls, John. 1970. *The Theory of Justice.* Cambridge, Mass.: Harvard University Press.

———. 1971. *Theory of Justice.* Cambridge, Mass.: Harvard University Press.

Reaves, Brian, and Andrew Goldberg. 1996. *LEMAS Data.* Washington, D.C.: Bureau of Justice Statistics, U.S. Department of Justice.

——. 2000. *LEMAS Data.* Washington, D.C.: Bureau of Justice Statistics. Department of Justice.

Reiner, R. 1992. *The Politics of the Police,* 2d ed. Brighton, England: Wheatsheaf.

——. 2002. *The Police in Oxford Handbook of Criminology,* ed. by M. Maguire, R. Morgan, and R. Reiner. Oxford: Oxford University Press.

Reiss, Albert J., Jr. 1992a. "Police Organization in the Twentieth Century." In *Modern Policing,* ed. by Michael Tonry and Norval Morris. Chicago: University of Chicago Press.

——. 1992b. "A Theory of Police Organizations." Delivered to American Society of Criminology, Phoenix, Ariz., November.

Reiss, Albert J., and David Bordua. 1967. "Organization and Environment" In *Police: Six Sociological Essays,* ed. by David Bordua. New York: John Wiley.

Reppetto, T. 1977. *The Blue Parade.* New York: Macmillan.

Rigakos, George. 2002. *Paramiliatry Policing.* Toronto: University of Toronto Press.

Roberts, Karlene, and Martha Grabowski. 1996. "Organizations, Technology and Structuring." *Handbook of Organizations,* ed. by S. Clegg, C. Hardy, and W. Nord. Pp. 409–23. Thousand Oaks, Calif.: Sage.

Robinson, C., and J. Scaglion. 1987. "The Evolution of Policing." *Law and Society Review* 21: 109–54.

Rose, N., and T. Clear. 1998. "Incarceration, Social Capital and Crime" *Criminology* 36: 441–80.

Rossmo, D. Kim. 2000. *Geographic Profiling.* Boca Raton, Fla.: CRC Press.

Roy, Donald. 1952. "Quota Restriction and Goldbricking in a Machine Shop." *American Journal of Sociology* 57: 427–42.

——. 1954. "Efficiency and 'The Fix': Informal Intergroup Relations in a Piecework Machine Shop." *American Journal of Sociology* 60: 255–66.

Sampson, R. 2002. "Transcending Tradition: New Directions in Community Research, Chicago Style." *Criminology* 40: 213–30.

Sampson, R., and W. Bryon Groves. 1989. "Community Structure and Crime: Testing Social Disorganization Theory." *American Journal of Sociology* 94: 774–802.

Sampson, R., and S. Raudenbush. 1999. "Systematic Social Observation of Social Spaces." *American Journal of Sociology* 105: 603–51.

Sampson, R., S. Raudenbush, and F. Earls. 1997. "Neighborhoods and Violent Crime." *Science* 277: 918–24.

Scheingold, Stuart. 1984. *The Politics of Law and Order.* New York: Longman.

——. 1991. *The Politics of Street Crime.* Philadelphia: Temple University Press.

Sellen, D., and R. Harper. 2002. *The Paperless Office*. Cambridge, Mass.: MIT Press.

Selznick, P. 1948. "Foundations of the Theory of Organization." *American Sociological Review* 13: 25–35.

Shaw, C., and H. McKay. 1942. *Juvenile Delinquency and Urban Areas*. Chicago: University of Chicago Press.

Shearing C., and R. Ericson. 1991. "Culture as Figurative Action." *British Journal of Sociology* 42: 481–506.

Sheptyki, James, ed. 2000. *Issues in Transnational Policing*. London: Routledge.

Sherman, L. W. 1987. *Repeat Calls to Police in Minneapolis*. Crime Control Institute Report #5. Washington, D.C.: Crime Control Institute.

———. 1990. "Police Crackdowns: Initial and Residual Deterrence" In *Crime and Justice*, vol. 12, ed. by M. Tonry and N. Morris. Pp. 1–45. Chicago: University of Chicago Press.

———. 1992. "Attacking Crime: Police and Crime Control." In *Crime and Justice*, vol. 15, ed. by M. Tonry and N. Morris. Pp. 159–230. Chicago: University of Chicago Press.

Sherman, L. W., P. Gartin, and M. Buerger. 1989. "Hot Spots of Predatory Crime." *Criminology* 27: 27–55.

Short, James F., Jr. 1963. Introduction to *The Gang*, by Frederick Thrasher. Chicago: University of Chicago Press.

Sica, Alan. 1998. *Weber, Irrationality, and Social Order*. Berkeley: University of California Press.

Silverman, D. 1971. *The Theory of Organizations*. New York: Basic Books.

Silverman, Eli. 1999. *NYPD Attacks Crime*. Boston: Northeastern University Press.

Singer, Peter. 2003. *Corporate Warriors*. Ithaca, N.Y.: Cornell University Press.

Skogan, W. 2006. *Community Policing: Three Cities*. New York: Oxford University Press.

Skogan, W., and S. Harnett. 1997. *Community Policing Chicago Style*. New York: Oxford University Press.

Skogan, W., et al. 1999. *On the Beat*. Boulder, Colo.: Westview.

Sparrow, Malcolm. 1993. *Information Policing and the Development of Policing*. NIJ Perspectives on Policing, Report #16. Washington, D.C.: U.S. Department of Justice.

Sparrow, Malcolm, Mark Moore, and David B. Kennedy. 1992. *Beyond 911: A New Era for Policing*. New York: Basic Books.

Staples, William. 1997. *The Culture of Surveillance*. New York: St. Martin's.

St. Clair, James. 1992. *Report of the Boston Police Department Management Review Committee*. Boston: Office of the Mayor.

Strachan H. 2004. *The First World War in Africa*. Oxford: Oxford University Press.

Suchman, Lucy. 1987. *Plans and Situated Actions.* Cambridge, England: Cambridge University Press.

Taylor, R. 2000. *Breaking Away from Broken Windows.* Boulder, Colo.: Westview.

Thacher, D. 2005. "The Local Role in Homeland Security." *Law and Society Review* 39: 635–59.

Thomas, Robert J. 1992. "Organizational Politics and Technological Change." *Journal of Contemporary Ethnography* 20: 442–77.

———. 1994. *What Machines Can't Do.* Berkeley: University of California Press.

Thompson, James. 1963. *Organizations.* New York: McGraw-Hill.

Thompson, V. 1962. *Organizations.* New York: Knopf.

Trojanowicz, Robert, and Bonnie Buqueroux. 1994. *Community Policing.* Cincinnati, Ohio: Anderson.

Van Maanen, John. 1973. "Observations on the Making of a Policeman." *Human Organization* 32: 407–18.

———. 1974. "Working the Street." In *The Potential for Reform in Criminal Justice,* ed. by H. Jacob. Pp. 83–130. Beverly Hills, Calif.: Sage.

———. 1983. "The Boss." In *Control in the Police Organization,* ed. by M. Punch. Cambridge: MIT Press.

———. 1988. *Tales of the Field.* Chicago: University of Chicago Press.

Venkatesh, S. 2000. *American Project.* Cambridge, Mass.: Harvard University Press.

Waddington, P. A. J. 1999. "Police [Canteen] Sub-Culture." *British Journal of Criminology* 39: 287–309.

Waegel, W. 1981. "Case Routinization of Investigative Police Work." *Social Problems* 28: 263–75.

Wakefield, Allison. 2003. *Private Policing.* Devon, England: Willan.

Walsh, William. 2001. "COMPSTAT: An Analysis of an Emerging Police Paradigm." *Policing* 24: 347–62.

Weber, M. 1947. *Theory of Economic and Social Organization.* Glencoe, Ill.: Free Press.

———. 1978a. *The Protestant Ethic.* New York: Scribners.

———. 1978b. *Economy and Society,* ed. by G. Roth and C. Wittich. Berkeley: University of California Press.

Weick, Karl. 1988. "Technology as Equivoque." In *Technology and Organization,* ed. by Paul Goodman and Lee Sproull. San Francisco: Josey-Bass.

———. 1995. *Sensemaking in Organizations.* Thousand Oaks, Calif.: Sage.

———. 2000. *Making Sense of the Organization.* Malden, Mass.: Blackwell.

Weick, Karl, and Karlene Roberts. 2002. "Collective Mind in an Organization." In *Making Sense of the Organization,* ed. by K. Weick. Malden, Mass.: Blackwell.

Weisburd, D., S. Bushway, C. Lum, and S. M. Yang. 2004. "Trajectories of Crime at Places." *Criminology* 42: 283–321.

Weisburd, D., and J. Eck. 2004. "What Can Police Do to Reduce Crime, Disorder, and Fear?" *Annals of the American Academy of Political and Social Science* 593: 242–65.

Weisburd, D., S. Mastrofski, A. M. McNally, R. Greenspan, and J. J. Willis. 2003. "Reforming to Preserve: COMPSTAT and Strategic Problem-Solving in American Policing." *Criminology and Public Policy* 2: 421–56.

Weisburd, D., and A. Braga, eds. 2006. *Police Innovation*. Cambridge, England: Cambridge University Press.

Weisheit, Ralph L., David N. Falcone, and Edward Wells. 1999. *Crime and Policing in Rural and Small Town America*. Prospect Heights, Ill: Waveland.

Weitzer, R. 2000. "Racialized Policing: Residents' Perceptions in Three Neighborhoods." *Law and Society Review* 34: 129–55.

Weitzer, R., and S. Tuch. 2005. "Can the Police Be Reformed?" *Contexts* 4: 21–26.

———. 2006. *Race and Policing in America*. Cambridge, England: Cambridge University Press.

Westley, W. [1950] 1970. *Violence and the Police*. Cambridge: MIT Press.

Wilensky, H. 1964. "The Professionalization of Everyone?" *American Journal of Sociology* 70: 137–58.

Willis, J. J., S. Mastrofski, and D. Weisburd. 2004. "Compstat and Bureaucracy." *Justice Quarterly* 21 (September): 463–96.

———. 2007. "Making Sense of COMPSTAT: A Theory-Based Analysis of Organizational Change in Three Police Departments." *Law and Society Review* 41: 147–87.

Wilson, J. Q. 1968. *Varieties of Police Behavior*. Cambridge, Mass.: Harvard University Press.

Wilson, J. Q., and G. Kelling. 1982. "The Police and Neighborhood Safety: Broken Windows." *Atlantic Magazine* 127: 29–38.

Wilson, O. W. 1942. *Police Records, Their Installation and Use*. Chicago: Public Administration Service.

Winship, C., and J. Berrien. 1999. "Boston Cops and Black Churches." *Public Interest* 36 (Summer): 52–68.

Wittgenstein, L. 1961. *Philosophical Investigations*. New York: Macmillan.

Wolff, K. 1993. *From Karl Mannheim*, 2d expanded ed. New York: Oxford University Press.

Young, Michael. 1991. *An Inside Job*. Oxford: Clarendon.

Zhao, S., N. He, and N. Lovrich. 2003. "Community Policing: Did It Change the Basic Function of Policing in the 1990s?" *Justice Quarterly* 20: 697–724.

Zuboff, S. 1986. *The Smart Machine*. New York: Basic Books.

# Index

American Criminal Justice Society, 145
American Society of Criminology, 145
Analytic categories, xi
ArcView, 75, 117–118, 148, 157, 160
Armed services, 7

Boston, ix–x, xiv, 165–166, 196, 245;
City Hall, 167; Common, 183; crimes in
2003, 183; Democratic National convention in, 32, 50, 293n. 3; neighborhoods, 268; shootings, 302–303n. 6;
suburbs of, 165
Boston crime-analysis meetings (CAMs),
xiv, 5, 12, 26, 164, 180, 185–187,
189–191, 196, 198, 285; "back-stage"
region/meeting, 217, 219, 223; and
Boston Regional Intelligence Center,
266; and "bureaucratic power," 245;
and death of an officer, 208–209; drama
in, 217; ecology of, 204–206, 248;
emotional tone of, 207; "front-stage
region," 217–218, 223; and gun crime,
212, 230; and information technology,
201–203; matters omitted from, 209–
211, 246; and mininarratives, 235–237;
rationality in, 202–203, 240; ritual of,
222–223; visual presentations in, 214–
216, 226
Boston Gun Project, 176
Boston Management Consortium, 172
Boston Police Department (BPD), ix, 5,
164, 167, 275, 298n. 4; Annual Report,
173, 182; commissioner-chief system of
organization, 170; democratic policing,
179; district level crime-analysis meetings (mini-CAMs), 182, 191, 221; five
districts of, 170; internal politics of,
168; neighborhood district stations of,

172; Office of Research and Evaluation,
181, 188, 190, 221, 223, 249; organizational chart of, 171; "same-cop-same-
neighborhood" scheme, 172; six landmarks of, 173; St. Clair Report, 174;
staff ratio of, 168; Stuart Murder, 173;
Ten Point Coalition (TPC), 176–179,
300n. 9, 303n. 6
Bratton, William, 40; and BPD, 174; and
management talk, 245
"Broken windows," 41

Case studies, x, 24; methods of, 271–273
Chicago, 4
Chicago Alternative Policing Strategy
(CAPS), 138
"Chicago School," 15
Civilian review boards, 29
Clinton, Bill, 34–35; and Boston, 300n.
10; Crime Control and Safe Streets Law
of 1994, 34
Cliques, 144
Community-Oriented Police Services
Agency (COPS), 34–35; in MDCPD,
139, 142, 145, 154, 156; in WPD, 105,
109, 116
Community-Oriented Problem Solving
Analysis Center, (COPSAC), 130; in
MDCPD, 141, 143, 145, 278; study of,
282–283
Compstat, 13; meetings, 16, 41, 91, 125;
NYPD's program, 39–40, 192, 197,
211, 288; and scientific rationality,
247
Computer-assisted dispatching (CAD), 36–
38, 83; in BPD, 192; database access,
76; introduction of, 52, 74; in MDCPD,
150; Printrak, 114; in WPD, 112

319

# About the Author

Peter K. Manning is Elmer V. H. and Eileen M. Brooks Chair in Policing, College of Criminal Justice, Northeastern University. He is the author of numerous books, most recently *Policing Contingencies* and, with Brian Forst, *Private Policing: Two Views.*